PROPERTY WRONGS

T0244329

PROPERTY WRONGS

The Seventy-Year Fight for Public Housing in Winnipeg

Doug Smith

Fernwood Publishing
Halifax & Winnipeg

Development editing: Wayne Antony
Copy editing: Sarah Michaelson
Text design: Brenda Conroy
Cover design: Evan Marnoch
Printed and bound in Canada

Published by Fernwood Publishing
2970 Oxford Street, Halifax, Nova Scotia, B3L 2W4
and 748 Broadway Avenue, Winnipeg, Manitoba, R3G 0X3

www.fernwoodpublishing.ca

Fernwood Publishing Company Limited gratefully acknowledges the financial support of the Government of Canada through the Canada Book Fund and the Canada Council for the Arts. We acknowledge the Province of Manitoba for support through the Manitoba Publishers Marketing Assistance Program and the Book Publishing Tax Credit. We acknowledge the Nova Scotia Department of Communities, Culture and Heritage for support through the Publishers Assistance Fund. The Social Sciences and Humanities Research Council, through the Manitoba Research Alliance, provided support for the production of this book.

Library and Archives Canada Cataloguing in Publication

Title: Property wrongs : the seventy-year fight for public housing in Winnipeg / Doug Smith.

Names: Smith, Doug, 1954- author.

Description: Includes bibliographical references and index.

Identifiers: Canadiana (print) 20230000274 | Canadiana (ebook) 20230000304 | ISBN 9781773635972

(softcover) | ISBN 9781773636245 (PDF) | ISBN 9781773636238 (EPUB)

Subjects: LCSH: Public housing—Manitoba—Winnipeg—History—20th century.

Classification: LCC HD7288.78.C32 W56 2023 | DDC 363.5/8509712743—dc23

CONTENTS

ACKNOWLEDGEMENTS

I owe particular thanks to Shauna MacKinnon, who asked me to undertake an analysis of proposed changes to the Manitoba Housing policy in 2020 for the Manitoba Research Alliance. At the time, Shauna asked if I could include a summary of the history of public housing in Manitoba. The thumbnail sketch contained in the report I wrote left me with many unanswered questions that this book seeks to address. The research on which this book is based was funded by the Social Sciences and Humanities Research Council of Canada through the Manitoba Research Alliance's Partnership Grant *Community-Driven Solutions to Poverty: Challenges and Possibilities.* I am grateful for the support given to this project by Molly McCracken of the Canadian Centre for Policy Alternatives (Manitoba), and Kirsten Bernas and Sarah Cooper of the Right to Housing Coalition.

I owe a huge debt to the people who have read and responded to this manuscript through the years: Jim Silver, Shauna MacKinnon, Lynne Fernandez, Wayne Antony, and Fernwood Publishing's anonymous readers. The infelicities and errors that follow are mine, any incision and flare are the products of their comradely advice. I would also like to thank the Fernwood's production team for their professional and sympathetic reception to this book. Thanks to Jo-Anne Douglas for the author photo.

Sarah Ramsden of the City of Winnipeg Archives was extremely helpful at key points in this work's history. Public libraries are almost as essential to society as public housing; I can only say that this book could not have been written without the resources made available by the Winnipeg Public Library system. Erica Smith assisted in the research by identifying thousands of newspaper articles dealing with housing in Winnipeg over the past century. Karen Botting and Lara Mazur provided me with documents and memories related to the role that their father, Skapti Borgford, played in the creation of co-operative housing in Winnipeg.

The notes for this book are extensive, but the works of Alan Artibise, John Bacher, Stefan Epp-Koop, David Hulchanski, and Jill Wade were essential in helping shape this project and merit a special acknowledgement.

Jason Martin of the Archives of Manitoba, James Kominowski of the University of Manitoba Archives, and Gordon Goldsborough of the Manitoba Historical Society were very helpful in locating historical images for use in the book. Bruce Owen kindly provided a photograph of his great-grandfather William Cooper.

Finally, over the past decade, Sandra Hardy has provided me with a ringside seat for the daily fistfight that is the creation of non-profit housing in this country. When the best combine conviction and passionate intensity, things don't fall apart, they come together.

This book attempts to explain why public housing took so long to come to Winnipeg. The history of the public housing that was built from the 1960s onwards still awaits its author. Such a history would attend to the myriad social and political questions that swirl around any discussion of public housing. These include decisions about where public housing is built, whether it is reserved for the poorest of the poor, or whether it is developed as some form of mixed-income community, the degree to which residents should shape the development and governance of housing projects, and the need to provide a range of supportive social services along with bricks and mortar. These questions are real and important—an examination of the history of public housing, not just in Manitoba, would do much to inform future housing policy decisions.

Introduction

DEMOCRACY, CLASS, AND HOUSING

In his memoirs, Humphrey Carver, a former official with the Central Mortgage and Housing Corporation and long-time public-housing advocate, observed during his career with the Corporation that "my many visits to Winnipeg were mostly concerned with the long succession of studies and plans for providing decent housing and a better way of life for the people who live near the railway tracks." When it came to looking after their own people, Winnipeggers, he feared, "needed a great deal more coaxing" than some other Canadians.[1] Carver was speaking, somewhat gently, of the fact that between the end of World War II and 1969, the City of Winnipeg developed only two public housing projects.

To be fair to the Winnipeggers who Carver was attempting to coax into building public housing, no Canadian city seriously engaged in the construction of public housing until 1949, when families began to move into the Regent Park North housing project in Toronto. And it was only with the amendment of the *National Housing Act* in that year, that federal funding was made available to support the construction and operation of public housing projects across the country. But no one could accuse the Manitoba government or Winnipeg city council of seizing this opportunity. Nearly fifteen years would pass before the Province and the City were able to overcome deeply rooted opposition to public housing. The two projects that they undertook—Burrows-Keewatin (now known as Gilbert Park) and Lord Selkirk Park—should be seen as important steps forward in the provision of quality housing for people with low incomes. But they were one-offs: unloved attempts by local elites to capture available federal money. The City did not attempt to learn from the experiences of public housing development in other provinces, and what it did spend on necessary social servic-es and recreational facilities was limited and provided grudging-ly. It was not until the election of Ed Schreyer's New Democratic Party government in 1969 that public housing was constructed in Winnipeg on anything close to the scale needed to address long-identified needs.

The need for public housing in Winnipeg can be traced back as far as the 1880s. By then, Winnipeg had identifiable shanty-towns located near the rail lines and east of Main Street on what was termed the Hudson's Bay Flats. In 1883, the *Winnipeg Daily Sun* reported that one shantytown was made up of "not less than three hundred little wooden shanties, varying in size from that of a large dog-house to a good-sized ash-house." (An ash house was a small shed that stored ashes used to make soap.) Shanties twelve by sixteen feet in size were advertised for sale in local pa-pers. Often located on the public roadways, these shanties were fire hazards, so flimsy a strong wind could literally pick them up and blow them away.[2] The shanties cost between $50 and $115 to build and were occupied by an estimated two thousand people (out of a population of sixteen thousand) who could not afford the local "high rents."[3]

From then on there was a portion of the city's populace that could not afford to rent, let alone buy, housing that was safe and healthy. Safe and healthy simply means housing that was warm enough, sturdy enough, properly ventilated, free from fire haz-ards, provided with adequate plumbing, and allowed for a modi-cum of privacy. A considerable portion of Winnipeg housing failed to meet these criteria when judged by the common standards of the day. What, then, did poor families do? They generally had two options: they cut down on what they spent on food and clothing, allowing them to pay rents that they could not otherwise afford, or they crammed more people than were healthy into barely ad-equate housing. Or they did all these things and still ended up liv-ing in substandard housing.

For each of these families, getting and maintaining housing was a crisis that dominated their lives. Could they find a house? Would they be evicted if a wage earner was injured? Were conditions so crowded that typhus or diphtheria would rip through the tenement, leaving a trail of sick and dying children? On a night when the temperature hit forty below, would a spark from a cheap stove set the whole building alight? Would anyone ever enjoy a moment's privacy? But it is not possible to say Winnipeg itself had a housing crisis, since that would imply that the shortage of good quality affordable housing was a rupture, a break from some normal condition in which modestly priced healthy housing was available for all. There was no golden age: the constant crisis that individual low-income households faced in the search for housing has been continuous throughout Winnipeg's history. From 1900 to 1970, it is possible to find reports from each decade that speak in sober, matter-of-fact tones of the extent of inadequate housing and the City's inability to enforce its housing and health bylaws, since to do so would be to force families onto the street.

The uninterrupted failure of the private housing market to provide adequate affordable housing is one of the central themes of this book. Historically, Canada has left housing to the private sector. And the private housing industry has been unable to deliver housing at a cost that is affordable to all Canadians. This is, in itself, not surprising. The ownership of urban land has often been concentrated: by controlling the rate at which land is developed, landowners have been able to keep house prices up. And good quality housing is not cheap to build or maintain. It is no surprise to discover that an industry that provides housing to make a profit fails people who cannot afford to pay for adequate housing.

Many of the people who lived in Winnipeg at the beginning of the twentieth century were immigrants from Great Britain. As such, they were painfully aware of the failure of the private housing industry in England, Scotland, and Wales. They did not have to have read Charles Dickens's *Oliver Twist* or Arthur Morrison's *A Child of the Jago*—to name but two popular nineteenth-century novels of London slum life—to know that crowded, poorly ventilated, unsanitary conditions had condemned thousands to a life of squalor. They had personally experienced these conditions; they had come to Canada in hopes of escaping such conditions. They were also aware that there was a growing public-health movement that was focusing on what we now call the social determinants of health. These advocates recognized that inadequate living condi-

"It was bad housing and bad milk that killed the baby" (J.S. Woodsworth). Children living in slum conditions in early twentieth-century Winnipeg. Unregulated, these buildings were poorly heated, poorly ventilated, and often overcrowded. Archives of Manitoba, L.B. Foote fonds, Foote 1492. Interior slum of dwelling, 1916, P7399/4.

tions created poor health, shortened the lives of slum dwellers, and served as a reservoir for diseases that could penetrate class lines, such as tuberculosis. Methodist minister and social reformer J.S. Woodsworth wrote of how, when officiating at an infant's funeral, the words "Forasmuch as it hath pleased Almighty God in His wise providence to take out of the world the soul of the departed" stuck in his throat. "In my heart, I said: 'That's a lie.' It was bad housing and bad milk that killed the baby." In his view, poor housing was one of the three major reasons why the infant mortality rate in the city was higher in the North End's Ward 5 than in the South End's Ward 1.[4]

Many of these immigrants played an active role in the city's labour movement and the various social reform movements that arose in response to the challenges of urbanization and industrialization. Aside from campaigns for public health, direct democracy, prohibition, votes for women, and proper sewage treatment, there were calls to address the problem of "slums," including, as early as 1908, calls for public housing. Public-housing advocates came from both the labour movement—many of whose members lived in or had lived in the city's slums and shanties—and from more economically comfortable social reformers like journalists, clergy, and, significantly, senior municipal health officials. J.S. Woodsworth is likely the most well known of these individuals, but E.W.J. Hague, Alexander Officer, Fred Austin, and William Courage, to draw only from the list of municipal officials, deserve to be better known. The chronicling of the work of these campaigners for public housing represents the second theme in this book. The first call for the creation of public housing was made by trade unionist William Cooper in 1908. The fact that fifty-five years would pass before the residents began to move into Burrows-Keewatin, the city's first housing project, is a sign of the tenacity of those who kept up the fight for public housing.

That gap is, of course, also a sign of the strength of those who opposed the creation of public housing. Proud, self-willed, and determined, Winnipeg's business elite was rarely less than visceral in its hostility to public housing. Its animus was grounded in ideology: to the city's elite, all housing should be provided by the market. And to force some citizens to subsidize the housing of others—whose poverty was doubtlessly the result of imprudent life choices—was unfair to those who must pay and would only further "demoralize" those who were being subsidized. Some members of the business community appear to have genuinely believed that with the right form of government incentives—usually low-cost loans to what were termed "limited dividend housing companies"—the housing industry could provide affordable low-cost housing. These beliefs were largely chimerical: they served to divert pressure away from the provision of public housing but failed to deliver housing at an affordable price. For that portion of the city's elite who were directly involved in the real-estate industry, the opposition to public housing was also pragmatic. They feared that a reduction in housing costs for low-income people would generate downward pressure on housing prices—and profits—in general. This fear led them to resist any government policies that might reduce housing costs. A classic example was the opposition of Winnipeg lenders to low-cost mortgages under the *Dominion Housing Act* in the late 1930s. Finally, the business community's opposition was partisan: it had come to associate public housing with socialism. Agreeing to public housing would, in effect, be seen as a capitulation to the socialist faction on city council, little more than letting the terrorists win, encouraging them to make even further demands on the rights of property. A third strand in this story, then, is an examination of the way the members of the Winnipeg business community stood shoulder to shoulder in their determination to block the construction of public housing in the city.

The business community was able to hold out for so long because the political deck was stacked against the proponents of public housing. In Winnipeg the rights of property and citizenship were at odds. In the city's early years, to be eligible to vote for the mayor or a member of council, "citizens" not only had to be male, over twenty-one, and a resident of the city, but they had to either own property or rent property of significant value. The right to vote on money bylaws—laws authorizing significant municipal borrowing and spending—was even more restricted: only those who owned $500 worth of property could cast a vote on a money bylaw. Property owners could vote in each ward in which they owned property: which meant in 1907, a person who owned property in each of the city's seven wards could vote seven times. In 1910, there were more than six thousand of these "plural voters." And no one could run for office unless they owned property, plenty of property. In 1905, when a house on Arnold Avenue in Riverview cost $1,700, one had to own $2,000 of property to run for mayor and $500 worth to run for council.[5] The rationale for these restrictions on the right to vote was simple: since the City raised its revenue through taxes on property, only people who owned property should have a say in city government. In 1909 Winnipeg city council went so far as to consider granting the right to vote to corporations. Mayor William Sanford Evans supported the idea, saying "Property is the whole basis of municipal voting and corporations own a large part of the property of Winnipeg."[6] Forty years later, a resident of River Heights felt no shame in asserting that "homeowners make the best citizens," when making an argument against building low-cost housing in his neighbourhood.[7] It was not until 1970 that all the property-based restrictions on the right to vote were lifted. The story of public housing is deeply embedded in a broader story of a struggle for greater democracy on the municipal level in Winnipeg and is very much a conflict between the rights of people and the rights of property.

Given the distribution of spending and taxing power in Canada, the story of public housing in any given city must address national and provincial housing policies. Building public housing requires large-scale long-term borrowing, as does the provision of operating subsidies. During those periods when the public-housing sector has expanded, the federal government has led the way, with provincial and municipal governments serving as junior partners. When the federal government turned away from non-profit housing, as it did in the 1990s, the sector's growth simply ceased. Up until the 1930s, no level of government was prepared to adopt an ongoing housing policy of any sort. When the federal government did enter the housing field in the 1930s, it did so to address the decline in construction prompted by the Great Depression. The limited supports that the government provided were intended to get construction workers back on the job, building homes for middle- and upper-income earners.

The dirty secret of Canadian housing policy is that more subsidies have been directed to homeowners and home builders than to low-income renters. These range from subsidized mortgages through the Canada Mortgage and Housing Corporation to the construction of highways and bridges that enable homeowners to live in the suburbs, to the exemption from capital gains taxes that homeowners enjoy. Although the 1962 Royal Commission on Taxation recommended that house sale capital gains be treated like other capital gains—on the sensible principle that a buck is a buck and that an exemption would be unfair to low-income Canadians—homeowners were exempted from paying this tax upon the sale of their homes. The cost to the Canadian government of this tax break for homeowners was $7.1 billion in 2021.[8] This is equivalent to the amount the federal government committed to spending on its entire National Housing Strategy in 2021, only a portion of which would be targeted to housing for low-income people.[9]

When, in 1949, the federal government agreed to fund public housing, it required provincial governments to contribute a quarter of the costs. Many provincial governments, including the government of Manitoba, chose to require municipal governments to pay a portion of the provincial costs. The funding of public housing under this model required that pro-housing governments simultaneously hold office at all three levels and be able to successfully negotiate complex three-cornered funding agreements in a short period. The election of the federal Conservative government headed by John Diefenbaker in 1958 meant that housing ceased to be a federal priority for five years, just as Winnipeg city council and the Manitoba provincial government were finally developing an appetite for development. It took the election of a reformist federal Liberal government in 1968 and a reformist NDP provincial government in 1969 to bring the public-housing stars into alignment. While the federal government provided the bulk of the needed mortgage money, the provincial government cleared away roadblocks by essentially relieving municipal governments of their funding role. The result was an explosion in the construction of public housing.

That period of growth in public housing created an important set of publicly owned assets. Those assets have been neglected and their residents have often been vilified. But public-housing developments were and are considerable improvements over the often-deplorable options that the private market offered to low-income people. The social problems that are associated with poverty should not be laid at the door of public housing, but of a society that has all too often scanted its responsibility to low-income people. As well, powerful forces sought to block the creation of public housing, while its advocates had to endure long years of frustration and defeat.

The immediate stimulus for the writing of this book was the housing policies that were embraced by the Conservative government of Brian Pallister and his housing minister, Heather Stefanson. They ended a tax credit for the construction of rental properties and issued no calls for proposals to construct new affordable rental housing. They did, however, seek proposals from organizations that might be interested in purchasing existing public housing. Slowly but surely, the Pallister government began to chip away at the public-housing sector: staff were reduced, programs were frozen, and construction was halted. The number of government-owned housing units declined by 2,600.[10] This was a dramatic break from the previous NDP administration of Greg Selinger, which had added five hundred units to the stock of government-owned housing and provided extensive support for affordable and social housing in partnership with local non-profit organizations, developers, and the federal government.[11]

Publicly provided health care and public education are crown jewels of the post-war welfare state. Public housing, on the other hand, is more like a neglected stepchild. Most Canadians believe, erroneously, that they provide themselves with their own housing free of any subsidy. The history of public housing should both serve as a reminder of the dangers of the current reversion to a model where the poor are obliged to rely on the mercies of the market for housing, and provide some succour for those who struggle to create better housing. There have been darker hours in the past, and while no victory is ever permanent, nor is any defeat.

NOTES

1. Humphrey Carver, *Compassionate Landscape: Places and People in a Man's Life*, Toronto: University of Toronto Press, 1975, 170.
2. "City and province," *Manitoba Daily Free Press*, November 8, 1883; "A phenomenon," *Manitoba Daily Free Press*, May 22, 1885; W.O. McRobie, "Of the doings of the fire brigade the past year," *Winnipeg Daily Sun*, December 27, 1884; "For sale," *Winnipeg Daily Sun*, January 14, 1884.
3. "Among the shanties," *Winnipeg Daily Sun*, January 31, 1883. See: "Winnipeg: The gateway of the Canadian West," in Alan A.J. Artibise (ed.), *Gateway City: Documents on the City of Winnipeg, 1873–1913*, Manitoba Record Society publications, Vol. 5. Winnipeg: Manitoba Record Society in association with the University of Manitoba Press, 1979, 267.
4. "Child death rate rouses ministers," *Manitoba Free Press*, May 27, 1913; J.S. Woodsworth, "Canadians of tomorrow," *Manitoba Free Press*, June 6, 1913.
5. An Act to Incorporate the City of Winnipeg, 37 Vic, Cap 7 Sections VIII and IX; Revised charter of the city of Winnipeg, 1918; Alan F.J. Artibise, *Winnipeg: A Social History of Urban Growth, 1874–1914*, Montreal: McGill-Queen's, 1975, 37–40. For house prices, see *Manitoba Free Press*, September 11, J.K. Moore and Company Advertisement, page 15.
6. "Fail to agree about franchise," *Manitoba Free Press*, February 17, 1909.
7. "City starts work on Howe's rental collection offer," *Winnipeg Free Press*, July 26, 1946; "Builders seek council committee to probe wartime houses set-up,"

Winnipeg Free Press, January 31, 1947.

8. "Canada's wild housing market is making the case for the country's most unpopular tax," *Globe and Mail*, March 2021.

9. Central Mortgage and Housing Corporation, National Housing Strategy, "What is the strategy?" <cmhc-schl.gc.ca/en/nhs/guidepage-strategy>, accessed March 18, 2022.

10. The Manitoba government owned 18,100 units of housing when Brian Pallister became premier in 2016. When he left office in 2021, the number was 15,500. Manitoba Housing owned 18,100. Manitoba Families, *Annual Report 2016–17*, n.d., 101; Manitoba Families, *Annual Report 20–21*, n.d., 120.

11. The Manitoba government owned 17,600 units of housing when Selinger became premier in 2009. When he left office in 2016, the number was 18,100. Manitoba Housing and Community Development, *Annual Report 2009–2010*, n.d., 18. Manitoba Families, *Annual Report 2016–17*, n.d., 101.

Chapter 1

SETTING THE STAGE: 1870–1900

In the fall of 1903, the *Manitoba Free Press* published a letter to the editor from "One who pays rent," which laid bare the problems that working-class families faced when looking for a place to live in Winnipeg.

> Many a weary stranger has tramped the streets of Winnipeg within the last two months, looking for a house of any kind to rent, and the landlord has simply tucked on the rent to the very last dollar that he thought it possible to wring from the unfortunate that must have an abiding place. Numbers of citizens have sent their families away to the east because they could not stand the rents asked for, be it ever remembered, salaries have not advanced in ratio to the cost of living. There are cottages of six rooms in Fort Rouge that have been taken on lease for a year at $40 per month; there are 7-roomed houses on Kennedy and such streets, and old houses at that, for which $45 has been asked and paid. It has been a common practice in Winnipeg this past summer to jump rents $5 per month at one time. In the matter of tenements and suite of rooms, 3-roomed suites in blocks in the less desirable neighborhoods of the city bring $20 to $22 the year round, and these rooms are simply bare walls. No sinks in the kitchen or sanitary conveniences, all these being located in public for the use of each floor at the end of a long corridor. Three-roomed suites with bath attached are renting for $35, and it is not unusual for applications to be 20 or 30 deep for any possible vacancy in such blocks. More than this there are suites

of two rooms without outside light or ventilation that bring in $18 a month to the landlord.[1]

To modern ears, a six-room cottage at $480 a year sounds like a bargain. But "One who pays rent" was writing at a time when most non-skilled labourers made less than $500 a year.[2] To put it plainly, by the beginning of the twentieth century, Winnipeg had a housing problem, one that would plague it well into the following century. This should not be surprising. The city's history, even in its early days, has been entangled with questions about the control and ownership of land. Winnipeg was a city deeply divided by class lines. Control over property gave the city's elite mastery over the cost of land, the cost of housing, along with control over workplaces and wages. This power was never total nor was it uncontested. In a direct challenge to the power of the propertied elite, workers created unions and political parties. In the workplace, they fought for shorter hours, better pay, and healthier conditions. Politically, they campaigned for fairer taxes, free access to education, health care, and welfare measures such as pensions. And they would fight for a reformed housing market: one viewed housing as a human right rather than an investment opportunity. From the outset, property and housing were deeply political issues in Manitoba.

THE POWER OF OWNERSHIP:
"AN OWNER OF THE SOIL IS A DIFFERENT PERSON"

Control over land lay at the heart of the struggle that culminated in the creation of the province of Manitoba in 1870. That was the year the residents of the Red River Colony, which was centred around the intersection of the Red and Assiniboine Rivers, staged what has come to be known as the "Red River Resistance." They prevented Canadian surveyors from measuring what they viewed as their land and blocked Canadian officials from entering the settlement. Their anger had been sparked by the fact that they had not been consulted when the British government bought Rupert's Land—a vast tract of North America that the Crown had granted to the Hudson's Bay Company in 1669—back from the Hudson's Bay Company for $1.5 million. The land was then transferred to the Canadian government, which made it clear that it was going to treat this newly acquired territory as a colony, governing it with appointed officials.

The agreement that ended the Red River Resistance included a legislated commitment to protect Métis land rights. The federal government was slow to make good on this commitment, while a corrupt political system favoured land speculators who bought up Métis claims at bargain prices.[3] As a result, Métis people were dispossessed of the land that they had sought to protect in 1870 and soon found themselves marginalized in the capital of the province they had helped create. By 1901 Métis families had begun settling in a community on un-serviced land on the southern edge of the city that came to be known as Rooster Town.[4]

In 1871 the federal government and local First Nations negotiated Treaty 1, which, from Canada's perspective, transferred Winnipeg (and a great deal more land besides) to the federal government. The government made sure that troops were present at the negotiations, instructed its negotiators to keep costs as low as possible, and, once the treaty was signed, did its best to ignore provisions that it was obliged to add in order to win First Nations' approval.[5] At the same time that the government gained control over First Nations land, it used legislation that would form the basis of the *Indian Act*, reducing First Nations to wards of the state. In other words, the struggle over property rights was present at the province's very inception.

Having gained political control of the west, the Canadian government set about recruiting settlers. In 1871 the city of Winnipeg had a population of 241. By 1901 it was 42,340.[6] This figure was to more than triple in the next decade. In 1910 a full-page article in the *Winnipeg Tribune* claimed to tell the thrilling story of "From trading post to metropolis in thirty-five years and how it all came about."[7] In 1911, there were 136,035 Winnipeggers, and the city was the third largest in the country. The First World War brought a temporary end to European immigration, but the population still rose to 179,087 in 1921.[8] From 1890 to 1914, immigration counted for 84 percent of the city's growth.[9] During roughly the same period, the percentage of the population that came from the Atlantic Isles (the islands that include England, Ireland, Scotland,

and Wales) declined from 83 percent to 67 percent, while the percentage that came from Eastern Europe increased from 1.4 percent to 13.1 percent. This did not include the Jewish population (many of whose members would have come from Eastern Europe, but were counted separately), which went from .3 to 8.2 percent of the population.[10] The business community, which was dominated by people involved in the real-estate and related industries, sought, and received, civic funding for campaigns to attract immigrants to Winnipeg and the west.[11] These same businesses and political leaders showed little interest in ensuring there was an adequate supply of decent, affordable housing for the immigrants they were so busy using public money to recruit since, in their minds, the rights of property took priority over the rights of people. And there were no profits to be made from building housing for low-income people.

*　*　*

The first regular issue of the *Manitoba Free Press*, published in November 1872, portrayed the city as a place where "the sober and industrious may, with the savings of a month or so, secure the purchase of a lot by a first payment, and in a few months have a home of his own; when, having become, for the first time, perhaps, an owner of the soil, he is a different person, and realizing that he can as easily gather rent from another as save his own, he kindles with the brilliant prospect of the future, and bends all his energies to save and accumulate." The ownership of property, in other words, was nothing less than transformative.[12] And in the mind of some, property rights were nothing less than divinely sanctioned. When workers at L.R. Barrett's Vulcan Iron Works sought to unionize, Barrett maintained, "God gave me this plant, and by God, I'll run it the way I want to!"[13]

The business community, which regularly boasted that Winnipeg would soon be the "Bull's Eye of Canada" or the "Chicago of Canada," led the drive to have the muddy, poorly populated settlement around Portage and Main incorporated as a city in 1873. At the time of incorporation, four people owned about a quarter of the taxable land in the city, while the Hudson's Bay Reserve, bounded by Notre Dame on the North, Colony Creek (now Colony Street)

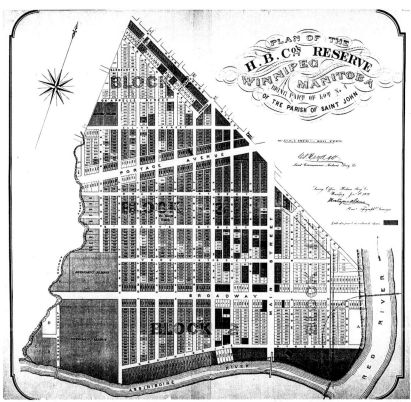

The Hudson's Bay Reserve was 465 acres of prime real estate in downtown Winnipeg, retained by the company when its lands were transferred to Canada in 1869. Library and Archives Canada. "The Canadian West: Plan of the Hudson's Bay Company's reserve in Winnipeg, Manitoba 1887, by C.V. Brydges." http://data2.collectionscanada.gc.ca/e/e001/e000007937.jpg.

on the west and the Assiniboine and Red Rivers on the South and East, accounted for another third of the land.[14] The Hudson's Bay Reserve was 465 acres in size and was land that the Hudson's Bay Company had been allowed to continue to own at the Red River Colony. The *Free Press* accused the company of slowing the city's growth by "holding their property at very high prices, and almost impossible terms."[15]

Winnipeg's early years were ones of ramshackle expansion. According to George Monro Grant, in 1872 Winnipeg "consisted of a few rickety-looking shanties that looked as if they had been dropped promiscuously on the verge of a boundless prairie."[16] Since the local construction workers had little or no training, employers were, according to another report, "not apt to criticize too closely the finish of a joint or the smoothness of a surface of paint."[17] By 1874 journalist George B. Elliott reported there were 903 buildings in Winnipeg, including 408 "dwelling houses," twenty-three boarding houses, and seventeen hotels. 421 buildings were simply classified as "miscellaneous." This category included stores, the upper stories of which, Elliott wrote, "were generally occupied as dwellings."[18] Real-estate speculation was rife: Alfred W. Burrows, who had left his position as the federal government's land agent to enter the real-estate field, had recently sold 400 city lots, while another local man's $50 investment in land was now worth $3,000.[19] The first type of multi-household dwelling in Winnipeg was the boarding house, which was generally a single-family home that had been subdivided. Rents were high, but board could be "obtained from $4 to $10 a week; $6 is the average for tolerably good board."[20] The development of apartment buildings awaited investors, architects, contractors, skilled labour, infrastructure, access to building materials, and demand.[21] The Cauchon Block at York Avenue and Main Street, constructed in 1884, was the city's first major apartment building. Built at a cost of $65,000, it was marketed as luxury housing and had steam heat, gas lighting, and a restaurant.[22]

THE COMING OF THE RAILWAY

In the early 1880s Canadian Pacific Railway, for a variety of sound reasons, considered placing its mainline cross of the Red River at the town of Selkirk. In response, Winnipeg city officials mounted a panicked, ongoing, effective, and very costly lobbying campaign. To get the CPR to run the line through Winnipeg, the City agreed to build a $300,000 rail bridge over the Red, grant the railway land for its marshalling yards, exempt the land from taxation forever, and provide the company with a grant of $200,000. These gifts were costly: the $200,000 grant alone cost the city an extra $17,000 over the next two decades, the tax holiday was only ended in the 1980s, and the rail yards remain an enduring insult to the city's geography. In coming years other railways would be lured to the city. And while they provided real economic benefit, no effort was made to control or direct their location. Instead, rail lines

The Canadian Pacific Rail yards divided the city in two: one either lived on the right side or the wrong side of the tracks. Archives of Manitoba, Archives of Manitoba photo collection, Winnipeg - Views 120. Winnipeg from the North West, ca. 1910, P1260.

and rail yards chopped the city up into a series of disconnected neighbourhoods, with industrial and residential neighbourhoods lumped cheek by jowl.[23] The railway gave physical expression to the ideological class lines that divided the city: one either lived on the right side or the wrong side of the tracks.

The coming of the railway sparked a sixteen-month real-estate boom that saw Winnipeg transformed, briefly, into "a community where almost everybody was dreaming rainbow-tinted dreams of sudden wealth from land gambling."[24] The population doubled, and, according to one observer,

> The city could not provide habitations fast enough to shelter the newcomers, but they accommodated themselves as best they could, sleeping in tents and hastily constructed shacks. There were hundreds of real estate offices in those days; plots of land were sold out in all parts of the country and land sold at fabulous prices. Men grew rich in a day and squandered their fortunes the next by extravagant living and rash speculation.[25]

Up until 1905, newly arrived immigrants were housed in a series of cramped, poorly insulated, and unsanitary sheds that were run by the federal government on a highly disciplined basis. The overflow was housed in tents, barracks, and warehouses. City council rejected federal requests for help in housing newcomers,

Up until 1905, newly arrived immigrants to Winnipeg were housed in a series of cramped, poorly insulated, and unsanitary sheds. Archives of Manitoba photo collection, Elswood Bole 6. Winnipeg Immigration Shed, ca. 1888, P1131, N13803.

responding that such would "diminish the energy or self-reliance of the new settlers." In 1882, the City finally built its own immigration shed, but unlike the federal government, it charged immigrants rent, and made an overall profit of $2,000.[26] In 1883, twenty-five Jewish refugee families were living in extreme poverty in the immigrant sheds. According to the *Winnipeg Daily Sun,* "the shed has been divided into little rooms about 10 x 12, like so many pens in a pig-stye." Many were there because illness made it impossible for them to work, while the cramped conditions meant that "all of the laws of health are most flagrantly violated."[27] At one point, the federal government was obliged to send 1,500 tents to house the city's surplus population.[28]

As early as 1886, there was a shantytown between Logan and the CPR tracks and another one on the Hudson's Bay Reserve.[29] When the land boom commenced, the Hudson's Bay Company began lobbying the city to have shanties removed from the Reserve, complaining that many of them were inhabited by "objectionable characters."[30] One of the defenders of the shanty dwellers pointed out that they were often poor and could not afford to move their shanties, let alone make enough to live. He also pointed out that far from being squatters, the shanty dwellers paid the HBC two dollars a month.[31] And, as the city engineer reported, there was no place to which the shanties, which were home to a variety of social outcasts, including, according to one listing, "C.P.R. laborers, Russian Jews, Icelanders, etc.," could be moved.[32] Other news reports make it clear that many of the shanty dwellers were Métis.[33] As it was cleared of shanties, the Hudson's Bay Company sold off its lots in the reserve, making an estimated $2 million. In the process, the reserve became the city's first exclusive neighbourhood: historian Randy Rostecki identified that twelve of the twenty-three "pretentious dwellings" in Winnipeg in 1886 were in the reserve.[34]

THE RIGHT TO VOTE: "PROPERTY IS THE WHOLE BASIS OF MUNICIPAL VOTING"

The council that spent a fortune to get the CPR to route its mainline through Winnipeg while refusing to provide support to immigrants was dominated by property owners. From the outset, the right to vote was restricted to people who owned or leased property of considerable value. Some members of the business community feared that the existing restrictions on the right to vote did not provide sufficient protection against democracy. In the wake of a collapse in property values in 1882 (the real-estate boom having been brought to earth by a flood of Biblical proportions), the city's leading property owners called for the creation of a three-person municipal executive and a dramatic reduction in the powers of the council. Under this scheme, the executive would be chosen by a truly property-based electorate: no one would be allowed to vote who did not own more than $500 worth of property, while property owners were to be given an increased number of votes depending on how much property they owned. Those who owned more than $100,000 worth of property would have six votes.[35] While the property owners failed to convince the legislature to adopt this draconian proposal, the existing restrictions meant that the business community was able to successfully dominate council.[36] So effective were these restrictions on the vote that up until 1914, only three candidates affiliated with labour parties were elected to the council.[37]

NORTH END/SOUTH END: "POOR AND FILTHY"/"NO CHEAP HOUSES"

The North End was dominated by the giant CPR yards, repair shops, station, and powerhouse, plus the various industries that located their operations along the edge of the CPR complex, including

Vulcan Iron Works, which would serve as one of the flashpoints for the 1919 General Strike. The CPR and these industries employed thousands of people who lived both north and south of the yards, starting each day awash in the soot and grime that drifted from the industrial giant that lay coiled in the heart of their neighbourhoods.

The North End was physically cut off from the rest of the city, reachable for many years by only an underpass at Main Street. It was the home to the city's Eastern European community. There were many members of the city's Anglo-Canadian elite who viewed the newcomers with undisguised disdain. An editorial in the *Winnipeg Telegram* of 1899 captures the flavour of the hostility towards Ukrainian immigrants. "Not only," the paper thundered, were the Ukrainians "poor and filthy, but their moral character is disgraceful." These were people who held "robbery and murder in very light estimation" and were "inveterate and unscrupulous perjurers."[38] The hostility expressed towards Eastern Europeans in the early twentieth century would be re-directed towards Indigenous people in the 1960s.

These communities were not only geographically segregated, but their residents also found themselves restricted to lower-paying industrial work. Jews made up 70 percent of the city's fur workers, 70 percent of its peddlers, and a third of its tailors.[39] The Ukrainian communities were located short distances from rail yards and the industries that operated on their fringes.[40] Although Winnipeg was not short of land, North End property developers, benefiting from the lack of any zoning laws, divided their holdings into lots that were rarely more than thirty-three feet wide and often as narrow as twenty-five feet, with houses being slapped up to the edge of the property lines. By 1906, 42 percent of the city's population was squeezed onto a third of its land.[41]

* * *

In the early twentieth century, the city's wealthier residents began to relocate, abandoning Point Douglas, once the home of the city's poshest residents, for points south. Their first stop was the former Hudson's Bay Reserve, where they built large mansions and luxury apartment blocks. For example, future Manitoba

Premier Duff Roblin grew up in a house on Smith Street in the early 1920s. Roblin's father was a lawyer and his grandfather was the former premier.[42] Hugh John Macdonald's home on Carlton, now the Dalnavert Museum, is one of the remaining examples of these mansions. Early in the century, many of these large homes were already being transformed into rooming houses. As real-estate developer C.H. Enderton warned, "The mansions of the town of 30,000 become the strictly private boarding houses of the city of 60,000 and the third-rate boarding houses of the city of 150,000."[43] By 1908 buildings in the Hudson's Bay Reserve that were once described as mansions were being termed "tenements." The *Tribune* reported, "The men who own the tenements are not paupers, but as a rule they are foreigners who have purchased dilapidated structures from former Canadian owners with a view to housing the foreign element. A low rental is exacted from the heads of the families, but on the whole the grand total is an enormous sum."[44] While contemporary readers tend to think of tenements as large apartment buildings filled with small suites, in early twentieth-century Winnipeg, the term was used to describe a wide variety of buildings from low-rise row housing—rarely more than two or three storeys in height—to residential homes that had been turned into rooming houses.[45]

When the elite left the Hudson's Bay Reserve, they kept moving west and south, some settling in Armstrong's Point, a peninsula created by a loop in the Assiniboine River. There were no bridges, no streetcars, and little traffic through this secluded community. To underscore the area's exclusivity, the streets in and out of the Point did not align with the neighbouring streets and were equipped with wrought-iron gates. The gates are gone, but the concept lingers on in the street names: East Gate, Middle Gate, and West Gate.[46] Others crossed the Assiniboine, building sumptuous piles along Wellington Crescent, the prestige street in Enderton's new development of Crescentwood. In this area, Enderton promised in 1902, "there will be no terraces, no cheap houses, no one building on the next lot out in front the line you had chosen for your building line."[47] And, obviously, no poor people. When they bought land from Enderton, purchasers had to agree to set their homes back from the street by a certain distance, not to take in boarders, and not to build homes that were worth less than $6,000.[48] In short, there was to be privately imposed planning in the South End to protect the neighbourhoods and investments of the rich but nothing to protect residents of the North End from the predations of speculators and landlords.

Due to the civic elite's lack of interest in planning and public services, Winnipeg frequently had one of the highest death rates in the country.[49] In 1890, the sewer and waterworks system for the city only reached to about 10 percent of the population. As late as 1902, only a third of the city's housing had a sewer connection. To no one's surprise, access was highest in South and West Winnipeg, and lowest in the North End.[50] Typhoid, sometimes referred to as "Red River fever," was linked to the reliance on outdoor toilets in many parts of the city. In 1904 and 1905 typhoid epidemics killed 133 people each year. In response, the City adopted a bylaw requiring sewage connections for all new buildings within the older part of the city. The bylaw was flouted, and fines were minimal, often as low as three dollars.[51]

THE NATIONAL AND INTERNATIONAL SCENE: "MUNICIPAL HOUSING IS POPULAR"

The housing problems that Winnipeg faced in the early twentieth century were hardly unique to the city. They were among the hallmarks of the rapid and expanding waves of urbanization and industrialization that had swept out from Europe since the beginning of the nineteenth century. The housing conditions faced by low-income Winnipeggers at the dawn of the twentieth century, and the responses to those conditions, are best understood in a national and international setting. For example, Friedrich Engels documented the horrors of the urban slum in his 1845 masterpiece of social investigation, *The Condition of the Working Class in England*. Engels's picture of the St. Giles neighbourhood is unforgettable.

> The houses are occupied from cellar to garret, filthy within and without, and their appearance is such that no human being could possibly wish to live in them. But all this is nothing in comparison with the dwellings in the narrow courts and alleys between the streets, entered by covered

passages between the houses, in which the filth and tottering ruin surpass all description. Scarcely a whole window-
pane can be found, the walls are crumbling, door-posts
and window-frames loose and broken, doors of old boards
nailed together, or altogether wanting in this thieves'
quarter, where no doors are needed, there being nothing
to steal.[52]

The novelist Charles Dickens's work was full of similar, if more
sentimentalized accounts of the lives of the poor, as they shut-
tled from orphanage to workhouse to debtors' prison to exile in
Australia.[53]

In the mid-nineteenth century, British philanthropists established corporations intended to provide low-cost housing while
paying investors a return of no more than 5 percent. Among the
first of these was the Metropolitan Association for Improving the
Dwellings of the Industrious Classes, founded in 1841. Thirty years
later nearly thirty such associations were operating in London
alone. While they increased the housing supply, they never operated on a scale that could meet the tremendous need for decent
housing. And these housing companies were plagued by the eco-
nomics of low-cost housing. If they provided adequate housing at
a cost that was affordable to the truly needy, they would not earn
enough to be able to pay the shareholders their 5 percent dividend.
If they charged enough to allow them to pay dividends, the housing
remained out of the reach of the poor, which is what happened.[54]

Improvement in affordable housing in Great Britain required
state investment. Initially, municipal governments led the way.
In 1847, Liverpool's campaigning medical officer William Henry
Duncan ordered the closing of 5,000 cellar dwellings.[55] Liverpool
city council drew up plans for low-cost housing, but when no
private investor stepped forward to actually build and run such
a project, the council went ahead and constructed the first municipally built public housing in Britain.[56] The 1890 *Housing of
the Working Classes Act* marked the beginning of what came to be
known as council housing. By 1914 the London County Council had
constructed over 10,000 units of council housing.[57]

Winnipeg newspaper readers were aware of these public-housing initiatives. For example, in the early twentieth century, the

Winnipeg press reported on municipal housing projects in Leeds, the work of the Glasgow Housing Commission, a "Garden City" development in Hertfordshire, and municipal housing in London.[58] A *Free Press* article from 1906 noted that in England "municipal housing is popular because there is something to show for the money, and it deals with frightful evils."[59] British journalists passing through Winnipeg gave reports on the prospect of public housing in the United Kingdom. In a 1903 interview with the *Tribune*, Harold Rylett, a Unitarian Church minister and radical journalist, overconfidently predicted that the Labour Party would soon be in a position to have the "housing question" dealt with.[60]

* * *

The forces that were transforming Winnipeg in the late nineteenth century were active across the country. From the mid-1890s to the start of the First World War, to use the title of a landmark history of this period, Canada was a nation transformed. Immigration, industrialization, export trade, and urbanization interacted in ways that remade the country. From 1891 to 1921, Toronto and Montreal, the country's two largest cities, doubled in size, while Winnipeg and Vancouver, the third and fourth-largest cities, experienced fivefold increases in population. Urban growth was unplanned and generated social inequality. Growing cities could point to their magnificent mansions, majestic legislatures and courthouses, dazzling department stores, cathedral-like train stations, and imposing office buildings.[61] But by the end of the nineteenth century, it was also apparent that there was a persistent housing problem in Canada's major cities. In 1901 the gap between the country's total housing stock and the number of households was 84,000.[62] Fourteen years later, a federal inquiry concluded that there had been a 50 percent rise in the cost of living in the first thirteen years of the century and a 60 to 70 percent rise in rents.[63] One could find slums in the downtown areas and shantytowns on the fringes of many of the country's cities.[64]

Instead of blaming an economic system that could not provide people with affordable housing, authorities at all levels held the poor, particularly if they were from Eastern Europe, to blame for their conditions. It was said that the newcomers were ignorant of hygiene, their diets were bad, their tolerance for poor conditions lamentable, and their lifestyles spendthrift.[65] Early "reform" methods often involved nothing more than knocking down slums without thought to where evicted tenants would live. This could lead to conflict between officials and the people who found their housing condemned and even demolished. Families were threatened with prosecution if they refused to move.[66]

Much of the work that was done to bring the emerging urban housing problem to public attention was done by people often referred to as middle-class reformers. Montreal businessperson Herbert Ames's *The City Below the Hill* pointed to conditions in Montreal's west end; child-welfare advocate J.J. Kelso's journalism called for the abolition of Toronto's slums; meanwhile, Winnipeg Methodist minister J.S. Woodsworth focused on the living condition of Canada's Eastern European immigrants.[67] A network of reformers began to identify the social causes of poverty and warn of the risks of not addressing inequality, including increased class conflict and crime, and the spread of contagious diseases. J.S. Schoales, the Chief of the Division of Housing and Industrial Hygiene for Toronto, wrote: "The slum is the mother of disease. There is in fact more pity for the slum child who lives than the slum child who dies. When a baby dies, the nation loses a prospective citizen, but in every slum child who lives the nation has a probable consumptive and a possible criminal."[68] Adherents of the social gospel movement in the Protestant churches, which was animated by a sense of spiritual mission to address the needs of the poor in this world, played a leading role in the reform movement.[69] They sought to convert Catholic immigrants to Protestantism, and few were able to shake off a determination to turn each immigrant into an Anglo-Canadian, if only for their own good. But they also called for basic public-health reform: sewers, water treatment, healthy milk supplies, adequate housing, and economic relief. This was a type of intervention that was new to Canada, and reformers often framed their arguments in terms that would appeal to the economic elite. A better housed and fed working class was a less militant working class, while a healthier working class presented less of a public-health risk to the entire city. They were more successful on the latter point than the former: public-health laws, improvements in drains, sewers, and waste collection came at a faster pace than efforts to reduce the cost or increase the quality of housing.[70] The movement was particularly vibrant in Winnipeg, where it brought together supporters of women's suffrage, electoral reform (often referred to as "direct democracy"), prohibition, and town planning.[71]

Following the British model, some Canadian housing reformers pinned their hopes on "limited dividend" housing companies that were intended to mix philanthropy with self-interest. Government would guarantee most of a housing developer's mortgage on the understanding that the housing would be made available at low rents and the developer would accept a limit on their annual return or dividend (usually between 5 and 6 percent). Labour unions were suspicious of limited dividend projects, fearing that they would not assist those in the greatest need. The fact that they were often proposed by interests that were generally hostile to labour only aggravated these suspicions.[72] Few provinces adopted legislation that would allow for limited dividend housing, and it was only in Toronto that it was attempted in a significant way. The Toronto Housing Company, an initiative spearheaded by Toronto industrialist Frank Beer, was intended to be a co-partnership in which tenants and private investors purchased shares. The company built over 240 units of housing, but never managed to bring rents down to a level that would make the housing affordable to the truly poor.[73]

The reformers' impact may have been limited, but the senior levels of government were missing in action when it came to housing. Before the total collapse of the Canadian residential construction industry in the 1930s, federal government housing initiatives were limited to modest efforts intended to prop up the construction industry in periods of economic recession. Provinces had constitutional responsibility for housing, but provincial assemblies were dominated by members from rural ridings who had little interest in housing. As a result, for decades neither the federal government—which had the taxing power to make an impact on housing—nor provincial governments—which had the legal authority to act—took any meaningful action to address the country's growing shortage of decent affordable housing.

It was far harder for municipal governments to ignore the housing crisis: their residents lived in slums or next to slums, and their residents were threatened by the public health hazards that arose when people lived in crowded unhygienic conditions. They were the governments to which local people turned for relief when they were evicted. But city councils were usually dominated by real-estate interests who sought to protect land prices, housing prices, and profits. They viewed measures that lowered rents or the prices of housing as little less than perverse.

DRAWING THE BATTLE LINES

The railways not only brought industrialism to Winnipeg, they also brought industrial workers and trade unions. As early as 1881, local typographers and carpenters had formed unions; soon after, they were followed by skilled trades workers, particularly railway and metal trades workers.[74] While these unions fought for better wages, hours, and working conditions, they also sought social improvements, including the provision of low-cost housing. After several false steps, a Winnipeg labour council was established in 1894. The council brought together most of the unions active in the city. In the coming years, it would play a leading role in coordinating the labour movement's political action. 1894 also saw the founding of one of the period's most successful labour newspapers. Published weekly, *The People's Voice*, soon shortened to *The Voice*, was filled with lively, literate, and often outraged, reportage and commentary on local and international labour and socialist issues.

Not surprisingly unionists were quick to realize that they needed to take political action. In 1894, they succeeded in electing Charles Hislop, a rail worker, to city council.[75] Hislop only served a single term, but a short-lived labour party was established the following year. Its initial focus was on education and propaganda, not electoral politics. But in 1900, it succeeded in electing to parliament Arthur Puttee, a printer and the editor of *The Voice*. Puttee and his supporters (who have been dubbed "labourists" by historians) proposed a series of moderate reforms such as improvements in public health and labour laws and modelled themselves after the British Labour Party.[76]

As the twentieth century dawned, the battle lines for a long struggle over public housing were shaping up. The city was governed by a class that viewed the ownership of property as the defining element of citizenship. The real-estate industry was failing to produce a sufficient supply of affordable housing. This left the lowest-income Winnipeggers, who were often disdained and denigrated by the elite due to their poverty and ethnicity, with no choice but to rent housing that was crowded and unhealthy. Furthermore, industrialization was summoning into existence political and social movements that would challenge the elite in the workplace and at the ballot box. When these actors confronted one another at the bargaining table, the struggle was over wages and working conditions. But when their representatives stared at each other across the floor at Winnipeg city hall, no issue more clearly defined their difference than housing.

NOTES

1. One who pays rent, "Rents in Winnipeg," *Manitoba Free Press*, November 30, 1903.
2. Alan F.J. Artibise, *Winnipeg: A Social History of Urban Growth, 1874–1914*, Montreal: McGill-Queen's, 1975, 226–240.
3. Alan F.J. Artibise, *Winnipeg: A Social History of Urban Growth, 1874–1914*, Montreal: McGill-Queen's, 1975, 106. It was not until 2013 that the Canadian Supreme Court ruled that the government had failed to honour its commitment to the Métis.
4. Evelyn Peters, Matthew Stock and Adrian Werner, *Rooster Town: The History of an Urban Métis Community, 1901–1961*, Winnipeg: University of Manitoba Press, 2018.
5. Wayne Daugherty, *Treaty Research Report: Treaty One and Treaty Two*, Ottawa: Treaties and Historical Research Centre, Research Branch, Corporate Policy, Department of Indian and Northern Affairs, Canada, 1981.
6. Alan F.J. Artibise, "Patterns of Population Growth and Ethnic Relationships in Winnipeg, 1874–1974," *Histoire sociale/Social History*, Vol. IX, No. 18, November 1976, 299.
7. "Winnipeg—Modern wonder of the world," *Winnipeg Tribune*, December 17, 1910.
8. Alan F.J. Artibise, *Winnipeg: A Social History of Urban Growth, 1874–1914*, Montreal: McGill-Queen's, 1975, 132.
9. Alan F.J. Artibise, *Winnipeg: A Social History of Urban Growth, 1874–1914*, Montreal: McGill-Queen's, 1975, 137.
10. Alan F.J. Artibise, *Winnipeg: A Social History of Urban Growth, 1874–1914*, Montreal: McGill-Queen's, 1975, 142.
11. Alan F.J. Artibise, *Winnipeg: A Social History of Urban Growth, 1874–1914*, Montreal: McGill-Queen's, 1975, 102–103; Don Nerbas, "Wealth and privilege: An

analysis of Winnipeg's early business elite," *Manitoba History*, 47 (Spring/Summer 2004): 42-64.

12. "Winnipeg: Size; growth, and development of the Metropolis of Manitoba and the Northwest," *Manitoba Free Press*, November 30, 1872.

13. Manitoba Historical Society, Vulcan Iron Works, <mhs.mb.ca/docs/features/timelinks/reference/db0131.shtml>, accessed June 4, 2021.

14. Ruben Bellan, *Winnipeg First Century: An Economic History*, Winnipeg: Queenston House Publishing, 1978, 13.

15. "Winnipeg: Size; growth, and development of the Metropolis of Manitoba and the Northwest," *Manitoba Free Press*, November 30, 1872.

16. George Monro Grant, "The Northwest: Manitoba," in George Munro Grant (ed.), *Our Picturesque Northern Neighbour: Historical and Descriptive Sketches of the Scenery and Life in and around Toronto, along the Canadian Shore of Lake Huron, in the Northwest Territories, and in British Columbia*, Chicago: Alexander Belford & Company, 1899, 208.

17. "Winnipeg: Size; growth, and development of the Metropolis of Manitoba and the Northwest," *Manitoba Free Press*, November 30, 1872.

18. George B. Elliott, *Winnipeg as it is in 1874, and as it was in 1860*, Ottawa: Ottawa Free Press Office, 1876, 10.

19. George B. Elliott, *Winnipeg as it is in 1874, and as it was in 1860*, Ottawa: Ottawa Free Press Office, 1876, 16.

20. George B. Elliott, *Winnipeg as it is in 1874, and as it was in 1860*, Ottawa: Ottawa Free Press Office, 1876, 24.

21. Dimitrios Styliaras, Arnold Koerte and William Hurst, *A Study of Apartment Housing in Winnipeg and Recommendations for Future Apartment Building in the Prairie Region*, Planning Research Centre at the Faculty of Architecture, University of Manitoba, 1967, 19-20.

22. Fred C. Lucas, *An Historical Souvenir Diary of the City of Winnipeg, Canada*, Winnipeg: Cartwright and Lucas, 1923, 194.

23. Alan F.J. Artibise, *Winnipeg: A Social History of Urban Growth, 1874-1914*, Montreal: McGill-Queen's, 1975, 61-76; Ruben Bellan, "Rails across the Red—Selkirk or Winnipeg," Manitoba Historical Society Transactions, Series 3, 1961-62 Season.

24. W.J. Healy, *Winnipeg's Early Days: A Short Historical Sketch*, Winnipeg: Stovel Company, 1927, 23.

25. William H. Carre, *Art work on Winnipeg, Manitoba, Canada*, W.H. Carre and Company, 1900, 19.

26. Alan F.J. Artibise, *Winnipeg: A Social History of Urban Growth, 1874-1914*, Montreal: McGill-Queen's, 1975, 178-181. The quote is from Winnipeg City Council Minutes, May 23, 1877, quoted in Alan F.J. Artibise, *Winnipeg: A Social History of Urban Growth, 1874-1914*, Montreal: McGill-Queen's, 1975, 180.

27. "Russian refugees," *Winnipeg Daily Sun*, January 8, 1883.

28. Ruben Bellan, *Winnipeg First Century: An Economic History*, Winnipeg: Queenston House Publishing, 1978, 23, 29.

29. Randolph Richard Rostecki, "The Growth of Winnipeg: 1870-1886," Master of Arts thesis, University of Manitoba, 1980, 105-106.

30. "The shanty question," *Winnipeg Daily Sun*, March 9, 1884; "He won't resign," *Winnipeg Daily Sun*, July 26, 1884; "Mr. Brydges complains," *Winnipeg Daily Sun*, June 10, 1884.

31. "Removing the shanties," *Winnipeg Daily Sun*, July 29, 1884.

32. "The shanty nuisance," *Winnipeg Daily Sun*, October 11, 1884; "The building record," *Winnipeg Daily Sun*, October 15, 1883.

33. "The shanty question," *Winnipeg Daily Sun*, March 9, 1884; "A brutal fellow," *Winnipeg Daily Sun*, December 2, 1884.

34. Randolph Richard Rostecki, "The Growth of Winnipeg: 1870–1886," Master of Arts thesis, University of Manitoba, 1980, 105–106.

35. Alan F.J. Artibise, *Winnipeg: A Social History of Urban Growth, 1874–1914*, Montreal: McGill-Queen's, 1975, 46–52.

36. Alan F.J. Artibise, *Winnipeg: A Social History of Urban Growth, 1874–1914*, Montreal: McGill-Queen's, 1975, 46–52.

37. Alan F.J. Artibise, *Winnipeg: A Social History of Urban Growth, 1874–1914*, Montreal: McGill-Queen's, 1975, 27.

38. *Winnipeg Telegram*, March 7, 1899, quoted in Peter Melnycky, "A Political History of the Ukrainian Community in Manitoba, 1899–1922," Master of Arts thesis, University of Manitoba, 1979, 50.

39. Gerald Tulchinsky, *Taking Root: The Origins of the Canadian Jewish Community*, Toronto: Lester Publishing Limited, 1992, 167.

40. Orest T. Martynowych, *Ukrainians in Canada: The Formative Period, 1891–1924*, Edmonton: Canadian Institute of Ukrainian Studies Press, University of Alberta, 1991, 138.

41. Alan F.J. Artibise, *Winnipeg: A Social History of Urban Growth, 1874–1914*, Montreal: McGill-Queen's, 1975, 158–162.

42. Duff Roblin, *Speaking for Myself: Politics and Other Pursuits*, Winnipeg: Great Plains Publications, 1999, 26.

43. "Crescentwood," *Manitoba Free Press*, September 13, 1902.

44. M. "Crowded districts," *Winnipeg Tribune*, August 29, 1908.

45. Joan Selby, "Urban Rental Housing in Canada 1900–1985: A Critical Review of Problems and the Response of Government," Master's thesis, University of British Columbia, 1985, 24–25.

46. Randy R. Rostecki, *Armstrong's Point: A History*, Winnipeg, Winnipeg Heritage Corporation, 2009, 96–98.

47. "Crescentwood," *Manitoba Free Press*, September 13, 1902.

48. Randy R. Rostecki, *Crescentwood: A History*, Winnipeg: Crescentwood Home Owners Association, 1993, 21–28; Rosemary Malaher, Manitoba Historical Society, Crescentwood, Winnipeg's Best Residential District, <mhs.mb.ca/docs/mb_history/24/crescentwoodtour.shtml>, accessed May 28, 2021; George Siamandas, "Charles Enderton and the great Crescentwood land auction, <timemachine.siamandas.com/PAGES/winnipeg_stories/CRESCENTWOOD.htm>, accessed May 28, 2021.

49. Alan F.J. Artibise, *Winnipeg: A Social History of Urban Growth, 1874–1914*, Montreal: McGill-Queen's, 1975, 223.

50. Alan F.J. Artibise, *Winnipeg: A Social History of Urban Growth, 1874–1914*, Montreal: McGill-Queen's, 1975, 226–227.

51. Alan F.J. Artibise, *Winnipeg: A Social History of Urban Growth, 1874–1914*, Montreal: McGill-Queen's, 1975, 226–227, 234.

52. Friedrich Engels, *The Condition of the Working Class in England*, edited with an introduction and notes by David McLellan, Oxford: Oxford University Press, 1993, 40.

53. Anthony S. Whol, *The Eternal Slum: Housing and Social Policy in Victorian London*, New Brunswick, NJ: Transaction Publishers, 1977, 37.

54. 54. Anthony S. Whol, *The Eternal Slum: Housing and Social Policy in Victorian London*, New Brunswick, NJ: Transaction Publishers, 1977, 144-164; John Boughton, *Municipal Dreams: The Rise and Fall of Council Housing*, London: Verso Books, 2018, 25-26.

55. S.P.W. Chave, "Duncan of Liverpool—and some lessons for today," *Community Medicine*, 6 (1984): 61-71.

56. John Boughton, *Municipal Dreams: The Rise and Fall of Council Housing*, London: Verso Books, 2018, 13.

57. John Boughton, *Municipal Dreams: The Rise and Fall of Council Housing*, London: Verso Books, 2018.

58. "Municipal ownership," *Winnipeg Daily Tribune*, July 16, 1902; Ben Nevis, "Scottish letter," *Manitoba Free Press*, August 20, 1904; "Our London letter," *Manitoba Free Press*, August 24, 1907; "Municipal ownership," *Winnipeg Tribune*, January 30, 1906.

59. "Municipal trading," *Winnipeg Free Press*, October 20, 1906.

60. "Preference in the old land," *Winnipeg Tribune*, September 8, 1903.

61. Robert Craig Brown and Ramsay Cook, *Canada, 1896-1921: A Nation Transformed*, Toronto: McClelland and Stewart Limited, 1974, chapters 4 through 6.

62. Joan Selby, "Urban Rental Housing in Canada 1900-1985: A Critical Review of Problems and the Response of Government," Master's thesis, University of British Columbia, 1985, 31.

63. "Prices and cost of living in Canada," *Monthly Review of the Bureau of Labour Statistics*, 2, 4 (April 1916), 53.

64. Joan Selby, "Urban Rental Housing in Canada 1900-1985: A Critical Review of Problems and the Response of Government," Master's thesis, University of British Columbia, 1985, 21.

65. Charles Hastings, *Report of the Medical Officer Dealing with the Recent Investigations of Slum Conditions in Toronto*, Toronto: Department of Health, 1911, 8, quoted in John C. Bacher, "Keeping to the Private Market: The Evolution of Canadian Housing Policy, 1900-1949," Doctoral thesis, McMaster University, 1985, 46-50. By the end of 1915, 1,007 houses in Toronto had been closed. By the following year, 500 of these homes had been destroyed, 200 remained closed, and 300 were "improved."

66. John C. Bacher, "Keeping to the Private Market: The Evolution of Canadian Housing Policy, 1900-1949," Doctoral thesis, McMaster University, 1985, 46-47, 50.

67. H.B. Ames, *The City Below the Hill: A Sociological Study of a Portion of the City of Montreal, Canada*, Toronto: University of Toronto Press, 1972; J.J. Kelso, "Can slums be abolished or must we continue to pay the penalty?" in Paul Rutherford (ed.), *Saving the Canadian City: The First Phase 1880-1920, an Anthology of Early Articles on Urban Reform*, Toronto: University of Toronto Press, 1974; J.S. Woodsworth, *My Neighbour: A study of city conditions*, Toronto: Missionary Society of the Methodist Church, 1911.

68. J.S. Schoales, "Importance of housing and lodging-house inspection," *Public Health Journal*, 7, 11, (1916): 472.

69. Sean Purdy, "Industrial efficiency, social order and moral purity: Housing

reform thought in English Canada, 1900–1950," *Urban History Review/Revue d'histoire urbaine*, 25, 2 (1997): 31.

70. Joan Selby, "Urban Rental Housing in Canada 1900–1985: A Critical Review of Problems and the Response of Government," Master's thesis, University of British Columbia, 1985, 35–36.

71. For an overview, see: Lionel Orlikow, "A survey of the reform movement in Manitoba, 1910 to 1929," Master of Arts thesis, University of Manitoba, 1955.

72. John C. Bacher, "Keeping to the Private Market: The Evolution of Canadian Housing Policy, 1900–1949," Doctoral thesis, McMaster University, 1985, 56–57.

73. Lorna Hurl, "The Toronto Housing Company, 1912–1923: The Pitfalls of Painless Philanthropy," *Canadian Historical Review*, XLV (March 1984): 28–53; Shirley Spragge, "A confluence of interests: Housing reform in Toronto, 1900–1920," in Alan F.J. Artibise and Gilbert A. Stelter (eds.), *The Usable Urban Past: Planning and Politics in the Modern Canadian City*, Toronto: Macmillan of Canada, 1979, 247–267; Catherine Mary Ulmer, "Introducing Canada to urban planning? Henry Vivian's Canadian Planning Tour, 1910," *Urban History Review/Revue d'histoire urbaine*, XLVI (Spring 2018): 51; Parliamentary Committee on Housing, "Minutes of Proceedings and Evidence of Special Committee on Housing," Ottawa: King's Printer 1935, quoted in John C. Bacher, "Keeping to the Private Market: The Evolution of Canadian Housing Policy, 1900–1949," Doctoral thesis, McMaster University, 1985, 49.

74. Bryan Dewalt, "Arthur W. Puttee: Labourism and Working-Class Politics in Winnipeg, 1894–1914," Master of Arts thesis, University of Manitoba, 1985, 29 and 68; Gerry E. Berkowski, "A Tradition in Jeopardy: Building Trades Workers' Responses to Industrial Capitalism in Winnipeg, 1880–1914," Master of Arts thesis, University of Manitoba, 1986, 86.

75. Ernie Chisick, "The Development of Winnipeg's Socialist Movement, 1900 to 1915," Master of Arts thesis, University of Manitoba, 1972, 20.

76. A. Ross McCormack, *Reformers, Rebels, and Revolutionaries: The Western Canadian Radical Movement 1899–1919*, Toronto: University of Toronto Press, 1977, 77–97.

Chapter 2

THE FIRST CALLS
FOR PUBLIC HOUSING:
1900–1915

In December 1914, E.W.J. Hague, a seventeen-year veteran of Winnipeg's health department, presented a lantern slide-show to the People's Forum, a weekly lecture series held at the corner of Jarvis and Main Street by the Methodist Church's All People's Mission. His topic for that evening was the "story of Winnipeg's struggle for better housing over the last quarter of a century."[1] Hague had been hired as one of the city's first housing inspectors in 1897 and became chief inspector in 1922.[2] His slides on that night in 1914 included images of houses that grew by an accretion of lean-tos and sheds until they came to house upwards of twenty families. In one case, five separate "dwellings" had been established on a sixty-six-foot-wide lot. The slides depicted "ventilation shafts virtually sealed up both at top and bottom, shafts so narrow that no sunlight could penetrate to the windows at the bottom, and areas the usefulness of which could be offset at any time by the construction of adjacent buildings."[3]

Over the previous twenty-five years, the worsening condition of the housing of low-income people received increasing attention. There had been calls for improved regulation—and the enforcement of regulation. Women's educational organizations, editorialists, and advocates of a newly emerging urban planning movement pointed to the social cost of not addressing the emerging housing crisis. The earliest calls for public housing appear to have come from labour activists, who, by the outbreak of the First World War, were making increasing progress both at the ballot box and in their efforts to build organizations that brought together skilled and unskilled workers.

"IT IS IMPOSSIBLE TO RENT
A HOUSE FOR MORE THAN A MONTH"

By the beginning of the twentieth century, newspapers were regularly reporting on the housing problems that would figure vividly
in Hague's presentation.[4] In 1903 it was estimated that there was
a shortage of between one hundred and two hundred homes in
the city.[5] The following year, the *Tribune* reported, "The housing
question at the present time is one of the most difficult problems.
Nearly everyone being struck with the sale craze, it is impossible
to rent a house for more than a month, and a tenant under these
conditions is not likely to make any repairs, but must be satisfied to
live in dirt and untidyness."[6] In 1905, the paper described a city in
the grip of a "house famine" so strong that every time a house was
vacated, "the landlord increased the rent by five to ten dollars."[7]
Supply was not the only problem. A 1906 report on construction
in the North End observed that many of the houses "were not all
worthy of half tone portrayal in newspapers columns: they are not
all triumphs of architecture." Indeed, they were often twelve-foot
by fourteen-foot lean-tos.[8]

In 1908, the *Free Press* ran a photo feature on slum housing in
the North End. Written by an "F.H.R.," the story noted that initial appearances could be deceiving. One newly painted building
gave "absolutely no indication of the throng of people housed in
this 'double-decker' of twelve homes." Another tenement teemed
"with people, each back door opening into a room where a family dwells." Upon entering the backyard of one building that he
thought looked pleasant, F.H.R. discovered "two shacks had been
built on, in each of which a household was living. The high rentals had been driving people into this mode of existence." A widow
with two children was living in one room along with five boarders.
The general atmosphere of a two-room household where two parents, three children, and ten boarders were living was, he wrote,
"better imagined than described."[9]

In 1909, inspectors uncovered a twenty-by-twelve-foot room
that had a continuous bed built around its walls. The room housed
forty-two men, one boy and one woman, each of whom was
charged ten cents a night and kept their belongings under their
pillows. Those who slept on the floor were allowed to pay only five

This photograph of housing on Lombard Avenue in downtown Winnipeg was part of a study conducted by city officials on the spread of typhoid from 1905 to 1908. "Telfer Block, 156 Lombard Avenue, ca 1905." City of Winnipeg Archives. Committee on Public Health and Welfare (A711 vol. 1), i01169.

cents a night. In another fourteen-room house, twenty-one men were living in a single room that could accommodate only six people. Although the City took action, the next time the inspectors visited, they found fifteen people living in the room. That year, Hague told the *Tribune*, "A house was found on Austin Street belonging to a prominent English-speaking citizen. The house consisted of two small rooms 17 x 18 x 4 feet high. There were found fourteen men although there was scarcely room for two. In such places there is hardly enough room even for a dog."[10] Five years later Hague reported on "a ten-roomed house, until recently occupied by one family, only, contained nine separate tenants (only one of whom had two rooms), each family living independently and doing their own cooking on gas stoves, and eating and sleeping in the one room." In this house:

> Not one of the gas stoves was provided with any hood or pipe for carrying off the product of combustion. Imagine the condition of the atmosphere in these rooms, containing from 500 to 1,000 cubic feet each, when fully occupied in the winter and with storm doors and sashes on all open-

ings to the house. Only one W.C. and one sink was provided for all these tenants.[11]

Memoirists have also left vivid pictures of what it was like to grow up in these conditions. Joseph Wilder moved to Winnipeg from Romania with his parent and siblings in 1904. They found a place to live south of the Canadian Pacific Railway yards.

> It was a small house located in the back yard of a larger residence which faced Patrick Street. Many homes were built that way to provide low-cost housing for friends and relatives who were continually arriving as immigrants. The front house stood next to Uncle Beresh's store, and he found the smaller one for us. His family lived in the store.
>
> The front house had running water, a toilet and a bath. Ours did not have any of these conveniences; we obtained our water from a pump just back of our house. Occasionally in winter the pump would freeze, and then it was necessary to melt snow on our wood stove and prime the pump to get the water flowing again. We had tiny bedrooms, a front room and a large kitchen. Each bedroom had two beds separated by an area hardly a foot wide.[12]

James Gray grew up in turn-of-the-century Winnipeg. His father's alcoholism was the source of endless economic instability for Gray, his brothers, and his mother. Having learned to write at an early age, Gray was obliged to employ this talent to beg his uncles for money when the family had, once more, been evicted.[13]

> We moved on an average of once a year, and in one two-year period moved from William to Giroux to Slater to Young streets. In this nomadic existence, we flitted from the North End melting pot to the fringe of Little Belgium in South St. Boniface and back again, then into the Italian district on Young Street, to the upper middle-class Westminster area and over the Anglo-Saxon heaven south of the Assiniboine.[14]

So great was the need for housing that in 1912 people were moving into a half-finished apartment block on McGee and Sargent to make sure that they could get a suite when the building was complete. According to the *Free Press*, "Practically every house in the west end has an increased rent since the first of last month and the raise has been accepted in most cases because the present occupiers realize that there is mighty little hope of securing another house."[15] In the following year, the city grew by 20,000 but only 3,000 new homes were built.[16] As a result, Winnipeg had "a scarcity of houses and flats unparalleled in the history of western Canadian cities." The city's rental offices were being stormed by "flathunters and prospective renters of four, five, and six roomed houses. Most of them are turned away, however, without getting what they are looking for."[17]

THE EMERGING CRITIQUE: "HOUSING— WHY HAS WINNIPEG A HOUSING PROBLEM?"

The growing housing shortage became a topic for general debate. The Social Science Study Club, an organization founded and led by women, held seven monthly meetings in 1913-1914 on social issues including one titled "Housing—Why has Winnipeg a housing problem?"[18] "Becky," the editor of "Woman's Empire," the women's page of the *Winnipeg Tribune*, wrote in 1907, "it would be an excellent plan if some of our Winnipeg ladies who have ample time to dispose of" were to "materially assist in the problem of better housing for the working classes."[19] In 1908 the woman's column in the *Tribune* ("Tea Table Talk") wondered sniffily "Who ... is going to educate the laboring classes on the necessity of healthful surroundings. Take for instance, the foreign element at the north end, where the people and their dwellings are none too clean."[20]

In 1908, the *Tribune* editorialized that if housing prices did not come down, there would be an exodus of skilled workers. It was, the paper wrote, "up to the contractors and businessmen in general to meet the demands and by erecting warm, well built and architectural terraces, which can be offered to families at from fifteen to twenty dollars a month, with the chance extended to the occupant of becoming the owner at an expense of not over fifteen hundred dollars."[21] *Free Press* readers in 1911 were warned, in an article on slum housing in Canada, that poor housing led to social catastrophe:

Low morals and life under unhygienic conditions are associated so often that we must admit their relation, although
we may not always be able to explain it. The uncomfortable
dwelling, ill-lighted, ill-ventilated, evil-smelling, drives its
occupants out to the pernicious influences of the street.
The nervous irritability, which bad air and poor lighting
engender, often does the same thing. The people from such
homes, when on the street naturally drift to places where
entertainment is cheap and apt to be demoralizing—the
saloon and the low theatre. And if they remain at home
they must still be affected by the subtle tendency of dirt,
foul air, and poor light to lower thought and moral standards, a tendency against which the best of men are not always proof.[22]

When a global economic downturn hit Winnipeg by late 1907,
the demand for railway workers and seasonal farmhands plum-
meted. To find work, the *Free Press* said a man "must be willing to
leave the city, and he must be willing to accept smaller wages."[23] In
the face of this mounting economic destitution, J.S. Woodsworth
called for the creation of a central organization to coordinate the
work of the city's various private charities. Such an agency would
keep a central record of clients, investigate need, help people find
employment, and, when that was not possible, operate a woodyard and laundry where those who could not find work would
be obliged to labour.[24] The idea won the support of Mayor James
Ashdown, who stressed that it was largely up to citizens, as opposed to government, to "relieve the present situation."[25] The following year the Associated Charities was formed, and a director
recruited from New York City. On his arrival, J.H.F. Falk stated
that one of the most important measures that could be undertaken
to ease the lives of low-income people was to improve tenement
housing.[26] The agency took over the delivery of the provision of relief to homeless men, in most cases placing them on farms where
they did chores in exchange for room and board. When farm work
was scarce, men were required to put in time at its woodyard in exchange for assistance. In the case of families, Associated Charities
might in certain conditions not only provide fuel, food, and cloth-

ing, but also money for rent; however, recipients had to agree to take any job offered to them.[27]

In the fall of 1908, a delegation led by Woodsworth and including Presbyterian minister J.W. MacMillan, Dr. A.J. Douglas (the city's public health officer), and Falk, requested that the City enact a tenement bylaw. Their proposals would restrict new tenements to 60 percent of any city lot, required windows in every room, made washrooms mandatory in every suite and ensured the provision of adequate fire escapes.[28] Douglas repeated the call in February of the following year, saying that apartment blocks and tenements were fast becoming "a favourite form of investment" in Winnipeg. As a result, regulatory authority was needed to ensure adequate light, ventilation, and fire protection. Poorly installed plumbing was also an ongoing problem, particularly in winter when fixtures froze.[29] Hague, for example, was in court in 1909 testifying against a landlord who refused to spend money on plumbing to address an insanitary condition.[30]

Pressure for a tenement bylaw also came from the Winnipeg Sanitary Association. Headed by William Bruce, an architect and sanitary expert who had trained in Great Britain, the association had been established in 1909 in response to health concerns related to the discharge of sewage into the Red and Assiniboine Rivers.[31] By the spring of 1909, there was still no sign of a bylaw. The *Tribune* noted:

> In the meantime permits are being issued almost daily for this class of building [tenements], and it is important that if there are to be any regulations they should be passed as soon as possible.[32]

It was summer before the council began to examine a draft tenement bylaw.[33] In a detailed critique of the bylaw's failings, Bruce said the proposed bylaw, which would have allowed tenements to be built within three feet of the lot line and cover an area of 70 by 40 feet, was "inviting and encouraging 'slum dwelling.'" The ventilation that the bylaw allowed was inadequate and the types of wooden construction allowed would result in dry rot.[34] The majority on council, however, dismissed Bruce's criticisms as "contrary."[35] In November Bruce wrote that council was determined to "force on the citizens a tenement bylaw that is certainly no improvement on present conditions, except to give a sort of legal status to badly lighted, deficiently ventilated and overcrowded erections, where friendly interests are at stake." The friendly interests being referred to were the relations between landlords and council members. The best clauses in the bylaw, he wrote, were dead for lack of enforcement.[36]

REGULATION AND INSPECTION: "THE ABSENCE OF ADEQUATE BUILDING LAWS"

In his capacity as Winnipeg housing inspector, E.W.J. Hague played a leading role in the national public-health movement, speaking at conferences and writing for industry journals. This work could not have pleased the boosterish majority on Winnipeg city council. In 1913 he told delegates to a health conference that:

> One of the many reasons why so many insanitary dwellings are found today in our large cities is the absence of adequate building laws and the superficial system of inspection of buildings which obtains. The extremely rapid growth of our Canadian cities has made it a well nigh impossible task for building inspection departments to provide an efficient system, even in places where the building bylaws are fairly good. Take the matter of cellars alone. Thousands of these have been constructed in a flimsy and inadequate manner with porus [sic] walls, no windows, no weeping drains; in fact, many of them are mere dug outs under the building and frequently under a bedroom. Such cellars, although not a nuisance when first constructed, rapidly become such. The walls cave in, the floors become covered with mud and they become generally a most insanitary place.[37]

In an article published the following year, Hague wrote that Winnipeg's overworked building inspectors often found that new buildings had been constructed in disregard to the building code. Older tenements were notable for their "narrow courts; dark rooms; non-fire proof construction; dark and damp basement suites" while courtyards, even in newer buildings, were "narrow and little sunlight reaches the suites that open to the courtyard on the lower floors."[38]

Since loan companies could not make a profit financing small affordable rental housing, he said "many persons are obliged to build larger houses than they need for their own families, and in order to meet expenses to take in boarders or even other families."[39] This led to a practice that came to be known as "house farming," in which tenants took in other tenants. According to city officials:

> The innocent looking couch by day is opened out at night to become a bed for two boarders. This disappearance of beds and bedding in the daytime is one reason why day inspections for overcrowding are not sufficient unless supplemented by night inspections. The ultimate effect of this dividing up of houses that taking in of lodgers is to raise rents all around.[40]

In July 1913 city housing inspector Alexander Officer was instructed to "prosecute a diligent campaign against every condition that has bearing on the establishment of slum districts in Winnipeg." The order was issued by the health department after Officer reported that five families were living in a nine-room, one-and-a-half storey, frame house. The landlord was receiving $93 a month for a property that should have been renting for $30 a month.[41] A City of Winnipeg report, likely written by Hague, recommended it would be a step in the right direction "if all lodging and boarding-houses were required to be licensed under stringent conditions regarding the buildings, their sanitary condition, equipment, and maintenance."[42] Such a regulation would be decades in coming.

To address overcrowding, the health department resorted to nighttime inspections, which often ended in people "climbing out by the windows, the hiding of men in cellars, toilet rooms under beds, and even in covered laundry tubs."[43] But prosecution often had limited impact. In April 1914, Fred Rekyt was convicted for the fourth time that year of violating the city's housing bylaw. He had been letting a dozen men sleep in an unventilated loft (average height two-and-a-half feet) over the kitchen of his home on Jarvis Avenue. He was fined five dollars—about $120 in 2021 dollars—plus court costs.[44] It was little more than a licensing fee.

While critical of landlords, Hague saw the growing immigrant population as needing public-health education, particularly during what he described as their period of assimilation. To this end, he said, his office had hired interpreters. Hague struggled with how to enforce the bylaws humanely. "In cases where a family, through stress of circumstances, have been unable to secure sufficient room, we have endeavored to be as lenient as possible, but in cases of over-crowding generally insisted on a partial or total reduction of boarders kept."[45] In January 1914 the *Free Press* reported that "the campaign of the city health department against bad housing conditions in Winnipeg is still active." Inspectors were finding many cases of "deliberate evasion of the building bylaws as well as the health bylaws." But officials continued to exercise leniency in enforcing the bylaws since it was apparent the tenants had no place to go.[46] This would be the eternal dilemma: without an adequate supply of low-cost housing into which people could be moved, housing officials would have no choice but to let their public-health regulations go largely unenforced.

THE PROMISE OF CITY PLANNING: "IT WILL BECOME EXPEDIENT TO INTRODUCE A SCHEME OF MUNICIPAL HOUSING"

By the turn of the twentieth century, reformers in both England and the United States were turning to city planning as a solution to the problems of urbanization.[47] There was a widespread if short-lived burst of interest in city planning in Canada after 1910.[48] In that year, Albert Henry George, better known as Governor-General Earl Grey, invited British parliamentarian Henry Vivian to come to Canada to give a series of lectures about town planning. Grey believed that town planning was needed to prevent the country from being engulfed by slums.[49] A carpenter by trade, Vivian was a proponent of what he termed "co-partnership," a form of management in which workers would become owners in the firms they worked, sharing profits and making business decisions. Elected to parliament as a Liberal in 1906, he played a role in the adoption of a Housing and Town Planning Act.[50] Vivian spent three months in Canada, travelling from coast to coast.[51]

Vivian visited Winnipeg twice on his 1910 tour of Canada. On his way out west, he addressed the Canadian Club, to whose members he stressed that slums bred small, underweight, and sickly people, and warned that overcrowding led to an increase in the death rate.[52] On his return trip, he spoke at the trades and labour hall, where, as a former trade unionist, he was given a warm welcome. He said that on his short visit he had "seen something in Winnipeg that looks very much like slums."[53] As in the other cities that he visited, Vivian's visit spurred the creation of a local town planning committee. The Winnipeg Town Planning Association was led by William Pearson, a leading figure in the real-estate industry and a person of considerable political courage. During the First World War, he lamented, "a small amount of the money spent to keep the British flag flying would suffice to save millions of lives now sacrificed to the sacred rights of housing."[54] On one occasion he observed that solving the housing problem was "not, as so many think, merely one of providing a certain quantity of houses at a certain rent, but also providing a good substantial workmanlike building at a reasonable rent.[55] Elsewhere Pearson wrote, "providing proper living accommodation for our people" would lead to "the reduction of bills for hospitals, and so forth, changing the expenses from one department to another, as it were, and to the great advantage of the public."[56]

At the behest of Pearson's Town Planning Association and the Industrial Bureau (an early version of the Chamber of Commerce), Winnipeg city council established a town planning commission and mandated it to develop a report for council. Having created the commission, city council did little to support it, providing only minimal funding. Despite this, its 1913 report amounted to what historian Alan Artibise described as "the most concise, objective and far-reaching document to come out of Winnipeg in the first forty years of its history."[57] Eight of the commission's top ten findings dealt with housing.[58] The commission recommended that business organizations invest in the construction of "low-priced, well constructed cottages for women, grouped in model suburbs, even though the net returns were only equal to the returns on the average investment bond. Better housing conditions mean better workmen and a more stable labor market." If the private sector was not willing to act, the committee recommended:

> for the sake of getting the correct standards of construction, it will become expedient to introduce a scheme of Municipal Housing. Experience has shown that many large cities such as London, Liverpool, Manchester, and new Industrial Towns such as Letchworth, have been forced to adopt Municipal Housing Schemes, while in rural districts the Local Government Board and the County Councils have found it necessary to relieve the situation by providing decent homes at fair rentals.[59]

The Voice editorialized, "within the limits set forth in the Commission, and still more within the limits imposed through the stupid antagonism of the city council in adopting a cheese-paring policy toward the Commission, the report is of a very thorough and comprehensive character." It noted that the council had hindered the commission in its work and cut back on its funding, concluding that unless council implemented the report's recommendations it would "deepen the suspicion that has been created very widely that its opposition is due to the fact that the Commission has had the interests of the community more at heart than the interests of real estate operators."[60] Suspicions were deepened a month later when council rejected six of the seven housing recommendations contained in the report, including proposals for mandatory room sizes and heights, ventilation, and limits on building footprints.[61] The only recommendation accepted was a call for an increase in building inspectors.[62] Council declined to even print the commission's report. While council did adopt a municipal building bylaw in 1914, it did not require permits for the conversion of a house from a single-family to a multi-family dwelling.[63]

In 1913 one council member, J.G. Munroe, recommended that the City follow Toronto's example and guarantee housing companies up to 85 percent of the total values of properties. The plans would have to be approved by the City and dividends would have to be no more than 6 percent.[64] The following year, the provincial government gave cities the right "to guarantee the bonds of companies which will provide adequate housing accommodation, and which are limited to a profit of six per cent."[65] Cities would first have to gain the approval of municipal property owners before issuing such guarantees.[66] In April 1914, labour member of council Richard Rigg unsuccessfully called on the City to take advantage of the new provincial legislation and guarantee the construction of workers' housing.[67] By the end of the decade, the town planning movement in Winnipeg was languishing. While the Province had adopted a planning act in 1916, the provincial director of planning was later to resign in frustration.[68] It would not be until after the Second World War that Winnipeg engaged in any planning.[69]

CALLS FOR PUBLIC HOUSING: "MUNICIPALLY OWNED WORKING CLASS HOUSES"

While church organizations, women's groups, professionals, and the members of the media had all concluded that Winnipeg not only had a housing problem, it fell to the labour movement to issue the first calls for public housing.

In 1908, union activist William Cooper told a public meeting, "We have arrived at a critical stage in the growth of Winnipeg with the growing congestion in the north end." According to the *Tribune*, Cooper went on to call upon the City to "break up the congested districts and take measures to erect dwellings of their own with larger spaces and better houses to accommodate those now living in the congested districts." A carpenter by trade, Cooper had been a Social Democratic Federation member of the Aberdeen city council in Scotland for eleven

William Cooper, an immigrant from Scotland and militant trade unionist, issued one of the first calls for public housing in Winnipeg. Photo courtesy of Bruce Owen.

years before coming to Canada in 1907. While on the Aberdeen council he chaired the city's public-health commission. According to his great-grandson, in that capacity, he made "great strides in improving the living conditions of many Aberdeen labourers." In Canada, he worked for the CPR and played an important role in the local leadership of the One Big Union in the 1920s.[70] His call for public housing drew upon his experience in Aberdeen: since the 1850s, that city's medical officers of health had been drawing attention to the link between slum housing and the spread of infectious diseases such as tuberculosis, smallpox, and typhus. Initially, the council's response focused on slum clearance, but with the appointment of Matthew Hay as Aberdeen's chief health officer in 1888, the council began to implement initiatives intended to improve housing. Having concluded that private builders were not prepared to build adequate shelter for low-income families, Hay became a staunch public housing advocate. His prodding led to the construction of the city's first housing project in 1897. The plan was only narrowly approved by the Aberdeen council. Cooper would have been one of the people who supported the measure.[71]

Housing was a regular topic of debate in Winnipeg's labour council. In September 1912, following a discussion of "the high rents charged for working class dwellings," labour council member A.A. Heaps moved that the labour council call on the City to go into the municipal housing business.[72] The following month the council directed its municipal committee to look into the benefit of "municipally owned working class houses."[73] These calls would be taken up in the coming years by labour political representatives on council.

LABOUR'S POLITICAL ADVANCES: "WE CAN DESTROY THE SLUMS BY CHANGING THE LAWS"

In the early years of the twentieth century, the labourists who had helped to elect Arthur Puttee to parliament clashed regularly with the more radical members of the Socialist Party of Canada, such as R.B. Russell, Dick Johns, and George and Helen Armstrong. An alphabet soup of left-wing political organizations struggled with each other for the support of the growing working class in the early years of the twentieth century, generally without success: Puttee himself was defeated in the 1904 federal election. Two years later, two labour candidates failed to win election to city council from North End wards.[74] While the British Labour Party served as a model for many Manitoba radicals, Eastern European immigrants created their own socialist institutions. In the early twentieth century, Ukrainian workers in Winnipeg established a Ukrainian branch of the Socialist Party of Canada and were also active in the formation of the Social Democratic Party in 1910.[75] Similarly, the Jewish community created a network of self-help, educational, political, and cultural organizations. A branch of the Arbeiter Ring (an international organization that proclaimed: "We fight against sickness, premature death, and capitalism"), for example, was founded in Winnipeg in 1907.[76]

Turn-of-the-century employers resisted unionization and could count on governments and the courts to back them in their disputes with their employees. A rail workers' strike was broken in 1902; a streetcar workers' strike in 1906 ended in a draw, but not before the troops were called out to protect the company from pro-union supporters; and in that same year metal workers saw their union not only broken in a strike but successfully sued by the employers. In 1911 the Great West Saddlery fired workers who refused to swear that they would not join a union.[77] Not surprisingly, working-class voters were increasingly prepared to vote for labour candidates. Despite internal conflicts and the restrictions that had been placed on the right to vote and run for office, the Winnipeg labour movement began to make political gains by the second decade of the twentieth century.

Richard Rigg scored a breakthrough victory when he won election to council in 1913. Born in Lancashire, England, Rigg had gone to work in a cotton mill at age ten, and later qualified to serve as a Methodist preacher. He immigrated to Canada in 1903 after abandoning the ministry. In Winnipeg, he worked as a bookbinder, served on the executive of his union, and was active in the Socialist Party of Canada and the Social Democratic Party.[78] Rigg believed strongly that housing was a labour issue. In 1912, Rigg, then secretary of the Trades and Labor Council, told a public meeting on housing, "little attention had been paid to the successive annual epidemics of typhoid fever until these had spread to the residential district in South Winnipeg." He considered that an injustice had been done in this regard to North Winnipeg, remarking "the slum district would hitch itself to Crescentwood sooner or later." He pointed out that "Tenement blocks were being built wholesale in the northern part of the city, forerunners of the poorest type of tenement slum, and people were being forced into crowded and unwholesome quarters, often at such an expense that the larger part of their salaries was swallowed up in rent."[79] Rigg, who saw reforms as merely a step on the road to socialism, said that while municipal housing and reformed land taxes would improve matters, "the problem was incapable of final solution until the ownership of all forms of capital was vested in the people."[80]

Rigg was soon joined on city council by John Queen and A.A. Heaps. Queen had emigrated from Glasgow in 1906. Years later he recalled that the first conversation he fell into with a Winnipegger was about profits to be made in real estate. The conversation taught him something about the ethos of the city, but having no money to invest, Queen was obliged to room in a crowded boarding house on Dorothy Street. A cooper by trade, he found work driving a delivery wagon for the North-West Laundry. He became increasingly involved in politics and the labour movement, joining the recently created Social Democratic Party. In 1915, he ran successfully for city council as a Labour Party candidate. According to Fred Tipping, another labour activist of the era, Queen's primary qualification for the nomination was the fact that he had "a huge mortgage." All the other potential labour candidates were renters, and therefore, were barred from running for municipal office.[81]

Abraham Albert (A.A.) Heaps was born in Leyland, the Jewish community in Leeds, England, in 1889. The child of immigrants from Poland, he had to leave school at thirteen to take work as an upholsterer's apprentice. Three years later he opened his own workshop, and at twenty he was running a furniture store. However, he felt that the prejudices of English society blocked his opportunities and he emigrated to Canada in 1910. The following year he found work as an upholsterer with the CPR and brought his fiancée over from England. Active in his union, he became the Winnipeg Trades and Labor Council's statistician in 1912 and was soon making friends with leading figures in the Social Democratic Party, including Queen.[82] He was defeated in 1915 in his first bid to serve on Winnipeg city council. His 1917 bid was initially unsuccessful, but he was able to have the results overturned after demonstrating that his opponent had stuffed the ballot box. He too was arrested and charged for his involvement in the 1919 General Strike but won an acquittal in a trial in which he defended himself. He remained on council until 1925 when he was elected to parliament as an Independent Labour Party candidate.[83]

The labourists found themselves drawn into an alliance with members of a now-forgotten reform movement known as the "single tax," which its adherents believed, if only implemented, could dramatically lower the price of housing. The author of a 1906 letter to the editor of the *Free Press* argued that high rents and low wages were the cause of mounting tuberculosis in the city. His solution was the introduction of a single tax on land speculation.[84] The single tax was a political theory popularized by the American political campaigner Henry George. Single-tax exponents argued that in industrial societies the major source of exploitation and inequality was land speculation. In their view, speculators who did not improve their land and kept it off the market drove up the price of other land. These same speculators were taxed on their land holdings at a different, and lower, rate than people who invested in their land. To the single taxers it was unfair that the investment of people who improved their land led to an increase in the value of the speculator's land. The solution lay in taxing all land at the same rate—in other words, a "single tax." This would encourage people to develop their land and increase the housing supply, rather than keeping it off the market and driving up the price of housing.[85]

Fred Dixon, a leading figure in the early twentieth-century reform movement in Winnipeg, was a fervent single taxer. The son of a coachman, he was born in 1881 in Berkshire. He left school at thirteen and immigrated to Winnipeg in 1903. He found work as an engraver with a bag company but became a full-time political campaigner for the League to the Valuation of Land Values.[86] In 1910 he wrote, "We can destroy the slums by changing the laws with regard to taxation; by abolishing all taxes upon buildings, and raising all our revenue by the taxation of land values. This will encourage the building of good houses, lower rents, and raise wages; and not only solve the housing problem but, if fully applied, as advocated by Henry George, banish involuntary poverty from our civilization."[87] *The Voice* regularly published columns supporting the views of the Land Values Taxation League.[88] A charismatic and courageous figure, Dixon ran unsuccessfully as a Manitoba Labour Party candidate for the legislature in 1910 before winning a seat in 1914.[89] In office, he helped expose the political corruption into which the provincial government had sunk and opposed Canada's participation in the First World War. Dixon led the labour group in the legislature from 1920 until his retirement in 1923.[90]

In the turbulent years that followed the outbreak of war in 1914, labour activists of all stripes took risky and outspoken positions against the war. In 1919 they stood together as a conflict between workers and employers exploded in a general strike that focused the world's attention on Winnipeg.

NOTES

1. "Struggle for better housing," *Winnipeg Free Press*, December 14, 1914; "Housing might be better here," *Winnipeg Tribune*, December 14, 1914; Manitoba Historical Society, "The People's Forum" <mhs.mb.ca/docs/features/timelinks/reference/db0043.shtml>, accessed on May 12, 2021.

2. "Struggle to save," *Winnipeg Morning Free Press*, September 14, 1897; "Who's who—in municipal election slate," *Winnipeg Evening Tribune*, November 16, 1932.

3. ""Struggle for better housing," *Winnipeg Free Press*, December 14, 1914; "Housing might be better here," *Winnipeg Tribune*, December 14, 1914; Manitoba Historical Society, "The People's Forum" <mhs.mb.ca/docs/features/timelinks/reference/db0043.shtml>, accessed on May 12, 2021.

4. "Scheme to house the wage earners," *Manitoba Free Press*, May 24, 1900.

5. "Building in Winnipeg," *Winnipeg Tribune*, March 7, 1903.

6. "The week in real estate," *Winnipeg Tribune*, April 30, 1903.

7. "Building notes," *Winnipeg Tribune*, June 17, 1905.

8. "Where builders are busy," *Manitoba Free Press*, June 2, 1906.

9. F.H.R., "Social settlement work in Winnipeg," *Manitoba Free Press*, July 11, 1908.

10. "Congestion in city tenement," *Winnipeg Tribune*, February 26, 1909.

11. Ernest W.J. Hague, "The housing problem," *Public Health Journal*, 5, 6 (June 1914): 375.

12. Joseph Wilder, *Read All About It: Reminiscences of an Immigrant Newsboy*, Winnipeg: Peguis Publishers Ltd, 1978, 18–19.

13. James Gray, *The Boy from Winnipeg*, Toronto: MacMillan of Canada, 1970, 20–34.

14. James Gray, *The Boy from Winnipeg*, Toronto: MacMillan of Canada, 1970, 11.
15. "Suites and houses scarce in Winnipeg," *Manitoba Free Press*, September 9, 1912.
16. "3,000 new homes erected in Winnipeg during the year 1913," *Winnipeg Tribune*, December 20, 1913.
17. "House hunters have busy time," *Manitoba Free Press*, April 26, 1913.
18. Mary Kinnear, *Margaret McWilliams: An Interwar Feminist*, Montreal and Kingston: McGill-Queen's Press, 1991, 57; "The little club among women's organizations," *Manitoba Free Press*, November 29, 1913.
19. Becky, "Woman's empire," *Winnipeg Tribune*, November 2, 1907.
20. "Tea table talk," *Winnipeg Tribune*, June 20, 1908.
21. "Homes for workingmen," *Winnipeg Tribune*, January 11, 1908.
22. "Unsanitary housing in Canadian cities," *Manitoba Free Press*, June 3, 1911.
23. Michael Goeres, "Disorder, Dependency and Fiscal Responsibility: Unemployment Relief in Winnipeg, 1907-1942," Master of Arts thesis, University of Manitoba, 1981, 6; "Labor conditions," *Manitoba Free Press*, November 30, 1907.
24. "Organized charity needed," *Manitoba Free Press*, December 5, 1907.
25. "Approve of centralization," *Winnipeg Tribune*, December 20, 1907.
26. "Fighting disease amongst the poor," *Manitoba Free Press*, September 24, 1908.
27. Michael Goeres, "Disorder, Dependency and Fiscal Responsibility: Unemployment Relief in Winnipeg, 1907-1942," Master of Arts thesis, University of Manitoba, 1981, 19-20, 27-28.
28. "Winnipeg tenements," *Manitoba Free Press*, October 20, 1908. For Falk's background, see: "Fighting disease amongst the poor," *Manitoba Free Press*, September 24, 1908.
29. "City's death rate is below norm," *Winnipeg Tribune*, February 5, 1909.
30. "Locked up in the wood-pile," *Winnipeg Tribune*, January 19, 1909.
31. "Sanitation is strongly urged," *Winnipeg Tribune*, September 25, 1909.
32. For start of talks, see: "Tenement regulations," *Winnipeg Tribune*, April 10, 1909. For delay, see: "Tenement bylaw," *Winnipeg Tribune*, August 13, 1909.
33. "Protect tenants," *Manitoba Free Press*, July 31, 1909.
34. "Tenement buildings," *Winnipeg Tribune*, August 25, 1909; "School by-law; patrol system," *Winnipeg Tribune*, August 31, 1909.
35. "Tenement by-law," *Manitoba Free Press*, October 27, 1909.
36. William Bruce, "Building bylaws of Winnipeg," *Winnipeg Tribune*, November 5, 1909.
37. "Crowding in the cities," *Winnipeg Tribune*, September 23, 1913.
38. Ernest W.J. Hague, "The housing problem," *Public Health Journal*, 5, 6 (June 1914): 372.
39. Ernest W.J. Hague, "The housing problem," *Public Health Journal*, 5, 6 (June 1914): 375.
40. "Night visit to foreign district," *Manitoba Free Press*, May 30, 1913.
41. "Five families in crowded quarters," *Manitoba Free Press*, July 5, 1913.
42. "Night visit to foreign district," *Manitoba Free Press*, May 30, 1913.
43. Ernest W.J. Hague, "The housing problem," *Public Health Journal*, 5, 6 (June 1914): 377-378. In May 1913 Police Magistrate Hugh John Macdonald accompanied the city's health officials on a midnight tour of north-end housing.

While the first boarding house they visited was not overcrowded, it was judged to be "not suitable for a boarding house." At the next house, boarders scrambled out of the rear of the house for fear of the level of crowding being discovered. Four people were living in a three-room shack in the backyard of this property. The litany continued: overcrowded conditions (five people living a single room), insufficient sanitary facilities, and no ventilation. "Night visit to foreign district," *Manitoba Free Press*, May 30, 1913.

44. "Housed 12 men in small loft," *Winnipeg Tribune*, April 29, 1914.

45. "Congestion in city tenement," *Winnipeg Tribune*, February 26, 1909.

46. "Campaign for better housing," *Manitoba Free Press*, January 5, 1914.

47. Thomas I. Gunton, "The ideas and policies of the Canadian planning profession, 1909–1931," in Alan F.J. Artibise and Gilbert A. Stelter (eds.), *The Usable Urban Past: Planning and Politics in the Modern Canadian City*, Toronto: Macmillan of Canada, 1979, 177–185.

48. Alan F.J. Artibise, *Winnipeg: A Social History of Urban Growth, 1874–1914*, Montreal: McGill-Queen's, 1975, 270.

49. Catherine Mary Ulmer, "Introducing Canada to urban planning? Henry Vivian's Canadian Planning Tour, 1910," *Urban History Review/Revue d'histoire urbaine*, XLVI (Spring 2018): 46–47.

50. Catherine Mary Ulmer, "Introducing Canada to urban planning? Henry Vivian's Canadian Planning Tour, 1910," *Urban History Review/Revue d'histoire urbaine*, XLVI (Spring 2018): 44–45.

51. Catherine Mary Ulmer, "Introducing Canada to urban planning? Henry Vivian's Canadian Planning Tour, 1910," *Urban History Review/Revue d'histoire urbaine*, XLVI (Spring 2018): 48.

52. "Protection will disband Empire," *Winnipeg Tribune*, September 6, 1910; "Home is principal factor in individual development," *Winnipeg Tribune*, September 6, 1910.

53. "Eradicate slums, improve humanity," *Winnipeg Tribune*, October 6, 1910; "Building cities," *Manitoba Free Press*, October 6, 1910.

54. "Should establish right values of life," *Manitoba Free Press*, July 15, 1915.

55. William Pearson, "Housing and town planning as an outlet for community service," *Manitoba Free Press*, May 30, 1914.

56. William Pearson, "Housing and town planning as an outlet for community service," *Manitoba Free Press*, May 30, 1914.

57. Alan F.J. Artibise, *Winnipeg: A Social History of Urban Growth, 1874–1914*, Montreal: McGill-Queen's, 1975, 270–277.

58. The City of Winnipeg, City Planning Commission, in Alan A.J. Artibise (ed.), *Gateway City: Documents on the City of Winnipeg, 1873–1913*, Manitoba Record Society publications, Vol. 5, Winnipeg: Manitoba Record Society in association with the University of Manitoba Press, 1979, 231.

59. The City of Winnipeg, City Planning Commission, in Alan A.J. Artibise (ed.), *Gateway City: Documents on the City of Winnipeg, 1873–1913*, Manitoba Record Society publications, Vol. 5, Winnipeg: Manitoba Record Society in association with the University of Manitoba Press, 1979, 225–264.

60. "Town planning commission," *The Voice*, January 13, 1913.

61. "Elaborate report on city planning," *Manitoba Free Press*, January 28, 1913.

62. Ernest W.J. Hague, "The housing problem," *Public Health Journal*, 5, 6 (June 1914): 372.

63. Alan F.J. Artibise, *Winnipeg: A Social History of Urban Growth, 1874-1914*, Montreal: McGill-Queen's, 1975, 243.

64. "Urge following Toronto's example," *Manitoba Free Press*, December 16, 1913.

65. "Education bill for committee," *Manitoba Free Press*, January 10, 1914.

66. "Kraf. Commission sittings open to public says Govt." *Winnipeg Tribune*, January 14, 1914; "For better housing," *Manitoba Free Press*, January 13, 1914.

67. "Would prevent slum districts," *Winnipeg Tribune*, April 17, 1914.

68. Alan F.J. Artibise, *Winnipeg: A Social History of Urban Growth, 1874-1914*, Montreal: McGill-Queen's, 1975, 278-279; J.D. Hulchanski, *The Origins of Urban Land Use Planning in Alberta, 1900-1945*, University of Toronto, Centre for Urban and Community Studies, Research Paper No. 119, 1981, 1; Michael Simpson, "Thomas Adams in Canada, 1914-1930," *Urban History Review/Revue d'histoire urbaine*, 11, 2 (1982): 9; "The city beautiful," *The Voice*, March 3, 1914; "Town planner's annual meeting," *Manitoba Free Press*, March 25, 1914.

69. Alan F.J. Artibise, *Winnipeg: A Social History of Urban Growth, 1874-1914*, Montreal: McGill-Queen's, 1975, 278-279.

70. "Music and drama," *Winnipeg Tribune*, June 4, 1908. For Cooper's career, see: David Edward Hall, "Times of Trouble: Labour Quiescence in Winnipeg 1920-1929," Master of Arts thesis, University of Manitoba, 1983, 44; Bruce Owen, "Angry voice faded away," *Winnipeg Free Press*, May 15, 1994.

71. Nicholas J. Williams, "Housing," in W. Hamish Fraser and Clive H. Lee (eds.), *Aberdeen: 1800-2000, A New History*, East Linton: Tuckwell Press, 2000, 303-307.

72. "House rents are abnormally high," *Winnipeg Free Press*, September 20, 1912; "Winnipeg trades council," *The Voice*, September 20, 1912.

73. "Municipally owned houses favored," *Manitoba Free Press*, October 18, 1912.

74. A. Ross McCormack, *Reformers, Rebels, and Revolutionaries: The Western Canadian Radical Movement 1899-1919*, University of Toronto Press, 1977, 77-97.

75. Jaroslav Petryshyn, *Peasants in the Promised Land: Canada and the Ukrainians, 1891-1914*, Toronto: James Lorimer and Company, 1985, 169.

76. Roseline Usiskin, "Toward a Theoretical Reformulation of the Relationship between Ideology, Social Class, and Ethnicity: A Case Study of the Winnipeg Jewish Radical Community, 1905-1920," Master of Arts thesis, University of Manitoba, 1978, 126-129; Arthur Ross, *Communal Solidarity. Immigration, Settlement, and Social Welfare in Winnipeg's Jewish Community*, 1882-1930, Winnipeg: University of Manitoba Press, 2019.

77. David J. Bercuson, *Confrontation at Winnipeg: Labour, Industrial Relations and the General Strike*, Montreal and London: McGill-Queen's Press, 1974, 11-21.

78. David Edward Hall, "Times of Trouble: Labour Quiescence in Winnipeg 1920-1929," Master of Arts thesis, University of Manitoba, 1983, 34.

79. "Rent question serious problem," *Manitoba Free Press*, October 14, 1912.

80. "The housing problem," *The Voice*, October 18, 1912.

81. A.B. McKillop, "Citizen and Socialist: The Ethos of Political Winnipeg, 1919-1935," unpublished Master of Arts thesis, University of Manitoba, 1970, 89, 107-108; Archives of Manitoba, C831, Fred Tipping oral history interview with Lionel Orlikow.

82. Leo Heaps, *The Rebel in the House: The Life and Times of A.A. Heaps, M.P.*, Markham: Fitzhenry and Whiteside, 1984, 1-3.

83. Leo Heaps, *The Rebel in the House: The Life and Times of A.A. Heaps, M.P.*,

Markham: Fitzhenry and Whiteside, 1984, 13–18.

84. A reader, "A suggested cure for consumption," *Manitoba Free Press*, June 1, 1906.

85. Ramsay Cook, *The Regenerators: Social Criticism in Late Victorian English Canada*, Toronto: University of Toronto Press, 1985, 107–121; Allen Mills, "Single tax, socialism and the Independent Labour Party of Manitoba: The political ideas of F.J. Dixon and S J. Farmer," *Labour/Le Travail*, 5 (January 1, 1980): 34.

86. Allen Mills, "Single tax, socialism and the Independent Labour Party of Manitoba: The political ideas of F.J. Dixon and S J. Farmer," *Labour/Le Travail*, 5 (January 1, 1980): 36–37.

87. Fred J. Dixon, "Land monopoly," *Winnipeg Tribune*, March 9, 1910.

88. See: "Land values," *The Voice*, April 24, 1914.

89. Allen Mills, "Single tax, socialism and the Independent Labour Party of Manitoba: The political ideas of F.J. Dixon and S J. Farmer," *Labour/Le Travail*, 5 (January 1, 1980): 36–37.

90. Allen Mills, "Single tax, socialism and the Independent Labour Party of Manitoba: The political ideas of F.J. Dixon and S J. Farmer," *Labour/Le Travail*, 5 (January 1, 1980): 33, 46, 47.

Chapter 3

THE 1919 GENERAL STRIKE AND ITS AFTERMATH: THE 1920s

On May 15, 1919, approximately 30,000 Winnipeg workers walked off the job. They were not striking for their own benefit, but to support metal trades and building trades workers who had been on strike since the first of the month. Negotiations had collapsed because the employers refused to meet with the bargaining councils that these workers had created. The Winnipeg Labour Council, hoping to force the employers back to the bargaining table, polled its membership on the question of whether they would take part in a general strike to support the metal and building trades workers. The vote was 11,000 in favour to 500 against. The resulting strike was a breathtaking and historic demonstration of working-class solidarity. It is estimated that roughly half of the 30,000 people who took part in the Winnipeg General Strike, as this conflict came to be known, were not even union members. The strike was not revolutionary in intent, but it did challenge the dominant rights of the city's propertied elites. It had been two decades in the making, and it would set the political stage for the next fifty years. And over that half-century, public housing would be one of the key issues on the political agenda at Winnipeg city hall. The attitudes of the political leaders who made the key decisions on public housing were shaped, in large measure, by their understanding of the General Strike.

* * *

In response to the General Strike, members of the city's business community established a Citizens' Committee of One Thousand, a secretive organization that certainly never had an enrolled membership of one thousand nor a democratic structure. One of the few documents that listed its leaders shows that they were all drawn from the city's economic elite: lawyers, manufacturers, grain merchants, former politicians, realtors, bankers, and insurance executives.[1] Convinced that the existing police force was too sympathetic to the strikers, the Citizens arranged to have most of the force replaced by "Special Police." At the Citizens' behest, amendments to the *Immigration Act* were rushed through parliament to provide the government with the power to deport those who were convicted of sedition. The Citizens demonized the strikers as traitors and foreigners, undercut efforts by elected officials to bring about a negotiated settlement, and convinced the federal government that the city was about to succumb to revolution.[2] When, to their surprise and horror, the Citizens discovered that a large portion of the returned soldiers supported the strike, they established their own anti-strike veterans' organization. If any group staged an illegitimate seizure of power in Winnipeg in 1919, it was this shadowy organization of "Citizens," not the strikers.

Socialists such as R.B. Russell and George Armstrong, who certainly believed a transformative social revolution was both necessary and inevitable, were strike leaders. But the leadership also included labourists such as John Queen and A.A. Heaps, single taxers such as Fred Dixon, and exponents of the social gospel such as J.S. Woodsworth. As pacificists or anti-imperialists, many of them had opposed Canada's participation in the First World War, and as democrats and socialists, they had cheered the Russian Revolution that had toppled the tsar and established a Bolshevik regime in Russia. But they did not harbour revolutionary aims for the strike: their conduct throughout the strike, particularly in face of the provocative tactics employed by the Citizens, was remarkably peaceful if tactically naïve. After holding firm for six weeks, the strike collapsed in the face of government repression. The leaders were arrested in midnight raids, a silent parade of pro-strike veterans was attacked by mounted police, strikers were killed, and the workers capitulated and returned to work. In many cases, employers used the end of the strike to break existing unions and fire union supporters. Eight strike leaders were tried for seditious conspiracy, a charge that was almost farcical given that many of them were members of political parties that were often at odds with each other. Seven of the leaders, including Russell, Armstrong, and Queen, were convicted, receiving sentences of six months to two years, while Heaps, who defended himself, was acquitted. Dixon, charged with seditious libel, successfully defended himself, while similar charges against Woodsworth were dropped. The prosecution's success rate can be attributed to the fact that the Citizens arranged, at government expense, for a private detective agency to interview the potential jurors to help screen out anyone who might be pro-strike.[3] The case against the strike leaders was pursued by the Citizens as a private prosecution. And while the Citizens portrayed themselves as public-spirited volunteers, the lawyers among them were well paid by the federal government to prosecute the strike leaders. As historians Reinhold Kramer and Tom Mitchell have revealed, the Citizen lawyers were better paid for their work in crushing the strike than the prime minister was paid for running the country. The money to pay them came from funds that had been earmarked for supporting returned soldiers, no small irony given the way the Citizens castigated the strikers for their lack of patriotism.[4]

The Winnipeg General Strike made headlines around the world: it was one of the largest strikes of its kind in an era marked by mass strikes. But it was not unique or exceptional. Labour historian Gregory Kealey described 1919 as the year of the "Canadian Labour Revolt." There were 458 strikes in that year, compared to 86 in 1915. Nearly 3.5 million workers participated in this revolt, compared to 95,232 involved in strikes in 1915.[5] The strike wave that engulfed Winnipeg was a social crisis long in the making: its causes were numerous and interrelated and went far beyond the refusal to negotiate. They extended to the brutal war, the suppression of civil liberties that accompanied the war, runaway inflation, the uneven distribution of basic civic services, the casual racism of the ruling class, the dangerous nature of industrialized work, and, most significantly for the topic at hand, the cost of housing. The federal government had ignored the advice of Thomas Adams, the head of its town planning branch, and chose not to follow the example of the British and American governments and create emergency wartime housing for munitions workers. As a result, the war led to inflation in housing costs and a precipitous decline in housing production.[6]

In early 1919, just as the "Labour Revolt" was taking shape, a worried federal government appointed Winnipeg judge Thomas Mathers to head up a Royal Commission into Industrial Relations.[7] In his final report. Mathers stressed the social and economic causes of the strike wave, noting:

> Another cause of unrest which we met with at practically every place we visited was the scarcity of houses and the poor quality of some of those which did exist. In nothing has production more significantly fallen off during the four years of war than in the building of dwelling houses. The existing condition for the worker is affected not only by the absence of sufficient housing accommodation, but also in the inadequacy of those that are in existence. Poor sanitary conditions and insufficient rooms are the chief complaints. The high price of building land and of building material has made it impossible for the worker to provide

Slum housing in early-twentieth-century Winnipeg. In January 1919, the city's Assistant Chief Health Inspector E.W.J. Hague reported that overcrowding was approaching "slumdom" in many parts of the city. Archives of Manitoba, Archives of Manitoba photo collection, Winnipeg - Streets – Dufferin 2, ca. 1904, P1253.

himself with a home, and some means should be adopted with as little delay as possible, to remedy this defect.[8]

These conditions were apparent in Winnipeg. In January 1919, the city's Assistant Chief Health Inspector E.W.J. Hague reported that overcrowding was approaching "slumdom" in many parts of the city. His report cited examples of six families living in one house, thirteen families living in twenty-eight rooms, and eighteen families living in thirty-six rooms. While Heaps and Arthur Puttee, a labour member of the board of control, argued that the report should be printed and its research extended, other council members were able to block its broader publication. Speaking for them, Mayor Fred Davidson, a former member of the Builders' Exchange (the construction industry's employers' organization), said that such bad publicity would hurt the city.[9] Six months later, at the height of the strike, the *Western Labor News*, the strikers' newspaper, urged readers to re-read:

> the report of actual conditions in Winnipeg by the health officer. Think who profits by this continuous war on women and children. Members of the committee of one thousand have permitted and encouraged such damnable conditions. They have grabbed the land of the city and thus prevent the worker from getting a site for a home—except he pays them an exorbitant price. They have supported a system of taxation under which the home builder is punished and the land speculator rewarded. By their sinister activities they have brought about a horrible condition of overcrowding which is the main cause of the high rate of infant mortality.[10]

In a report on the strike that was prepared for the Manitoba government, Justice Hugh Robson observed the strike was the result of rampant inequality and an ever-hardening sense of class division in the city. "Labour has seen manufacturers and the merchandising class prosperous during the war, and in too many cases self indulgent, whereas the condition of the very labour essential to the prosperity, instead of improving grew worse." Robson betrayed his own frustration with the Winnipeg elite in his summary of labour's position, writing, "There has been, and there is now, an increasing display of carefree, idle luxury and extravagance on the one hand, while on the other is intensified deprivation. The generally cold indifference of the one section to the condition of the other and the display of luxury aggravate this feeling of social disparity into one of active antagonism by the one class against the other."[11]

While the strikers' boasts that they would soon be turning the mansions of River Heights into boarding houses were simply rhetorical flourishes, the city's elite did feel threatened. After all, barely a year had passed since the mansions of St. Petersburg in Russia had indeed been confiscated by revolutionaries, and their previous occupants counted themselves lucky if they had only been evicted.[12] In the eyes of the elites, the leading figures of the labour movement were quite literally criminals. They had defeated them in the streets and in the courts, but they were fearful that labour could emerge victorious at the ballot box. And the issue that they were most fearful of labour succeeding with was the estab-

"There has been, and there is now, an increasing display of carefree, idle luxury and extravagance on the one hand, while on the other is intensified deprivation" (Justice Hugh Robson on the causes of the General Strike). Winnipeg Public Library, Mansions, 200 Block of Wellington Crescent, Crescentwood. Past Forward: Winnipeg's Digital Public History, Public Historical Postcards.

lishment of public housing. As result, in 1919, the elite throttled a labour-backed proposal to use federal money to establish public housing, transformed the Citizens' Committee of One Thousand into a permanent "non-partisan" political party at the municipal level to secure victory in that year's political election, and campaigned for a redrawing of the political map of Winnipeg to limit labour's opportunities for political success in the future. It was class struggle, and the ruling class was fully engaged.

THROTTLING THE LABOUR HOUSING PLAN: "THE RELIEF AFFORDED TOUCHED A RELATIVELY SMALL CLASS"

Thomas Adams had not been able to convince the federal government to build housing for wartime workers, but he did manage to alert it to the fact that the housing shortage would only increase when, at the war's end, tens of thousands of soldiers returned to civilian life.[13] By the end of 1918, the government had the elements of a temporary housing program in place. Under the program, $25 million was being made available as low-cost, twenty-year loans to stimulate the construction of homes that would be sold to private owners. The homes were to cost no more than $3,000 to $4,500 depending on size and construction materials, with the purchasers required to make a 10 percent down payment. Provincial governments were expected to provide additional loan money. In keeping with the prevailing belief in the political and moral benefits of homeownership, there was no support for rental housing. To no avail, unions protested the exclusion of rental housing from the program and called for support for co-operative housing.[14] The federal government argued that it was only entering the housing field on a short-term emergency basis to deal with a war-related, and therefore national, housing crisis. Once the war-related crisis was over, it would be up to the provinces and municipalities to deal with housing.[15]

Winnipeg labour leaders and labour politicians sought to have the money earmarked for Manitoba used to build public housing. In the months before the outbreak of the General Strike, A.A. Heaps, who was at that time a member of Winnipeg city council, led this fight. In January 1919, he called on the City to build three hundred units of housing on thirty acres of land off Selkirk Avenue, on what was termed the Old Exhibition Grounds.[16] Both the federal government and the local business community were adamant that the money could not be used to build rental housing. Federal interior minister Arthur Meighen felt obliged to lecture Winnipeg union leaders that the whole point of the government housing plan was to make homeownership universal.[17] A Winnipeg Board of Trade's Industrial Development Bureau pamphlet claimed, "The solution of the housing problems will have to be largely met by people building their own homes" and the board dismissed Heaps for simply "catering only to the floating population, that exploits a community as long as it is to their benefit, moving on when problems present themselves."[18] It was the perennial class-based argument: only homeownership could turn renters into citizens. And those who could not save up enough for a down payment were little more than rootless vagabonds.

At a public meeting held in February 1919, several speakers recognized that the federal government program "would not solve the problem of getting small, comfortable homes for the class it was desired to benefit on terms compatible with the income they received."[19] At a following meeting, a clear division emerged between those like Heaps who wanted the federal money used to build low-cost housing that could be rented and those, like realtor N.T. MacMillan, who wished to see the money loaned to returned soldiers to buy homes. Heaps pointed out that those who objected to council becoming a landlord had no objections to council being turned into a mortgage corporation.[20] At the beginning of May 1919, Heaps proposed that the City use the federal money to build one thousand houses: such a plan, he argued would "solve the labor difficulties now confronting the city."[21]

But as Heaps was putting this plan forward, the metal trades and building trades workers had walked off the job, and within two weeks the General Strike was underway. Just as the business community took control of municipal government in the city during the strike, it also began to involve itself directly in the city's financing and construction of housing.[22] On June 17, the Northwest Mounted Police derailed Heaps's housing plan when it arrested him and fellow councillor John Queen. Later that month, city council rejected the Heaps plan, recommending instead that a group of councillors meet with a group of "citizens" to develop a new housing plan.[23] J.K. Sparling, David Finkelstein, and Ed Parnell put together a very different housing plan: the *Free Press* described it as the work of "a joint conference of city fathers and citizens."[24] These were not just any councillors and citizens. Sparling, while technically not a member of the Citizens' Committee of One Thousand, had served as its handmaiden on council, proposing motions, such as the

John Queen, convicted for his role as a leader of the Winnipeg General Strike, went on to become a strong advocate of public housing when he served as mayor of Winnipeg in the 1930s. Archives of Manitoba, Archives of Manitoba photo collection, Personalities - Queen, John, ca. 1935, P1280.

one demanding that striking civic workers be fired. When called as a witness during one of the post-strike trials, he brushed off a question about the role the Citizens' Committee played in directing the civic response to the strike, ingenuously asking "was there a committee of one thousand at that time?"[25] Finkelstein was a Winnipeg real-estate developer and longtime mayor of the elite suburb of Tuxedo that he developed and controlled.[26] Parnell was the owner of Speirs-Parnell, the city's largest bakery, and a leading spirit behind the Winnipeg Citizens' Alliance, founded in 1917 as an anti-labour business lobby, the Winnipeg Citizens' Committee of One Hundred, which was created to oppose a 1918 civic workers' strike, and the Winnipeg Citizens' Committee of One Thousand.[27]

The housing plan that these three developed focused on creating a civic housing authority that would "be run on strictly business lines and that the character of each applicant would have to be looked into the same as is done by private mortgage and loan companies."[28] In other words, it would only finance houses that were to be sold to private individuals who had good credit. The Winnipeg Housing Commission, the agency established to administer the program in Winnipeg, would eventually lend $2.76 million, financing the construction of 712 homes. The home buyers were required to supply the land, further limiting the number of people who could afford to take part in the plan, while the commission took out a first mortgage and supervised construction.[29]

The national loan program, which contributed to the construction of 6,200 units of housing across the country, was wound up in 1923. It was viewed by most observers as having been a failure. Federal government limits on the value of the housing that it would finance meant that many contractors could only make a profit by skimping on quality, sometimes building houses without proper foundations.[30] Mismanagement of the program in the municipality of Assiniboia, on Winnipeg's western border, left the local council immersed in a conflict when labour member of the provincial legislature W.D. Bayley charged that the money lent for housing had been used for speculative purposes and profiteering.[31] A legislative committee concluded that the privately owned City and District Land Company in Assiniboia had been allowed to sell "a lot of land which was unsaleable."[32]

In contrast, the program enjoyed a generally positive reputation in Winnipeg. This was in large measure because city council succeeded in having the federal and provincial governments increase the allowed construction costs for homes built in Winnipeg, placing the maximum cost at $7,500.[33] As a result, the Winnipeg Housing Commission was able to demand higher construction standards than were required by the city's bylaws, and there were few complaints about house quality.[34] The program financed the construction of bungalows throughout the city: houses were built, for example, on Morley, Clare, and Balfour in Riverview, Arlington, Garfield, Sprague, and Lipton in the West End. The *Free Press* reported that Beaverbrook in River Heights was being opened up by "salaried young men who have decided to become homeowners early in life, and who are being assisted to ownership by loans from the civic housing commission."[35]

Longtime city housing official Alexander Officer would later tell a parliamentary committee that while the Winnipeg Housing Commission managed to build houses for "white collar" purchasers, it did nothing for "the working man."[36] *Tribune* municipal editor A. Vernon Thomas concurred: "Everyone agrees that the Commission made a great success of its job. However, the relief afforded touched a relatively small class, and left a major housing problem unsolved."[37] Not everyone, however, who took advantage of the plan was a white-collar worker: F. Wilde, an electrician with Winnipeg Hydro, was able to build his own home. F.R. and H.R. Hooper, two brothers who were carpenters, built their own homes side by side.[38] Labour members of the Manitoba legislature, including George Armstrong, likely the most radical member of the labour caucus, supported the program and sought to double the provincial contribution to one million dollars in 1921.[39]

In January 1924 the Housing Commission's directors, having concluded that the "house shortage problem in Winnipeg has been largely solved," chose not to seek authority for continued borrowing and Commission staff were laid off in the spring.[40] Housing, as the *Free Press* noted, would once more "be left in the hands of private individuals and firms."[41] The labour members of council, who had sought to have the federal money used to build rental housing, also opposed the winding down of the Housing Commission. Labour member of council W.B. Simpson claimed the Housing Commission was being put out of business because it was loaning money at a lower rate than the loan companies. He claimed that 500 of the 700 plus homes financed by the Commission would not have been built without its support.[42] Closing the Commission's doors would not only raise house prices but would also reduce quality, heralding a return to the days, Simpson said, where "any kind of shack" could be constructed.[43] His motion to have $400,000 budgeted for a revived Housing Commission was defeated by an eight-to-seven vote.[44] The continuously observant and outspoken E.W.J. Hague attributed the shutdown of the Housing Commission to "a reluctance to interfere with private enterprise."[45]

In 1926, the Commission's vice-chairman W.H. Carter said he was disappointed that "some other body" had not continued the Commission's work. "Men in smaller positions will never be able to own their own home under the ordinary working of loan and mortgage companies." H.C. Thompson, the Commission's chair, said that anyone making less than $175 a month was condemned to be a lifelong renter, which was a shame since the man who owned his own home "was a better citizen for that fact."[46] One cannot help wondering if Carter and Thompson were crying crocodile tears for the poor renter, since they were the ones who in 1924 recommended that the Commission stop making loans.[47] Throughout the twenties, the revival of the Commission would be a staple of the labour movement's municipal campaign platform.[48] When running for council in 1928 as a Labour candidate, for example, J.A. Cherniack not only called for a renewal of the Winnipeg Housing Commission but a municipal takeover of the actual construction of the houses.[49]

The civic elite's success in crushing Heaps's efforts to see federal housing money used to build public housing, was only one prong in a post-strike re-assertion of the power of property. Of greater significance was the establishment of a political party at the municipal level that would defend the rights of property and the rewriting of the election rules to ensure that party's electoral dominance.

REDRAWING THE POLITICAL MAP OF WINNIPEG: "PERMANENTLY CARRY ON THE WORK OF THE CITIZEN'S COMMITTEE OF ONE THOUSAND"

Having crushed the strike, the Citizens' Committee girded itself for the fall 1919 municipal election, in which one-half of the council's fourteen aldermen were up for election. Of the remaining seven, who were serving the second year of a two-year term, four were labour supporters, while only three came from the business community. Alarmed at the prospect of labour gaining control of city hall, the elite worked to establish a Citizens' League that would "permanently carry on the work of the Citizen's Committee of One Thousand."[50] In the coming years, this league underwent a series of name changes: the Citizens' League, the Citizens' Campaign Committee, the Civic Progress Association, and so forth. For simplicity's sake, this party (which always declined to be recognized as a party) will be referred to as the Citizens.[51]

Both the Citizens and labour viewed the 1919 election as a rematch of the strike. Incumbent mayor Charles Gray, who had the support of the Citizens, termed the campaign a battle between the "sane and the Reds" while labour candidate for mayor Seymour J. Farmer called it the "second round of the strike that took place last May and June." Farmer also sought to make housing a central issue by advocating a program of "municipal house building." He proposed that when land came into the possession of the City due to a failure of the owners to pay taxes, the City should build on it and rent the houses out at cost. He also sought to ease the burden on small property owners by removing property tax on property worth less than $3,000. The lost revenue would be covered by taxing the $42 million worth of untaxed land owned by the federal government, the railways, and the churches.[52] In a subsequent campaign, he said there was no reason why "a municipal housing scheme cannot be financed and made self-supporting like other enterprises such as the light and power plant."[53] The 1919 labour platform also called for the reinstatement of civic workers who had been fired for supporting the General Strike, the public ownership of utilities, and the abolition of property restrictions on the right to vote in municipal elections.[54] The Citizens campaign sought to portray the labour candidates as dangerous revolutionaries: the headline on one advertisement, "Just one issue now; 'Red' or white," exemplified the approach.[55] *Free Press* editorials warned readers that while the labour candidates might seem acceptable, they should remember that if labour won, they would be living in a city where "The Bolshie pulls the string."[56] On election day, the Citizens elected four candidates, labour three, leaving a seven–seven deadlock on council, with Mayor Gray, who had been re-elected as the tiebreaker. Labour leaders noted that fighting their way to a tie was a victory of sorts since property restrictions meant that many working people could not vote, while approximately ten thousand property owners had the right to cast more than one vote.[57]

The results left both labour and the Citizens clamouring for a change to the voting system. John Queen, still on council and awaiting trial for sedition, proposed that council move to adult suffrage and do away with property restrictions on the right to vote and the right of property owners to vote in every ward in which they owned property (plural voting). Heaps favoured the abolition of wards, with all councillors being elected at large through a system of transferrable ballots. The Citizens by contrast sought to further restrict the right to vote: in 1920 they proposed people not be allowed to vote unless they had passed an education test. This, in the view of the labour councillors, was a measure intended "to protect the landlord interests."

In March 1920 the provincial government proposed what it termed a compromise between the labour and Citizen proposals: a three-ward system (to replace the existing seven-ward system), the continuance of plural voting, and a transferrable ballot within the wards. Speaking for labour, S.J. Farmer said the proposal was not a meaningful compromise since it did not include the principle of one person, one vote. Without advance notice, the Citizen councillors forced the changes through council rapidly in March. Queen said, "[the] Citizens' League was afraid of the growing power of labor in the council and this re-distribution was intended to make it certain that labor could never gain a majority." The same day that council adopted the new electoral system, Winnipeg lawyer A.J. Andrews completed his address to the jury in the trial of seven General Strike leaders, including Queen and Heaps, accusing them of attempting to overthrow the government and impose an "autocratic soviet government" on the city.[58] The changes in the electoral system yielded the kind of results that the Citizens had been looking for: in the 1920 election, the Citizens elected twelve candidates, while labour elected six, even though the labour vote had increased from the previous election.[59] Farmer, the labour candidate, was able to win election as mayor in 1922 and re-election the following year. However, the failure of labour to win a majority of seats on council made it impossible for him to implement a public housing program.

Throughout the 1920s labour councillors sought without success to have the property restrictions on the right to vote in municipal elections eliminated.[60] In calling for adult suffrage in 1924, Farmer said, "by dividing the community into property and non-property owning classes, the opponents of labor were the direct propagators of class distinction."[61] Not that the Citizen representatives on council were completely opposed to expanding the franchise: in 1928, they approved a motion asking the Province to give the right to vote in municipal elections to corporations.[62]

Labour was internally divided during the post-strike period, which saw the outbreak of a civil war between radical supporters of the newly created One Big Union, which sought to organize all workers—skilled and unskilled alike—into a single union and a more traditional form of craft unionism, one that focused on creating separate unions for each skill or craft. The crushing of the General Strike allowed employers to play both sides off against one another, and often to demand that workers pledge not to join any union at all if they wanted to keep their jobs. Various political factions and parties had always been courting the labour vote. In the years following the Russian Revolution of 1917, these differences hardened and were institutionalized. The 1921 election of J.S. Woodsworth to parliament gave the moderate socialists, referred to successively as the Independent Labor Party and the Cooperative Commonwealth Federation (and from the 1960s onwards as the New Democratic Party) a national platform. More radical labour activists gravitated toward the Communist Party (which also ran candidates for office under a variety of names including the Labour Progressive Party). The party elected Wasyl Kolisnyk to Winnipeg city council in 1926, but it was not until the 1930s and the election of Jacob Penner that Communist representatives had a continuous and effective presence on council. The hostility that the socialists and communists displayed toward one another hampered their ability to make common cause on many issues, and the conflict was heightened by the communists' willingness to let the leadership of the Communist Party of the Soviet Union provide them with political direction.

THE WINNIPEG HOUSING SHORTAGE
IN THE 1920S: "THE DEATH RATE FIGURES
FOR THE AREA WERE ASTOUNDING"

The years following the end of the First World War were ones of economic collapse in Winnipeg. Factories closed, construction stopped, and workers who had been employed in resource industries flocked to the city, further increasing the demand for low-cost housing. Municipal officials were not prepared for the wave of unemployment. Previously the city had required that unemployed people chop wood in the city's wood yard to qualify for relief: but there was not enough wood to keep the army of unemployed busy.[63] The City's Social Welfare Commission had no choice but to temporarily drop this work test and issue relief based on need. It would only, however, provide funds for rent (up to $25 a month) if the applicant was two months behind on their rent. While the City was not prepared to build public housing, the City was, very reluctantly, taking the first steps toward the social provision of housing by subsidizing landlords.[64] Labour councillor W.B. Simpson claimed that the City was not paying rent until the bailiffs were at a welfare recipient's door.[65] In 1924 the policy of paying rent if the relief recipient was two months in arrears was dropped. Instead, an applicant who was in arrears had to work at the wood yard, where he would be paid $1.75 for every cord of wood cut, with the money being applied to rent.[66] By then there were 2,229 married men on relief; 87 percent of them were renters, 15 percent of these households were living in one-room suites, while another 40 percent had only two to three rooms.[67] In January 1925 a delegation from the Trades and Labor Council and the unemployed themselves told councillors that the "wood yard test was unfair, that the unemployed were housed under unsanitary conditions and that a foreman at the wood yard used filthy language to the men."[68] These meagre levels of relief were restricted to families.[69] The single unemployed were encouraged to get out of town or bunk down in jail: in the winter of 1928–1929, 4,000 single men had been forced to seek a bed for the night from the Winnipeg police.[70]

Whether they were on relief or not, low-income Winnipeggers would find it harder and harder to find adequate housing. In

January 1921 the city's health department announced it would be initiating a series of annual housing surveys.[71] In May, Hague reported that conditions were worse than they had been in 1918 when the last housing survey had been conducted. In the five districts that were surveyed, more than a quarter of the one-family houses were being occupied by more than one family. There were 539 families living in single rooms and 650 families living in two-room units. These houses were characterized by a lack of sanitary facilities, poor light, poor ventilation, and limited fire safety provisions.[72] In his report, Hague called on the City to build and rent housing to "persons who cannot afford to buy."

> What I have in mind is a district laid out in an attractive manner with good streets, boulevards, trees, park school site, library, picture theatre, and a few necessary stores, all built and designed as part of one harmonious plan. The houses need not be large, but the architectural features should be just as pretty as those of the Crescentwood district, in fact it would be a wage earners Crescentwood. People say, "Oh, but the working man does not want to live in a segregated Area." On[e] does not hear the Crescentwood or Armstrong's Point residents objecting to segregation, though they none the less are so.

Hague also drew attention to successful co-operative housing developments in the United States.[73]

That year, the city was estimated to have a housing shortage of between two and three thousand homes.[74] The number of vacant houses in the city declined by 500 from 1919 to 1924. Of the 1,002 vacancies, only 479 were deemed fit for occupation.[75] The following year, the city's housing vacancy rate was 2.7 percent, down from 9.8 the year before. In a report on housing Hague wrote:

> The situation as regards these houses does not improve and quite a few cases of new conversion of dwellings to tenement use have come to our notice during the year. I am of opinion that in some parts of the city, at all events, conditions are becoming worse instead of better. Rents charged for these rooms tend to increase, and the effect of this is

many families who formerly rented two or three rooms now live in one room.[76]

The vacancy rate declined again in 1926. In reporting on the continued tightening of the housing market, Hague said there was a growing tendency for families to live in a single room. He also thought more children were living in single-room suites and that these children were increasingly being hospitalized. He pointed to a fifteen-room house on Balmoral which had housed two children in 1919 and was housing ten in 1925.[77] In 1927 Hague reported that the city had a housing vacancy of 1.86 percent and a suites vacancy of 4 percent.[78] Labour member of council Jack Blumberg pointed to a recently discovered case of a house that was occupied by eleven different families as a concrete example of what such a vacancy rate meant.[79]

Labour councillor James Simpkin noted in 1926 that while the city's slums used to be confined to the North End, the Hudson's Bay Reserve was turning into another "slum district." In one case, seventeen families were living in a single house in the area, which was fast becoming the city's rooming-house district.[80] Two years later, Simpkin told a labour meeting that nothing had been done by council to address the "deplorable condition" that existed in the rooming-house district. "These places were over-crowded and the death rate figures for the area were astounding. Congestion was practically double that of any other part of the city and as well as the high death rate, the birth rate was practically double."[81] In the coming decades Blumberg and Simpkin, both of whom had first-hand experience of slum housing, were staunch advocates of public housing. Born in England, Blumberg immigrated to Winnipeg in 1910, worked as a streetcar motorman, served overseas during the First World War, and was active in the One Big Union. First elected to council as a labour candidate in 1919, he served until 1956.[82] Simpkin, born in Lancashire, England, had gone to work in a cotton factory by the age of ten. He emigrated in 1907, working as a carpenter until his 1923 election to Winnipeg city council, where he served until 1946.[83]

Hague continued to advocate for improved standards in housing and to deliver reports that Citizen councillors could only view as more "bad publicity." Since at least 1913, city officials had been calling on the City to license rooming houses, yet Hague's January 1928 call for regulating rooming houses fell, once more, on deaf ears.[84] At the end of the year, eleven men died after drinking wood alcohol at a party held in a rooming house at the Coronation Block at 238 King Street in downtown Winnipeg. A coroner's jury recommended not only regulating the sale of wood alcohol but more vigilant inspection of rooming houses, since the "sanitary arrangements" in the King Street rooming house were judged to be in a "most unsatisfactory state."[85] The city's sanitary inspection report of 1928 stated, "We see little, if any change in the condition of a large number of one-family dwellings now occupied unlawfully as tenements." There were also "too many families housed in the so-called rooming-houses. Notwithstanding the large number of dwellings built during the past few years, there is still a serious shortage of single-family dwellings." For the city as a whole, the number of infant deaths per 1,000 live births was nine. However, in the four sections of the city that bordered the Canadian Pacific Railway yards, the rate was thirty-three per 1,000.[86] Hague was no one-trick pony: upon his retirement from the city in 1930, he served for four years as an Independent Labor Party member on the Winnipeg school board, where he opposed what he termed "false economies" such as firing the city's only kindergarten teacher, cutting teachers' wages, dropping medical and dental services for students, and charging students for textbooks.[87]

Alexander Officer, who had come to Canada after receiving training in sanitation and inspection in Scotland, replaced Hague as the city's chief housing officer.[88] He was well aware of the city's failure to regulate housing conditions. In 1916, when he was inspector, he had reported on a two-and-half-storey frame house that had been divided into twenty-six rooms. It was housing thirteen families—a total of thirty-nine people—and did not count the families living in the cellar (height six feet eight inches) or the attic (height at maximum, seven feet). Orders for improvements and evictions were issued. Ten years later Officer inspected the house again. Once more there were families in the cellar and attic, the windows were frozen shut, and the rooms were so small that families slept on mattresses that were rolled up during the day.[89]

Like Hague, Officer played a national role in public-health inspection, using this position to speak forthrightly on the need for public housing, ending a 1927 speech to the Annual Convention of the Canadian Public Health Association by quoting American housing reformer Lawrence Veiller's 1910 *Housing Reform: A Handbook for Practical Reform in American Cities.* "No housing evils are necessary; none need be tolerated; where they exist they are always a reflection upon the intelligence, rightmindedness and moral tone of the community."[90] In the same speech, he identified the key elements of any meaningful low-cost housing program: "There will always be a large number of people who cannot afford to purchase a home, and it becomes the business of somebody—civic, provincial, or federal—to see to it that a sufficient number of suitable and sanitary dwellings are available." This would require "providing for the borrowing of money at low rates of interest, and the power to condemn old and insanitary tenements in order that large parcels of land may be acquired at reasonable prices."[91] In what amounted to a valedictory speech to the annual convention of the Social Services Council of Canada in 1929, Hague was "emphatic in his advocacy of some government housing scheme." There already were "many successful schemes in various parts of the world."[92]

By the end of the 1920s, the groundwork for public housing would appear to have been laid. There was an established need, successful international examples, the precedent of federal intervention in a national housing crisis, and local advocates with professional credibility. One might have expected that when the economic crash of 1929 plunged the country into a decade-long economic depression, public housing's moment would have come. What followed instead was a decade of political failure on a scale that surpassed the failure of the global economy. When Winnipeg city councillors met to debate housing, some members looked across the council chambers and saw men who had tried to have them deported and had succeeded in having them arrested and sent to jail. Their opponents saw reckless radicals who were prepared to demolish the pillars of established order. Property was to assert its rights with a vengeance.

NOTES

1. Reinhold Kramer and Tom Mitchell, *When the State Trembled: How A.J. Andrews and the Citizens' Committee Broke the Winnipeg General Strike*, Toronto: University of Toronto Press, 2010, 61–64.
2. Reinhold Kramer and Tom Mitchell, *When the State Trembled: How A.J. Andrews and the Citizens' Committee Broke the Winnipeg General Strike*, Toronto: University of Toronto Press, 2010, 44, 52, 54.
3. Reinhold Kramer and Tom Mitchell, *When the State Trembled: How A.J. Andrews and the Citizens' Committee Broke the Winnipeg General Strike*, Toronto: University of Toronto Press, 2010, 299.
4. Reinhold Kramer and Tom Mitchell, *When the State Trembled: How A.J. Andrews and the Citizens' Committee Broke the Winnipeg General Strike*, Toronto: University of Toronto Press, 2010, 289–292.
5. Gregory S. Kealey, "1919: The Canadian labour revolt," *Labour/Le Travail*, 13 (Spring 1984): 16.
6. John C. Bacher, "Keeping to the Private Market: The Evolution of Canadian Housing Policy, 1900–1949," Doctoral thesis, McMaster University, 1985, 72–77.
7. Gregory S. Kealey, "1919: The Canadian labour revolt," *Labour/Le Travail*, 13 (Spring 1984): 16.
8. Royal Commission on Industrial Relations, *Report of Commission appointed under Order-in-Council (P.C. 470) to enquire into Industrial Relations in Canada, together with a Minority Report and a Supplementary Report*, Printed as a supplement to the *Labour Gazette*, July 1919, 13.
9. "Housing survey exposes slum conditions here," *Winnipeg Evening Tribune*, January 1, 1919; "Want limelight on housing conditions," *Manitoba Free Press*, January 1, 1919; Manitoba Historical Society "Frederick Harvey 'Fred' Davidson" <mhs.mb.ca/docs/people/davidson_fh.shtml>, accessed May 5, 2021.
10. "The war on women and children," *The Strike Bulletin*, June 10, 1919.
11. Hugh Amos Robson, *The Royal Commission to Investigate the Cause, Effects, Methods of Calling and of Carrying on the General Sympathetic Strike*, Winnipeg: Government of Manitoba, 1919, 27.
12. Hubertus F. Jahn, "The housing revolution in Petrograd 1917–1920," *Jahrbücher Für Geschichte Osteuropas*, 38, 2 (Franz Steiner Verlag, 1990): 212–227.
13. John C. Bacher, "Keeping to the Private Market: The Evolution of Canadian Housing Policy, 1900–1949," Doctoral thesis, McMaster University, 1985, 74–77.
14. John C. Bacher, *Keeping to the Market: The Evolution of Canadian Housing Policy*, Montreal and Kingston: McGill-Queen's University Press, 1993, 58–61; John C. Bacher, "Keeping to the Private Market: The Evolution of Canadian Housing Policy, 1900–1949," Doctoral thesis, McMaster University, 1985, 86–89; J. David Hulchanski, "The 1935 Dominion Housing Act: Setting the stage for a permanent federal presence in Canada's housing sector," *Urban History Review/Revue d'histoire urbaine*, 15, 1 (1986): 22.
15. John C. Bacher, "Keeping to the Private Market: The Evolution of Canadian Housing Policy, 1900–1949," Doctoral thesis, McMaster University, 1985, 80–81.
16. "Urges city to build 300 houses at once," *Winnipeg Evening Tribune*, January 23, 1919; "Six hundred new houses," *Manitoba Free Press*, March 7, 1919.

17. "Frank discussion on many matters," *Manitoba Free Press*, January 23, 1919.

18. "Housing situation and our industries," *Manitoba Free Press*, February 1, 1919.

19. "Citizens discuss housing problem," *Manitoba Free Press*, February 15, 1919.

20. "Oppose city entering building proposition," *Manitoba Free Press*, March 29, 1919; Manitoba Historical Society, "Neil Thomas MacMillan" <mhs.mb.ca/docs/people/macmillan_nt.shtml>, accessed June 10, 2020; "Summer time by-law defeated by council on second reading," *Winnipeg Evening Tribune*, April 29, 1919.

21. "Heaps' housing plan favored," *Winnipeg Evening Tribune*, May 3, 1919.

22. "Board of Trade and council talk housing," *Manitoba Free Press*, April 25, 1919.

23. "Again defer action on housing scheme," *Manitoba Free Press*, July 10, 1919.

24. "Latest housing plan is believed feasible," *Manitoba Free Press*, July 11, 1919.

25. Reinhold Kramer and Tom Mitchell, *When the State Trembled: How A.J. Andrews and the Citizens' Committee Broke the Winnipeg General Strike*, Toronto: University of Toronto Press, 2010, 63–64.

26. For details on David Finkelstein's career, see: James Stephen Pask, "Myth, Money, Men and Real Estate: The Early Years of Tuxedo, Manitoba," Master of Arts thesis, University of Manitoba, 1981.

27 27. Reinhold Kramer and Tom Mitchell, *When the State Trembled: How A.J. Andrews and the Citizens' Committee Broke the Winnipeg General Strike*, Toronto: University of Toronto Press, 2010, 46–51.

28. "Latest housing plan is believed feasible," *Manitoba Free Press*, July 11, 1919.

29. A.V. Thomas, "Housing certain to be big civic election issue," *Winnipeg Tribune*, October 19, 1935.

30. John C. Bacher, *Keeping to the Market: The Evolution of Canadian Housing Policy*, Montreal and Kingston: McGill-Queen's University Press, 1993, 58–61; J. David Hulchanski, "The 1935 Dominion Housing Act: Setting the stage for a permanent federal presence in Canada's housing sector," *Urban History Review/Revue d'histoire urbaine*, 15, 1 (1986): 22; Shirley Spragge, "A confluence of interests: Housing reform in Toronto, 1900-1920," in Alan F.J. Artibise and Gilbert A. Stelter (eds.), *The Usable Urban Past: Planning and Politics in the Modern Canadian City*, Toronto: Macmillan of Canada, 1979, 260; Thomas I. Gunton, "The ideas and policies of the Canadian planning profession, 1909-1931," in Alan F.J. Artibise and Gilbert A. Stelter (eds.), *The Usable Urban Past: Planning and Politics in the Modern Canadian City*, Toronto: Macmillan of Canada, 1979, 183; Joan Selby, "Urban Rental Housing in Canada 1900-1985: A Critical Review of Problems and the Response of Government," Master's thesis, University of British Columbia, 1985, 44–45.

31. "Independent farmer on old party politics," *Manitoba Free Press*, March 2, 1921.

32. "Legislature refused to nullify decisions," *Manitoba Free Press*, May 6, 1921. The former Assiniboia assistant housing inspector told the inquiry, "The plans and specifications were insufficient. I have seen more elaborate plans used to put up a dog kennel than were used for some of the houses built under the Assiniboia scheme." His reports on the inadequacy of construction were ignored and sometimes altered. An architect testified that many of the houses were poorly built and not "durable;" the plaster was cracking, the doors and windows were not fitting, and the floors were shifting. In January 1921 one man had his Assiniboia home repossessed: it had been built for

less than $2,000 on land worth $150 but sold to him for $3,400. In September 1921 seven of fourteen houses financed by federal loans on one street in Assiniboia were sitting vacant. See: "Tells housing probe reports were altered," *Manitoba Free Press*, January 10, 1921; "Want wider inquiry," *Manitoba Free Press*, January 12, 1921; "Assiniboia housing inquiry is resumed," *Manitoba Free Press*, January 17, 1921; "Provincial treasurer challenged by Bayley," *Manitoba Free Press*, October 6, 1921.

33. "What city council did," *Manitoba Free Press*, April 27, 1920; "Citizens tackle housing problem," *Manitoba Free Press*, April 16, 1921.

34. "City council favors Elmwood stub line," *Winnipeg Evening Tribune*, February 26, 1924.

35. "Housing Commission on inspection visit," *Manitoba Free Press*, October 17, 1921; "Satisfaction shown by new home owners," *Manitoba Free Press*, June 24, 1921; "Beaverbrook is street of homes," *Manitoba Free Press* July 2, 1921.

36. Charles Bishop, "Needs of homes for Winnipeg workers cited," *Winnipeg Tribune*, March 21, 1935.

37. A.V. Thomas, "Housing certain to be big civic election issue," *Winnipeg Tribune*, October 19, 1935.

38. "Housing Commission on inspection visit," *Manitoba Free Press*, October 17, 1921; "Satisfaction shown by new home owners," *Manitoba Free Press*, June 24, 1921; "Beaverbrook is street of homes," *Manitoba Free Press* July 2, 1921.

39. "Capital expenditure estimates go through," *Manitoba Free Press*, April 26, 1921.

40. "Winnipeg housing scheme," *Manitoba Free Press*, January 14, 1924; "Housing staff dismissed," *Manitoba Free Press*, March 28, 1924.

41. "Prospects bright for big building year in Winnipeg," *Manitoba Free Press*, February 22, 1924.

42. "Mud streets, housing and power pact are theme of Simkin's election appeal," *Winnipeg Evening Tribune*, November 20, 1926; "Municipal questions laid before electors," *Manitoba Free Press*, January 30, 1924.

43. "Housing report adoption will be opposed," *Winnipeg Evening Tribune*, January 26, 1924.

44. "Mayor Farmer wavers in council rulings," *Manitoba Free Press*, January 28, 1924.

45. "Vacant houses show decrease in past year," *Winnipeg Evening Tribune*, January 28, 1926.

46. "Many young men buying homes, states report," *Winnipeg Evening Tribune*, January 28, 1926.

47. "Year's housing loans $500,000," *Winnipeg Evening Tribune*, January 23, 1924.

48. "Civic candidates represent variety of political views," *Winnipeg Evening Tribune*, November 26, 1926; "Declares auditorium needed in Winnipeg," *Manitoba Free Press*, November 23, 1927; "John Queen reserves discussion of policy," *Manitoba Free Press*, November 16, 1927; "City council names board to classify civic service," *Winnipeg Free Press*, February 7, 1928.

49. "Ward 3 candidates address electors," *Manitoba Free Press*, November 15, 1928.

50. "Citizens unite in organizing strong league," *Manitoba Free Press*, August 21, 1919.

51. Alan F.J. Artibise, *Winnipeg: An Illustrated History*, Toronto: James Lorimer and Company, 1977, 207.

52. "See chance for labor alderman in Ward One," *Manitoba Free Press*, November 8, 1919.

53. "Refers to mall as automobile drive," *Manitoba Free Press*, November 27, 1920.

54. J.E. Rea, "The politics of conscience: Winnipeg after the strike," *Historical Papers/Communications historiques*, 6, 1 (1971): 278–280; Morris Mott, "The 'Foreign Peril': Nativism in Winnipeg, 1916–1923," Master's thesis, University of Manitoba, 1970, 56.

55. Advertisement, *Manitoba Free Press*, November 21, 1919.

56. "Labor in the civic elections," *Manitoba Free Press*, November 6 and "Bolshie pulls the strings," *Manitoba Free Press*, November 19, 1919.

57. J.E. Rea, "The politics of conscience: Winnipeg after the strike," *Historical Papers/Communications historiques*, 6, 1 (1971): 278–281.

58. "Council to provide for adult suffrage," *Manitoba Free Press*, October 15, 1919; "To drop plural voting in civic election fights," *Manitoba Free Press*, November 8, 1919; "Ward system nears an end in Winnipeg," *Manitoba Free Press*, November 12, 1919; "Mayoral elections may be abolished," *Manitoba Free Press*, November 22, 1919; "Labor mass meeting to protest franchise changes," *Manitoba Free Press*, February 7, 1920; "Changes proposed in Winnipeg civic rule," *Manitoba Free Press*, March 5, 1920; "Winnipeg may decide its own charter needs," *Winnipeg Tribune*, March 12, 1920; "Vote for three wards and four more aldermen," *Manitoba Free Press*, March 16, 1920; "Crown calls strike committee autocratic Soviet government," *Winnipeg Tribune*, March 16, 1920; "Crown's presentation of case concluded," *Manitoba Free Press*, March 16, 1920.

59. J.E. Rea, "The politics of conscience: Winnipeg after the strike," *Historical Papers/Communications historiques*, 6, 1 (1971): 284; Morris Mott, "The 'Foreign Peril': Nativism in Winnipeg, 1916–1923," Master's thesis, University of Manitoba, 1970, 68.

60. "Housing Commission motion is delayed for four weeks," *Manitoba Free Press*, February 22, 1927; "City council names board to classify civic service," *Winnipeg Free Press*, February 7, 1928.

61. "Municipal questions laid before electors," *Manitoba Free Press*, January 30, 1924.

62. "City council names board to classify civic service," *Winnipeg Free Press*, February 7, 1928.

63. Michael Goeres, "Disorder, Dependency and Fiscal Responsibility: Unemployment Relief in Winnipeg, 1907–1942," Master of Arts thesis, University of Manitoba, 1981, 57–61.

64. "Unemployment Relief Before Council," *Manitoba Free Press*, December 6, 1921; Michael Goeres, "Disorder, Dependency and Fiscal Responsibility: Unemployment Relief in Winnipeg, 1907–1942," Master of Arts thesis, University of Manitoba, 1981, 61–62, 74.

65. "Council to prepare for vote on street railway," *Winnipeg Evening Tribune*, February 24, 1925.

66. Unemployment Relief Committee, *Report on Unemployment Relief Covering Winter 1924–25*, 3, cited in Michael Goeres, "Disorder, Dependency and Fiscal Responsibility: Unemployment Relief in Winnipeg, 1907–1942," Master

of Arts thesis, University of Manitoba, 1981, 135.

67. Unemployment Relief Committee, Table 16, cited in Michael Goeres, "Disorder, Dependency and Fiscal Responsibility: Unemployment Relief in Winnipeg, 1907–1942," Master of Arts thesis, University of Manitoba, 1981," 131.

68. "Demand rescinding of welfare appointments," *Manitoba Free Press*, January 13, 1925.

69. Michael Goeres, "Disorder, Dependency and Fiscal Responsibility: Unemployment Relief in Winnipeg, 1907–1942," Master of Arts thesis, University of Manitoba, 1981, 93.

70. "Aldermen make move to reduce hours of labor," *Winnipeg Evening Tribune*, November 13, 1929.

71. "Health department to start housing survey," *Manitoba Free Press*, January 20, 1921.

72. "Crowded conditions in Winnipeg houses," *Manitoba Free Press*, May 12, 1921.

73. Ernest W.J. Hague, *Report on Housing Survey of Certain Selected Areas*, City of Winnipeg Health Department, 1921, City of Winnipeg fonds, Committee on Public Health and Welfare, Communications, Box 590 File 29, 108, 118.

74. "Citizens tackle housing problem," *Manitoba Free Press*, April 16, 1921.

75. "Vacant houses less this year," *Winnipeg Tribune*, January 26, 1924.

76. "Vacant houses and suites in city decrease," *Winnipeg Tribune*, February 26, 1925.

77. "Vacant houses show decrease during year," *Winnipeg Evening Tribune*, January 28, 1926.

78. "Vacant houses show decrease during year," *Manitoba Free Press*, January 27, 1927.

79. "Committee hears of overcrowded houses," *Manitoba Free Press*, February 10, 1927.

80. "Independent Labor Party candidates in Ward Three outline civic platforms," *Manitoba Free Press*, November 18, 1926.

81. "Municipally owned bakery advocated," *Manitoba Free Press*, February 6, 1928.

82. David Edward Hall, "Times of Trouble: Labour Quiescence in Winnipeg 1920–1929," Master of Arts thesis, University of Manitoba, 1983, 114.

83. Manitoba Historical Society, "James Simpkin" <mhs.mb.ca/docs/people/simpkin_j.shtml>, accessed June 1, 2021.

84. "To consider control of rooming houses," *Manitoba Free Press*, January 6, 1928; "Committee favors rooming house bylaw," *Winnipeg Free Press*, January 12, 1928.

85. "Coroner's jury advocates rooming house inspection," *Manitoba Free Press*, January 5, 1928. The Coronation Block had served as Winnipeg's city hall from 1883 to 1886. It will be familiar to some Winnipeggers as the long-time home of the Shanghai Restaurant; Heritage Winnipeg, "City Hall: The Heart of Winnipeg's Decision Making" <heritagewinnipeg.blogspot.com/2018/06/city-hall-heart-of-winnipegs-decision.html>, accessed June 1, 2021.

86. "Winnipeg's war for health," *Manitoba Free Press*, July 5, 1928.

87. "Results at a glance," *Winnipeg Free Press*, November 26, 1932; "Farmer scores Hydro contract as grave error," *Winnipeg Evening Tribune*, November 24, 1932; "How the votes were transferred," *Winnipeg Free Press*, November 26, 1934; "Official first count," *Winnipeg Free Press*, November 30, 1936.

88. "Congratulations," *Winnipeg Tribune*, August 21, 1943; Family search, "Alexander Officer" <ancestors.familysearch.org/en/KLGK-WK1/alexander-officer-1878-1973>, accessed July 7, 2021.

89. Alexander Officer, "The Sanitary Inspectors' Association of Canada: Housing and public health," *Public Health Journal*, 18,. 6 (1927): 288–289.

90. Alexander Officer, "The Sanitary Inspectors' Association of Canada: Housing and public health," *Public Health Journal*, 18,. 6 (1927): 290.

91. Alexander Officer, "The Sanitary Inspectors' Association of Canada: Housing and public health," *Public Health Journal*, 18,. 6 (1927): 284–285.

92. Winnipeg Downtown Places, "95 MacDonald Avenue—Point Douglas Presbyterian/Our Lady of Lourdes Church" <winnipegdowntownplaces.blogspot.com/2013/03/95-macdonald-avenue-point-douglas.html>, accessed July 8, 2020; "Responsibility for youth is discussed," *Manitoba Free Press*, April 5, 1929.

Chapter 4

"NO ACTION TAKEN": THE 1930s

"Low-cost housing scheme again debated by council but no action taken." This headline from the *Winnipeg Tribune* of April 4, 1939, not only summed up the previous evening's city council meeting but was an apt and accurate summary of a decade-long failure to address the city's ever-intensifying shortage of low-cost housing. There had been plenty of talk at the national and local levels. Over the course of the decade, a parliamentary committee had been convened to inquire into the national housing situation, two separate national housing acts had been adopted, and in Winnipeg, at least four "housing schemes" had been proposed and debated. Yet, in Winnipeg at the end of the Great Depression, not a single unit of government-sponsored low-cost housing had been built. The Great Depression of the 1930s created a housing crisis throughout the country and for tens of thousands of households. Mass unemployment had forced thousands to seek shelter in crowded dangerous rooming houses or had banished them to dormitories, farms, and work camps. At the federal level, neither the Conservatives nor the Liberals were prepared to work with municipalities to create and subsidize low-cost housing. Provincial governments, dominated by rural electorates, turned their backs on urban problems of any sort. It was left to socialists, social reformers, and their allies to prod cash-strapped city councils to take action. They were up against the entrenched power of property: the real-estate industry, landlords, and investors saw public housing as a direct assault on the rights of property. They fought off this assault with every tool at their command. In the end, they prevailed with the support of a political system that privileged the rights of property over the rights of people.

THE GREAT DEPRESSION HITS MANITOBA

The decade-long international economic collapse known as the Great Depression devastated the Canadian economy. In some years one in three workers was unemployed. On the prairies, falling grain prices were compounded by drought and crop failure. By 1930, farmers' incomes were only a third of what they had been in 1928. In the face of the government's revenue crisis, Manitoba Premier John Bracken increased taxes, cut expenditures, and cancelled construction projects.[1] The measures only served to undercut any chance of economic recovery.[2] As the Depression worsened, the federal government agreed to contribute to relief payments, as welfare was termed in that period, but only if the Province matched every federal dollar and the municipalities agreed to shoulder 50 percent of the costs. This meant that civic governments had to cover most of the cost of meeting the needs of the unemployed, the homeless, the dispossessed, and the bankrupt.

The Manitoba government showed little interest in addressing the needs of the urban poor and unemployed.[3] This should not be surprising: Winnipeg was under-represented in the legislature. In 1936, the city, with a population of 200,000, had only ten seats in the fifty-five-seat provincial legislature, at a time when the provincial population was 680,000.[4] Historian John Kendle's biography of John Bracken, who was premier throughout the Depression, makes scant reference to urban issues and none to housing, a reflection of the attention that the provincial government paid to these concerns.

Municipal relief—which was the only kind of relief available—was only granted to those who could demonstrate severe need and those who qualified had to agree to a highly intrusive level of scrutiny of their personal lives. They could not own a car, have a phone, nor purchase liquor, were subject to random home visits, and had to requalify every month.[5] By December 1932 there were 8,050 Winnipeg families on relief.[6]

To pay the relief bill, the City of Winnipeg had to borrow from the provincial government: by 1936, it owed $3.6 million.[7] Over 90 percent of civic revenues came from property taxes but thousands of homeowners were unable to pay their taxes.[8] City revenue fell by 12 percent between 1931 and 1936, by which time the city was owed $12 million in tax arrears, double the amount it collected.⁹ The following year, 1,175 Winnipeg properties were set to go on sale for tax arrears.¹⁰ If they could not be sold, they became the property of the city.

A 1937 *Tribune* editorial noted that at the start of the Depression "the unemployed were herded into the city's available supply of tumble-down houses, and the rack-renting landlord, due to the general disappearance of income among his clients, having no other alternatives, was compelled to accept rents approximately equal to the taxes."¹¹ As in the past, rent subsidy to people on relief was not given until families were three months in arrears. An appalled Independent Labor Party (ILP) member of council, Morris Gray, commented, "The only time the [Social Welfare] commission will pay rent before the time is when the people are thrown out of their homes."¹² By 1936 the City was giving families on relief between $10 and $20 a month for housing, with the average payment being $12.66. At that time Statistics Canada estimated the average national rent to be at $21.76 a month. In addition, families were provided with $11.60 a month for utilities, a figure that everyone agreed was below the cost of the services. In that year there were 5,433 tenants on relief, with an average household size of 4.8 people.¹³

THE SINGLE UNEMPLOYED

The single unemployed—a largely male population—received even less support. In 1929, the federal government opened the immigration halls on Main Street and Water Street (now called Sir William Stevenson Way) to house the single unemployed, and the following year, the Canadian National Railways immigration hall was converted to a dormitory that would sleep 350 single men.¹⁴ These halls were large imposing buildings that had been constructed in the early years of the twentieth century to replace the earlier immigrant sheds.¹⁵ The men were given vouchers for meals in five dining halls the city set up for the single unemployed.¹⁶ To qualify for this relief the men were required to chop firewood in the city wood yard. Later the single unemployed were put to work digging the Grassmere Ditch, a drainage project north of the city. There they were housed on site in railway bunk cars that housed twelve men a car.[17]

Politicians viewed the single unemployed as a social threat: the policy goal was to drive them out of the city. In 1931 the federal government, the Province, and municipalities placed 1,600 single unemployed men on Manitoba farms. Each man got five dollars a month while the farmer got five dollars a month for providing room and board.[18] The Province also opened nine rural work camps where the unemployed cut brush, built roads and created the infrastructure for what would become Manitoba's cottage country, all for ten cents a day. The federal Department of National Defence established a similar network of national work camps in 1934 that eventually came to house over 25,000 men in remote locations across the country. The Manitoba camp was in what is now Riding Mountain National Park. One of the men sent this description of the windowless, 1,896 square foot shack that he and eighty-seven other men were living in: "There is a marked resemblance to a hog pen or dog pound. At times the place reeks of the foul smell and at night the air is simply fetid. The floor is dirty and the end of the shack where men wash... is caked with black mud."[19]

The farms, immigration sheds, and work camps could not absorb all the single unemployed. In 1936, Winnipeg was providing the single men with 85 cents a week in rental relief and vouchers for two meals a day. According to the Single Men's Unemployed Association, an organization created by the unemployed, "This situation brings about overcrowding and lack of sanitation. Householders cannot supply sufficient heat, room and cleanliness as required by the board of health for 85 cents a week."[20] At the end of the decade J. Kensington Downes, a former member of the Manitoba legislature, compared the treatment of two lions at the Assiniboine Park Zoo with that of the single unemployed. Each day Downes could see the unemployed sifting their way through garbage bins throughout the city in search of scrap paper they could sell for a half-cent a pound. The knowledge that the City had spent $6,000 on a new lion house at the zoo led him to contemplate poisoning the lions to free up additional shelter for the poor wretches reduced to scavenging for a living.[21]

THE FAMILIES ON RELIEF

Through the 1930s housing conditions in the city of Winnipeg continued to worsen. The city's chief housing official Alexander Officer spoke out on the issue clearly and bravely throughout the decade. In one public address, he described the fire hazard in Winnipeg's boarding houses as so extreme that hundreds were at risk of being "burned like rats." It would, he said, "make your heart bleed to see some of the conditions under which many of the people in this city have to live."[22] A 1934 civic administration report concluded, "there are far too many families crowded to-gether in houses originally designed and constructed for one fam-ily, without any attempt being made to partition off rooms." Of the 352 houses inspected, 111 were occupied by single families. In one case, a 19-room house was occupied by 11 families and in another, a 15-room house was occupied by 11 families. Nine families were sleeping in basements and 111 in attics.[23] In the area bounded by Portage Avenue, Kennedy Street, Broadway, and Main Street, 3,728 people were living in 352 houses.[24]

There was little new housing. While twelve apartment buildings were built in Winnipeg in 1931, only one was built the following year. In 1933, 124 houses and three apartment block had been built in the city, when just five years prior, in 1928, those figures were 838 and 20.[25] Many buildings were foreclosed upon, larger suites were broken up into smaller ones, and single-family houses were converted into rooming houses.[26] In 1935, seventy-two units of housing were constructed, but this was only equal to the number of houses that were torn down in that year.[27]

Thousands of people were sentenced to a life of misery, conflict, and even tragedy. It took James Gray three attempts to overcome his sense of shame and walk the three miles from the home that he was living in on Ruby Street with his wife Kay, his daughter Patty, his parents, and two brothers, to the City of Winnipeg relief office on Elgin Street. It was, he later wrote, the most humiliating experience of his life. But he had to do it. "We were almost out of food, we were almost out of fuel, and our rent was two months in arrears." It was February 1931 and Gray had been out of work since November. He had come to the "ego-shattering discovery that there was not a single employer in all Winnipeg who would give me a job." Gray, who was twenty-five years old, and had been working since he was fifteen, would spend the next two years on relief, showing up at the city wood yard every Tuesday to chop cordwood to earn his relief payment.[28] Qualifying for relief was not easy. In *Laugh, Baby, Laugh*, her memoir of life as a young single mother, Winnipeg writer Ann Henry told of how, after briefly moving in with her father in St. Boniface, she was banned from welfare in either Winnipeg or St. Boniface. She did not qualify for relief in Winnipeg because she was living in St. Boniface, but St. Boniface officials said she had not met their residence requirements either. She and her children ended up spending a winter in the living room of a kind-hearted landlady, who managed to bully Winnipeg welfare officials into providing her with a small housing allowance.[29]

Gray, his wife, and daughter eventually moved out of his parents' Ruby Street house and established their own household. A $13-a-month housing-relief voucher allowed them enough to rent a single room in a house on Furby Street, whose seven rooms were home to seven families, with the landlord and his wife sleeping in the kitchen. There was no privacy. In winter:

> the strain involved in keeping children cooped up in a rooming-house began to tell. Patty had a five-year-old playmate who lived downstairs. When they played together it had to be in the halls and on the stairs. When they played they naturally fought and cried, so the other tenants complained and shooed them out of the hallways. In an effort to keep peace in the house, Kay and I took turns riding Patty around the block in the sleigh, a Spartan regimen in a Winnipeg winter.

Washday conflicts between boarders could boil over to the point that half the tenants were not speaking to the other half. One landlord's habit of keeping the washroom locked up led the Grays to retaliate by never turning off the hot water.[30] While landlords were at first reluctant to take in people on relief, they soon became highly prized tenants, since the rent, however minimal, was guaranteed. The turnover was such that landlords rarely bothered to take down a "Rooms for Let" sign.[31] David Burley and Michael

Maunder's history of life on Furby Street, which was transformed into a rooming-house row in the 1930s, shows that in 1931 a third of the families on Furby had moved in during the previous year, and nearly a third would move out in the following year. It was a pace that would continue for the rest of the decade.[32] Even though Gray was often locked in endless wearying conflicts with his landlord, he recognized that in a poorly insulated rooming house where every tenant was cooking on hotplates the utility bills quickly ate up the overworked landlord's potential profits, with little or nothing left for maintenance.[33]

In a memoir published in 1970, Ann Henry wrote:

> During the Depression, people spoke of a "room" the way they now speak of a house. We didn't say people had nice houses. We said they had nice rooms. A whole social structure sprang up. The well-to-do might have two, or even three, rooms, which, with ingenuity and imagination, could be made into a real apartment.[34]

Like James Gray, Henry recalled the ongoing wars between roomers and landlords.

> Rooming-house landladies schemed to keep tenants from coming in with mud on their feet, from wasting water or burning lights. They booby-trapped their houses with signs: "Remove Your Rubbers," "Lights Out at Ten O'Clock," "No Visitors," "No Cooking (or Light Housekeeping)," "Turn Off the Light When Leaving Bathroom," "Phone Calls, Five Cents," and "No Peddlers."
>
> Tenants fought back, plugged phones and toilets, muddied floors, sneaked visitors in on tiptoe past the landlady's door and traded insults with her. Women argued over washdays, the use of bathrooms, hot water. The loss of clothes-pins could generate wars that raged for weeks. In countless attic rooms, old men with serpent eyes muttered incantations.[35]

There was also generosity. Adele Wiseman's parents turned their home on Burrows into a rooming house:

There was one winter when the three-bedroom house had roomers in at least two and sometimes all three of those bedrooms. To sleep, we [Adele, her mother, and her siblings] were moved around in the living room and in the dining room, just wherever we could sort out places. My dad was in Vancouver looking for work and a down-and-outer came to the door. Mom told him if he looked after the furnace he could sleep downstairs. He put up some boards on four logs. Mom gave him bedding and he slept down there for the whole winter.[36]

C.H. Enderton had predicted that the prestige homes of turn-of-the-century Winnipeg would be eventually transformed into third-class boarding houses. During the 1930s, his prediction came true as once-elite neighbourhoods became part of a vast and deteriorating rooming-house district. In 1937 the *Free Press* ran a series of articles highlighting conditions in the city's rooming houses. According to the reporter in Point Douglas "a tenement known as 'The Ship'—a two-story architectural monstrosity containing 16 suites in which lived 35 adults and 16 children. Every suite, upstairs and down, is heated by a wood stove. It has no fire escape."[37] Another rooming housing in Point Douglas had:

11 wood stoves scattered through its 19 tiny rooms. The stoves supply the heat in winter and make the place a veritable inferno in the summer. There are only two toilets in the building. The 12 men in the basement and 10 adults and seven children on the first floor share one, while the 11 roomers on the second floor have one of their very own.

The lack of even one sink in the building causes such congestion, a housewife said that they have to stand in line to pour the dishwater into the toilets.[38]

In a Logan Avenue tenement, the *Free Press* found forty-four people living in thirty rooms.[39] Slum conditions also existed south of Portage Avenue in the old Hudson's Bay Reserve. "On Smith Street a *Free Press* reporter and cameramen found 19 people living in one eight-roomed terrace section. In another terrace a couple of blocks away a man and his wife and three children were confining their lives in a single room—cooking there on a gas stove, eating there, washing their clothes and sleeping there." The three-storey terraced housing units that the reporters visited were all lacking in fire escapes and most had a gas stove in each room. Tenants stored perishable food in boxes hung from their windows or between the inner window and the storm window. A woman who had been living in the Higgins area for five years said she had never been able to find "a house free of bed bugs, mice and other vermin." Relief officials had told her she should move if she did not like the place she was living in. The owners, she said, were "'milking' the houses of every penny they could get out of them before they were condemned by the city health department. Under no condition would they make even the smallest repair."[40]

Some were driven to the brink and beyond. On December 17, 1934, William Morris, an unemployed electrician, returned from yet another unproductive visit to the local employment office to the small house his family was renting on Valour Road in West End Winnipeg. The doors to the house were locked and Morris, lacking a key, climbed through a window to discover a holocaust: his wife Emma had committed suicide by drinking carbolic acid. Before killing herself, she had strangled their five-year-old daughter and drowned their two-year-old son. The family had moved into their Valour Road home ten months earlier, their second move since William had lost his job with the Canadian National Telegraph Company in 1931. Their conditions were so reduced that Emma had bought the carbolic acid from a local pharmacy on credit. According to the news reports, her shame at going on relief had led her to live the life of a recluse, particularly after a "cruel neighbour" had "thrown" her family's dependence at her.[41]

RESISTANCE

People on relief did fight back. On April 15, 1930, six thousand people gathered at the Manitoba legislature to support the demands made by Communist Party activists for some form of unemployment insurance. At one point, police charged the demonstration, which had been denied a police permit. Nine demonstrators were

knocked unconscious by the police and an additional fifteen required hospital treatment. Four of the nine were arrested as soon
as they were released from hospital. At least three of them were on
relief (the fourth, according to the *Winnipeg Tribune*, spoke little
English).[42]

In 1933 a picket led by Mitch Sago, a leading figure in the
Winnipeg Communist Party, prevented bailiffs from seizing the
furniture of Mike Skomorak, who was being evicted from his
home at 539 Pacific Avenue. Skomorak was allowed to keep his furniture on the condition that he move out. Sago announced that the
Neighbourhood Council movement would picket all future evictions under the slogan, "No evictions, no furniture seized."[43] James
Gray participated in a Communist-organized anti-eviction demonstration at city hall. "Some aldermen got shoved around, some
small rocks were thrown, and a few heads were cracked. It was not
much of a riot, but it was enough to get some small attention paid
to our clothing problem." By then, all his clothing was worn out.[44]
In 1937 a group of men on relief went on strike, demanding to be
paid the going rate of 42 cents an hour for their work. The strike
failed and they were struck off the relief rolls and evicted from the
housing that the City had found for them and their families.[45]

A national campaign to end the relief camps culminated in the
On-to-Ottawa Trek of 1935, which saw thousands of men leave the
camps in Western Canada, hop freight trains, and head for Ottawa
to put their case before the federal government. The federal government resolved to halt the Trek in Regina where the arrest of
the Trek's leadership sparked a conflict that left two people dead
and hundreds wounded.[46] A thousand men from Manitoba relief
camps had gathered in Winnipeg, waiting to join the Trek. In late
June they occupied a municipal dining hall on Princess Street.
Much to the frustration of the Citizens members on council, deputy mayor John Blumberg arranged to have the military provide the
men with tents, while the City provided the men with meals. After
several tense and uncertain days, the Manitoba trekkers left the
city in rented buses but were turned back by police at the Ontario
border, bringing the Trek to an end.[47]

PRESSURE FOR A NATIONAL HOUSING POLICY

Similar stories of poverty, suffering, and conflict could be told about every city in the country. The Canadian residential construction industry collapsed at the outset of the Great Depression in 1930. The number of new housing starts in 1933, for example, was a third of the 1929 figure.[48] The high levels of unemployment contributed to homelessness, overcrowding, evictions for non-payment of rent, and declines in building maintenance.[49] Nationally the gap between housing stock and households jumped from 120,000 to 188,000 during the 1930s.[50] In 1934, the Lieutenant-Governor's Committee on Housing Conditions in Toronto reported that poor housing conditions threatened the health of between 2,000 and 3,000 Torontonians, leading the commission to call for the establishment of a national housing commission.[51] A growing recognition that the private market could not meet the housing needs of low-income people led to an increasing number of calls for the construction of government-funded low-cost housing.[52]

Political parties and social reformers took up the issue. In 1935, the Co-operative Commonwealth Federation, under the leadership of J.S. Woodsworth, called for the development, ownership, and operation of low-rent nonprofit housing.[53] The League for Social Reconstruction's 1935 reform manifesto, Social Planning for Canada, recommended the establishment of a federal housing authority to address the needs of low-income households through subsidized publicly owned housing developments.[54] These were and remain the two essential pillars of any effective public-housing program. In 1938 the Canadian Federation of Mayors and Municipalities used its brief to the Royal Commission on Dominion–Provincial Relations to call for a national low-rental housing program.[55]

HOUSING ACTS, BUT NO HOUSING ACTION

The Depression had broken out in the fall of 1929, leading to the election of the Conservative government of Prime Minister R.B. Bennett the following year. Housing conditions worsened with each passing year, but it was only in 1935, with a federal election just months away, that Bennett appointed a special parliamentary committee to investigate and report on housing issues. At the end of the committee's hearings, its Conservative chairman, Arthur Ganong, admitted to having been converted to the views of people he had once viewed as "housing cranks."[56] The committee's unanimous report recommended that a national housing authority be established to build low-cost housing and loan money to municipalities to carry out similar projects.[57] Winnipeg member of parliament A.A. Heaps served as a committee member and would have been one of the cranks who brought Ganong around to the need for public investment in housing. Another was Alexander Officer, who after painting a grim portrait of housing conditions in Winnipeg, stressing the dangers that arose from jamming people into unsanitary, poorly lit, poorly ventilated rooms, issued a call for federal funding of municipal housing projects.[58]

The government, however, was not prepared to adopt measures that would put it into competition with private industry.[59] Instead, Bennett's government brought in a three-page *Dominion Housing Act*.[60] To the degree that it sought to have a concrete impact, its focus was on stimulating the construction of private homes by providing economic incentives to mortgage lenders. No attention was directed to the housing needs of low-income people.[61] Under the Act, the federal government was prepared to provide a mortgage for 20 percent of the cost of a house, if a purchaser could come up with a 20 percent down payment and find a private lender who would provide the remaining 60 percent. To sweeten the deal, the government was prepared to guarantee the private lender's risk. But the lender had to agree to a limit on the interest charged to the home buyer.[62]

The *National Housing Act*'s government-subsidized mortgages were only available to the top 20 percent of Canadian income earners.[63] W.C. Clark, the federal deputy minister of finance, was unapologetic about the blatant class bias of the act, noting, "We desire to encourage building, and I suppose the building of high cost houses meets this objective more effectively than the building of low cost houses."[64] One of the first homes financed under the program was an $8,000 mansion in the exclusive Westmount neighbourhood of Montreal.[65] Despite the government guarantees, private lenders declined to make any of what they viewed as high-risk loans and generally avoided making loans in the

Prairies, which were seen as a risky region.[66] By the end of 1937, only fifty *Dominion Housing Act* loans had been issued in the prairie provinces.[67]

Because the Act did not allow the federal government to make direct loans to municipalities, cities could not use the act to finance low-cost housing.[68] Nor was there anything in the *Dominion Housing Act* for renters.[69] An outraged A.A. Heaps pointed out that the *Dominion Housing Act* bore as much resemblance to the Housing Committee's recommendations as a pig did to pig iron.[70] William Irvine, another ccrer, issued a robust challenge to the federal government's do-nothing approach. "The people need homes and the government should provide them. Whatever is physically possible is financially possible."[71] This may have sounded economically naïve, but in fact, it does a pretty good job of describing the attitude the government took to military spending upon the outbreak of the Second World War.

The *Dominion Housing Act* was one of a series of last-minute reforms that failed to rescue the political fortunes of R.B. Bennett's Conservative administration, which went down in defeat in 1935. When it came to housing, the incoming Liberal government of Mackenzie King did not depart from the policies of the Bennett government. It waited three years before bringing in its own *National Housing Act*, which like the *Dominion Housing Act*, focused on stimulating the construction of high-end housing.[72] The *National Housing Act* did have a provision for the funding of non-profit housing that would have allowed the federal government to make loans of between 80 and 90 percent of the cost of a project. The provisions, however, were so restrictive that during the two years they were in effect, not a single unit of housing was constructed under them.[73] The 1938 Act did not have any provision for the subsidization of rents—a key element of any public-housing program—because the federal government believed this to be a municipal responsibility.[74]

THE CONTENDING FORCES ON COUNCIL

In the absence of meaningful federal policy and the provincial government's complete disinterest in housing, the struggle over public housing would be fought out in city councils across the country.

In Winnipeg, the political conflict between the Citizen and labour councillors was continuous. From 1933 to the end of the decade, four different major housing proposals emerged from council. Three focused on creating large-scale low-cost housing developments, while one, proposed during a period when the Citizens dominated council, sought to use the *Dominion Housing Act* provisions to establish a private-limited dividend housing company that was intended to focus on the construction of lower-priced houses. The first plan was rejected by the federal government, after initial acceptance, in response to pressure from Winnipeg's property industry; the second was defeated in a referendum in which the right to vote was restricted to property owners; the limited-dividend plan was torpedoed by the provincial government, whose actions were in keeping with the local property industry; and the fourth died because the Citizen caucus insisted that it be subjected to a property-owners referendum, a requirement that led the plans' supporters to simply abandon it. The trajectory of these four doomed projects is best understood in light of the contending forces on council and the broader social forces that pushed for and against public housing.

For much of the decade, John Queen led the labour contingent on council. Queen had been elected to the Manitoba legislature in 1920 while he was in jail for his participation in the Winnipeg General Strike and continued to serve as a member of the legislature until 1941. He was the ILP's unsuccessful candidate for mayor in 1932 and 1933, making sure to include a commitment to establish a "municipal housing scheme" in each campaign platform. After being elected mayor in 1933, Queen would serve in that position, with one interruption, until 1942.[75] The leading ILP city council members were Jack Blumberg, Morris Gray, Matthew Stobart, and James Simpkin. Blumberg and Simpkin were veteran councillors, but Gray had been elected in 1930 and Stobart in 1934. Gray was born Moishe Gurarie in Goroditz, Russia, and orphaned at a young age. He was radicalized by the failed 1905 Russian revolution, coming came to Canada in 1907. He was elected to council after serving on the school board for four years. He left council in 1941 to sit as a CCF and later NDP MLA until his death in 1966. He was heavily involved in Jewish community service organizations including the Jewish Children's Aid Society.[76] Matthew Stobart was a painter by trade, working for the Winnipeg school board.[77]

In 1933, Jacob Penner, a bookkeeper with the Workers' and Farmers' Cooperative Company and a former organizer of the Winnipeg General Strike, won election to council as a Communist candidate. Born in Ukraine, Penner immigrated to Canada in 1904. His experience of life in Tsarist Russia, which culminated in his participation in a steelworkers' strike that was crushed by force, made him a lifelong radical. In 1921 he was a founding member of the Communist Party of Canada. First elected to represent a North End ward on Winnipeg city council in 1933, he sat on council until his retirement in 1961 with only one major interruption: the twenty months that he spent in a Canadian government internment camp during the Second World War. His job as an accountant paid him twenty-five dollars a week, enough to allow him to rent a house on Polson Avenue in the North End. (According to Jacob's son Roland, the family always rented and never owned, moving almost annually.) However, once elected to council, he felt compelled to serve as a full-time councillor and quit his job. This was highly unusual because council members only received a thirty-dollar-a-month honourarium at the time, since politics was expected to be reserved for members of the business community.[78] Following the 1934 election, Joseph Forkin joined Penner as the second Communist member of council.[79] The two men were unswerving supporters of public housing.

Until his defeat in 1934, Mayor Ralph Webb led the conservative faction on council. A veteran of the Great War, Webb was known for the violent language he used in criticizing the political left, at one time championing the idea of throwing "the Reds" into the Red River or shipping them to Russia.[80] The other leading establishment figures were John McKerchar, Cecil Gunn, and Cecil Rice-Jones. A successful grocer, McKerchar had been first elected to council in 1920, where, as chair of the finance committee, he had developed a reputation as the "watchdog of the treasury." A central element of his 1934 election platform was easing the burden of taxation on property owners.[81] Gunn was an engineer by profession and the president of the Winnipeg Builders' Exchange.[82] Rice-Jones was a former rancher who had risen to be the vice president of the United Grain Growers Association and later head of his own investment firm.[83]

While Webb, McKerchar, Gunn, and Rice-Jones were the dominant figures on council, Frederick G. Thompson and Charles Simonite were the shock troops in the fight against public housing. A lawyer by training, Thompson had served in the Winnipeg Grenadiers and been wounded in the Amiens campaign in the First World War. He served on the executive of the Citizens' Committee of One Thousand during the General Strike, founded the anti-General Strike Returned Soldiers' Loyalists Association, lobbied successfully to have the Winnipeg police force fired because it was not sufficiently anti-strike in attitude, and organized the violence-prone Special Constables that were hired to replace the police.[84] Elected to council in 1935, Thompson once criticized a municipal proposal to have the federal government relief money used to build housing because the tenants would be "of the type who would not give their homes proper care."[85]

In 1929, Charles Simonite was one of "a number of Winnipeg business and professional men [who] were asked to run in the civic election on a slate promising sound business practices." He would serve on council from 1930 to 1955 with one two-year break, spending seventeen years as chair of the finance committee. As his obituary stated, he was a "firm believer in private enterprise and private initiative." Born in Paris, Ontario in 1879, he moved to Manitoba with his parents the following year. He went into the real-estate business in the early 1900s and eventually served as the chair of the real-estate board.[86] A 1931 election advertisement in the Free Press included, among Simonite's qualifications, the fact that he was "a large taxpayer."[87] Shortly after his election to council Simonite joined with Mayor Webb in an unsuccessful attempt to have relief for the single unemployed men reduced to a daily allowance of bread and cheese.[88] The only form of housing support he would countenance was an increase in the amount paid to private landlords who housed families on relief, a measure that he proposed annually in the later years of the decade.[89]

The occasional councillor tried to find some middle ground between the Citizen and labour councillors, the most prominent of these being Margaret McWilliams.[90] While McWilliams was a

Liberal who represented south Winnipeg, she was open to leftist ideas.[91] In her speeches, she regularly pointed to the lack of home construction, the increase in family formation, and the health and social problems arising from communities characterized by poor housing.[92] At one point she recommended the construction of what was dubbed a "honeymoon hotel," that would rent suites to newlyweds while they sought to establish themselves. "A marriage that doesn't start in a self-contained unit," she said, "has only a 50-50 chance of success."[93] These, it turned out, were far better odds than any public-housing proposal had at city council.

FRIENDS AND ENEMIES

While Winnipeg city council was the cockpit in which Citizen and labour councillors fought out their battles over public housing, each side had its allies. Unions, professionals, church leaders, and journalists emerged as prominent supporters of public housing. Arranged against them were the broader business community and the Home and Property Owners' Association.

Many of the ILP politicians such as Queen, Blumberg, Simpkin, and Stobart had roots in the labour movement, and it is of little surprise that unions were strong supporters of any measures intended to create public housing. In 1931, for example, the Independent Labor Party and the Winnipeg Building Trades Council presented a plan for the construction of moderate-priced housing that was rejected by the City.[94] The Building Trades Council could be depended on to raise a vociferous and often eloquent voice in favour of public housing. In commenting on the failure of a 1934 proposal to building a public-housing complex in downtown Winnipeg, the Building Trades Council, in a letter to the editor, reminded readers, "The tall buildings of Winnipeg, the Tyndall stone banks, the marble stores and picture houses, are merely a screen around a cesspit. Take them away from one or two of our best streets, and you reveal an appalling sight, which has been accumulating horror at compound interest for many years."[95]

Women's organizations affiliated with the labour movement also spoke up in favour of public housing. In 1937 the Labor Women's Federation of Manitoba called on council to "institute a proper housing scheme."[96] Labour member of the Winnipeg school board,

Jessie Maclennan, told a 1939 International Women's Day meeting held at the Peretz School, a left-wing school operated by Winnipeg Jewish community, that women could "do much to improve education and housing conditions if they protest to the governments responsible."[97]

The firm Green, Blankstein, Russell, and Ham, a dynamic group of young architects, produced innovative and creative proposals for low-cost integrated public housing developments. Lawrence Green and Cecil Blankstein, two recent graduates of the University of Manitoba School of Architecture, created the firm in 1932 and were joined shortly afterwards by three other U of M graduates: Leslie Russell, Ralph Ham, and Herbert Moody. The boldness of the low-cost housing projects that they designed reflected global trends in modernist design. The fact that the design sought to make creative use of green space and natural light reflected the architect's social values.[98] Sadly none of these proposals ever got off the drawing boards.

While no local leader of J.S. Woodsworth's stature emerged during this period, the Protestant churches, particularly those with roots in the city's core area, regularly drew attention to the conditions in the city's rooming-house district. James W. Clarke of Knox United Church was horrified by what he found when he surveyed housing conditions in two neighbourhoods close to his church in 1936. South of Portage between Sherbrook and Main Street, in what Clarke termed the city's rooming-house district, there were 402 houses, of which 111 were occupied by single families. The average was 4.1 families per house. There were ninety-six families living in attics and nine families living in basements. In total, 731 families slept and cooked in the same room. Clarke said that by tolerating these conditions, "We are guilty of a major crime."[99]

Social service groups also drew attention to the need for housing reform: the Winnipeg Youth Council passed a motion in 1937 calling for a national housing program and held an educational meeting later that year featuring films about slum clearance in Britain and slum conditions in eastern Canada, along with presentations from architect Leslie Russell and city councillor R.A. Sara. James Cowan headed a Youth Council committee that developed its own housing scheme for Winnipeg. While he later served as a Citizens member of council in the 1940s, Cowan remained an advocate of low-cost housing.[100]

In 1937, an editorial in the *Winnipeg Tribune* called federal housing plans "at best timid steps in the right direction," concluding that slum conditions would not be addressed until "Ottawa shakes itself out of its comfortable nineteenth-century belief that the average Canadian can, if he tries, make himself a home and attain the modest degree of economic security which that implies."[101] This was one of many insightful editorials that identified the need for housing for low-income people and the failure of government policy to address those needs. These editorials were likely the work of the paper's municipal editor in the 1930s, A. Vernon Thomas, who paid close attention to international housing trends. In 1934 he wrote a feature article on a proposed, but never executed, "garden city" development for Elmwood that would have included seven playgrounds. Most of the land was vacant and City-owned: speculators had once owned it but had surrendered it rather than pay municipal property taxes. Thomas noted, "It is a curious thing that we in Winnipeg are almost unanimously of opinion that the taking over by the city of so much property is an unmitigated evil." But he noted by engaging large-scale landholding, German cities such as Frankfurt and Cologne controlled land speculation and were able to direct urban development. In Thomas's opinion, there should be no tears "for the speculator who lets go his holding at the first sign of bad weather, recognizing no obligation to support the civic administration and leaving others to bear the burden."[102] In the spring of 1935, Thomas wrote a long feature on the "magnificent housing effort" of British municipal councils over the previous quarter-century. "Since the war well over 2,000,000 new homes have been provided, half of which have been built by the municipalities with government assistance."[103] The British-born Thomas had been an early supporter of Woodsworth's People's Forums and the Single Tax League.[104] In 1917 the *Free Press* fired him from his position as a legislative reporter after he burst into applause for one of Fred Dixon's anti-war speeches.[105] He and his wife, the suffragist Lillian Beynon Thomas, briefly moved to New York but returned to Winnipeg where both continued with careers as writers and journalists.[106]

Not surprisingly, there were organized opponents to public housing. In the spring of 1934, leading members of the city's real-estate and construction industry formed the Home and Property Owners' Association (HPOA). One of the founders would later write that the association members came together "for the sole purpose of hoping that by united action, homeowners like themselves should eventually be able to force a tangible reduction of city taxes on their homes and vacant lots."[107] Among the founders were realtors J. Feilde, W.J. Christie, and Charles Simonite, contractors J.E. Parker, R.C. Pinnell, and D.E. Wright, hardware store owner W.A. Templeton, shoe store owner James Affleck, and Dr. J.R. Thompson, the medical superintendent of Victoria Hospital.[108] Travers Sweatman, one of the leading figures of the Citizens' Committee of One Thousand, addressed the Association's first public meeting, where he spoke on the "Excessive burden of taxation."[109] The HPOA, which by 1935 claimed a membership of two thousand, was run out of secretary-treasurer Feilde's real-estate office at 210 Kennedy.[110]

Feilde, along with Wright, the association's first president, regularly contributed letters to the editor, calling for a reduction in property taxes and civic spending. In 1935 the HPOA opposed free Grade 12 in the public schools, called for cuts to the fire department, the public swimming pools, and golf courses, protested a 10 percent increase in the municipal food allowance for the unemployed, and opposed increases in wages to municipal employees and to the extension of the right to vote in municipal elections to renters.[111] Feilde, who was said to have "many years experience in the real estate business," told the Free Press that all levels of government needed to balance their budgets. To do this, "Some of our costly services, and this includes that of education, must be reduced."[112] About the only form of government spending the HPOA approved of was the provision of low-interest renovation loans to homeowners.[113]

The HPOA portrayed public housing as taxpayer-funded, and therefore unfair, competition with private contractors and realtors.[114] The fear that public housing could lower the cost of housing was overblown, but it lies at the heart of much opposition to public housing. Its implications need to be drawn out, since its underlying premise is that in order to protect the property investments of people who own housing, decent housing must always be out of the financial reach of a portion of the population. Such a politically unpopular view, in turn, needed the protection of a restricted electoral franchise.

To draw attention away from the underlying unfairness of its position, the HPOA claimed that property taxes were the problem because they discouraged people from buying homes. The suggestion that the only thing that kept the James Grays and Ann Henrys of the world from buying houses was the prospect of having to pay property taxes was ridiculous. The barrier, of course, was their poverty and unemployment: when the Depression lifted and the Grays and Henrys of the world got jobs, they bought homes despite the existence of even higher property taxes. In January 1935, Wright said that the best housing plan would be to "lower the tax burden on homes of all kinds so that the Winnipeg business man, clerk, teacher, artisan or laborer, can be induced to see that it is in his interest to own a home in the city."[115] Feilde argued that if property taxes were cut, "the housing condition will soon remedy itself by private initiative."[116]

These then were the forces that were arrayed against one another in the 1930s, when four separate housing proposals were brought before council: each of which was to meet with defeat.

1934: A VISIONARY PROJECT CRUSHED

After all the ballots had been counted in the November 1933 municipal election, Winnipeggers awoke to discover that the city council was now evenly divided between labour and Citizen councillors, with Mayor Webb holding the tie-breaking vote.[117] Independent Labor Party city council member Morris Gray decided to test the limits of labour's influence when, in February 1934, he proposed that the City seek provincial authority to borrow $1.5 million to build new housing and repair existing housing.[118]

Gray succeeded in getting council to support an ambitious public housing plan: it was to cover sixteen and three-quarter acres on land a mile-and-a-half from the city's downtown. The project would include 588 housing units in a series of duplexes and two-

The 1934 proposal for a public housing development to the northwest of Arlington Street and Notre Dame was bold, innovative, and blocked by the Winnipeg property industry. "City Visionaries: For Decades, Architectural Firm GBR Transformed Winnipeg's Skyline and Neighbourhoods," Winnipeg Architecture Foundation. Green Blankstein Russell fonds. [photo of model, 1934 housing project] (GBR_3.30).

and three-storey buildings. The proposed rents would make it affordable for households with incomes of between $80 and $150 a month. This, in the opinion of the architects, was "an income group never provided for properly by private enterprise, and who could not possibly build or support individual houses on individual lots."

No buildings were to be more than three storeys in height and the design included playgrounds, vegetable gardens, a pedestrian mall, a shopping area along with office space for doctors and other professionals, and a day nursery that the architects proposed be operated as a free service. The estimated total cost was $1.75 million, which included the cost of the land, 90 percent of which was City-owned. The mortgage for the project would be paid down over thirty-five years.[119] The project was the first major proposal to emerge from a newly formed architectural firm: Green, Blankstein, Russell, and Ham. The architects, recognizing that public housing was highly politicized, warned that "there would be a great deal of opposition to the scheme from the real-estate and speculative building interests." As a result, the firm campaigned for the project and sought out allies, winning the support of the Manitoba Association of Architects, the Building Trades Council, and the Trades and Labor Council, all of whom briefed Premier John Bracken on the proposal.[120] The Building Trades Council enthused that the project would create six months of full-time employment for 2,500 workers.[121] Public meetings in support of the proposal were also held around the city.[122]

City administrators and Citizen members of council opposed the plan, arguing that the costs had not been properly estimated, that the site was too far from downtown, and that the thirty-five-year payback period was too long.[123] Citizen council member Cecil Rice-Jones argued the project would merely transfer people from old houses to new ones, leaving the city with more vacant houses.[124] The fact that the newer houses would be of better quality hardly seemed to register with Rice-Jones.

It is no surprise that Premier Bracken offered no support for the plan. However, Mayor Ralph Webb embraced it. At first blush, Webb was a very unlikely champion of public housing, but he appears to have been genuinely distressed by housing conditions in the city, calling them a "disgrace" and adding, "We are pushing people into places unfit to live in, and the one-half fit are overcrowded."[125] In May 1934, Webb travelled to Ottawa to make Winnipeg's case to have the housing development funded as a federal government's public works project.[126] Initially, it appears that he was successful: in a telephone call from Ottawa, Webb informed the architects that the proposal had been included in the federal public works plans.[127] When by late June there had been no further word on the plan and Webb had yet to return to the city, Building Trades Council President J.B. Graham telegraphed the prime minister for an update. Bennett's response was terse: "Lack of support from Winnipeg made it impossible to proceed with the project." Graham was told that as soon as the proposal had been announced, "75 messages were at once dispatched to Ottawa against the scheme. They came from real estate interests and other selfish sources."[128] The HPOA claimed responsibility for blocking the housing proposal, which its president D.E. Wright described as a "hair-brained [sic] idea of building a shack town and calling it a Garden City."[129] It appears the HPOA was fully justified in taking credit for blocking a visionary housing plan.[130] In 1935 Bennett told parliament that after being initially supportive of the project, he had backed away because "petitions came to us asking that we should not go forward with the work, because it might interfere with the renting of properties in the city in question."[131] In 1937, Webb, then a Conservative member of the provincial legislature, told his fellow legislators that Bennett had dropped his initial support for the housing plan in response to a "deluge of telegrams" from the "real estate bodies, the Board of Trade and other groups like that, who don't have to live in these conditions."[132]

1935: JOHN QUEEN AND THE REFERENDUM

Dizzy with their success in getting the federal government to drop its support for the 1934 housing project, the HPOA leaders convinced the Citizen members of council to support their call for a reduction in property taxes. Commissioned by council, Thomas Bradshaw, the president of North American Life Insurance, prepared a report that called for a reduction in commercial property taxes and residential property taxes on houses in commercial areas. To pay for this reduction, he recommended the introduction of a 10 percent tax on rent, a 10 percent increase in the water and electricity rates, fees for school textbooks, and fees for Grade XI in public schools.[133] The report would hang like an albatross around the neck of Citizens' next mayoral candidate, John McKerchar, and paved the way for John Queen's victory in the 1934 campaign.[134]

Queen characterized the Bradshaw Report as a gift to land speculators. The new taxes and the cuts to education were particularly odious. There were, he said:

> thousands of homes in the city where the breadwinner is working short time and at reduced wages or salary. These people are engaged in a bitter struggle against a poverty that threatens their very existence, denying themselves oftentimes the very necessities of life that they might keep off relief. Yet Mr. Bradshaw says that these people should be further taxed.[135]

The Citizens could mount no effective response to this critique and Queen won the 1934 mayoral election in a very tight race.[136] The election also returned nine labour councillors (including two Communists) and nine right-wing councillors.[137] Now it was Queen who held the balance of power. This was the moment the ILP had been working towards for two decades.

In the first months of 1935, the ILP pursued three goals: a tax reform that would provide council with additional revenue to address the needs of the unemployed, an extension of the right to vote to all adults, and the establishment of a municipal housing project. All three initiatives were an assault on the rights of property since they would increase the taxes on some of the city's most profitable businesses, grant the vote to people who did not own property, and insert the government into the property market. And all three required the support of the provincial government. John Bracken's rural-based government generally had little interest in urban issues and appears to have been happy to take its direction from the city's economic elite. It probably did not help Queen's case that he continued to serve as an ILP member of the legislature during this period. Bracken could be forgiven for declining to co-operate with John Queen, the mayor of Winnipeg, when the same man was his most persistent critic in the Manitoba legislature.

Queen and the Labour caucus sought provincial approval to move away from a flat business tax to one that would allow the City to tax large businesses more heavily and reduce taxes on small businesses. This move was attacked by the business community, including the Board of Trade and the HPOA.[138] Small business was more receptive: H.B. Scott, a future maverick city councillor, presented a brief on behalf of the Retail Merchants Association in favour of the differential tax rate.[139] Bracken's government eventually agreed to a compromise: while it refused to give Queen the right to tax business property at a variable rate that could go up to 40 percent of assessed value, it did increase the tax ceiling to 15 percent, leading to a near doubling in the City's business tax revenue.[140]

Queen made less headway in extending the right to vote. In 1931, renters constituted 56 percent of Winnipeg households. These renters were paying, on average, 26 percent of their income on rent. Many were paying far more.[141] Many had no right to vote for mayor or council because they were deemed to be roomers as opposed to tenants. As James Gray pointed out:

> A man who brought his bride home to share his mother's
> house, and who kept the whole house going, could not vote.
> Thousands of young married couples who live with rela-
> tives cannot vote. Nor can sons and daughters who support
> widowed mothers.[142]

Gray was writing from experience: he and his wife were denied the vote when they lived with his parents on Ruby Street and when they lived in a single room in a Furby Street boarding house. But their lives, particularly the relief rates they received, were governed by the rules created at city hall. And whether they lived in one room or half a dozen, no renter could vote in plebiscites on money bylaws. These plebiscites were required by the City's charter—and were intended to ensure that property owners retained control over all major spending decisions. And, as we shall see, they served as a near-impenetrable barrier to the construction of public housing.

In both 1935 and 1936, the Queen-led council asked the provincial legislature to do away with property restrictions on the right to vote and to eliminate plural voting in Winnipeg elections.[143] If approved, the 1935 measure would have given the vote to "Roomers or those doing their cooking in a common kitchen in a house divided into several suites," thereby adding 30,000 Winnipeggers to the voters' list.[144] L.T. Hartley of the HPOA argued that plural voting should remain in place "as long as class politics was a factor in civic elections"—a clear, if unwitting, recognition of the leaders of the HPOA that they were engaged in a form of class warfare.[145] Citizens councillor Frederick Davidson opposed the extension of the vote to non-property owners since it meant "Anybody could come into Winnipeg, occupy a shack and after one year have a vote." While Queen was able to get the measure through council, he could not convince the legislature to make the needed amendments to the city charter. Conservative member of the legislature Sanford Evans spoke for the majority in that assembly when he said that the vote was already granted "to all those who had homes and a real stake in the city."[146] In 1936 the HPOA made its own proposal for a change in the way council was elected. Along with a call to reduce the number of councillors, a standard conservative cost-cutting proposal, it recommended that the 30,000 resident owners and 4,500 non-resident owners should elect half the council, while the 70,000 tenants should elect the other half. In other words, the HPOA thought a property owner should have two votes for every tenant vote.[147] It is hard to believe that the proposal was more than a provocation: in any case, neither the council nor the legislature exhibited much interest.

In December 1934, before he had been sworn into office as mayor, Queen told the *Tribune,* "There is undoubtedly a strong case for a housing scheme."[148] Because the *Dominion Housing Act* had not authorized the federal government to lend money to municipalities to develop low-cost housing, the City would have to finance any project by borrowing. And such largescale borrowings, in turn, had to be approved by a referendum in which the right to vote was restricted to the city's 30,000 property owners.

Quite correctly, Queen and company believed the odds of winning such a vote to be quite slim. Their only option was to convince the provincial government to exempt a housing project from the requirement to hold a referendum. Such exemptions had been granted in the past to ensure the construction of large-scale infrastructure projects such as bridges.[149]

In March 1935, the city housing committee, under the leadership of ILP councillor James Simpkin, proposed the construction of $2 million in public housing. Simpkin said he was prepared to seek provincial approval to develop the housing without putting the proposal to a referendum. "If the ratepayers don't like our methods, they can kick us out at the next civic election." ILP councillor Morris Gray pointed out that every candidate who came out in favour of public housing in the last election had won his seat. That, he said, was referendum enough for him. Margaret McWilliams said she was not opposed to the City getting into housing, noting that "Every city in Great Britain was renting homes." But, she said the idea of going ahead without a referendum would leave the council open to the accusation that it was indulging in a "wide open spending campaign."[150] While she had commissioned a report that outlined the social costs of poor housing, she tended to blame the failure to make progress on the provision of public housing on a lack of political will.[151] She never was able to take the next step and acknowledge that the restricted franchise meant that the majority of the city's citizens had no opportunity to voice their will on the need for public housing.

Not surprisingly, the Bracken government turned down Queen's request for an exemption, leaving the labour councillors with no option but to hold a ratepayers' vote in conjunction with the November 1935 municipal election.[152] In early October 1935, ILP city council members Morris Gray and M.W. Stobart proposed that the City invest $500,000 in building four-room housing units that would rent for $25 a month. They would be built on City-owned land, amortized for thirty-five years, and administered by the Winnipeg Housing Commission.[153] The plan's supporters noted that 80 percent of the funding would be paid in wages, which they predicted would create $2 million worth of business in Winnipeg.[154] Stobart said the council was planning to provide "sanitary, airy, well lit, comfortable homes with lawns and garden space for people earning moderately low wages at a rent which they can afford to pay."[155]

The Citizens candidate for mayor in 1935, Cecil Gunn, opposed the plan, claiming to prefer funding rehabilitation of existing buildings—in other words, a subsidy to homeowners and landlords.[156] Cecil Rice-Jones, another Citizens representative on council, objected to the City taking on what he viewed as a federal responsibility, while C.E. Simonite said that any houses that the City built would quickly turn into slums: an argument that ignored the fact that the existing slums had been built by private builders.[157]

Labour member of council Victor B. Anderson noted that rehabilitation would simply favour landlords who could then charge higher rents for their property, leaving the City with the responsibility for housing those households that could not afford the new rents. John Blumberg agreed that housing was a federal responsibility, but, he said, the previous Conservative government had done nothing for housing, and he did not expect the newly elected Liberal government "will do any better." He had his doubts about rehabilitation since many of the homes that might be rehabilitated for low-income people had been "jerry-built" to begin with and were not worth fixing.[158] Despite these reservations, the ILP-dominated council agreed to a proposal that would authorize the borrowing of $500,000 to fund both constructing 120 four-room homes and housing rehabilitation.[159]

The business community was not interested in this compromise and continued to campaign against the bylaw. The Winnipeg Board of Trade claimed that it was not "economically sound," although it was prepared to support the federal government in making low-cost loans to landlords to renovate existing rental properties.[160] HPOA secretary-treasurer J. Feilde said that property owners should vote down the City's housing proposal, which he termed "a huge joke."[161] Gunn made opposition to the housing proposal a centrepiece of his mayoral campaign, claiming that Queen and his labour supporters were financially irresponsible. At one rally he asked, "Who is going to pour money into Winnipeg while it is controlled by a vigourous minority group? We know the city is going back, costs increasing and revenue decreasing."[162] Rice-Jones exhibited a hitherto hidden solicitude towards the housing needs of the poor when he said the rooms in the proposed project would not be big enough to "swing a cat in." Up until then, Rice-Jones has been silent about the limited cat-swinging opportunities available to families living in single rooms. Rice-Jones also questioned the ILP's commitment to rehabilitation, saying it had only been added to the bylaw to improve the likelihood of it being adopted by the voters.[163] To summarize, the Citizens argued that the plan did not provide enough housing—but refused to propose measures that would provide more housing. They argued that the housing would be of poor quality but did not argue for the construction of better-quality housing. They argued that the houses would turn into slums, but they did not argue for slum clearance. They argued that the federal government should be providing housing but had nothing to say to people whose lives were being blighted by federal inaction. They argued for rehabilitation, and when they got it, they said the ILP would not live up to its commitment.

Both the *Free Press* and the *Tribune* editorialized in favour of the housing bylaw, with the *Free Press* observing, "If the bylaw is passed, some very necessary action can be taken." The endorsement was qualified, with the paper limply observing, "There would be no justification, of course, for the city or the Housing Commission building houses to rent if there were any way of solving the housing crisis without doing so." But there wasn't any other way.[164] The *Tribune* made it clear it preferred to see the money used to rehabilitate existing buildings since this would "cause no dislocation of present values."[165]

The Winnipeg Building Trades Council backed the proposal—and the *Tribune* printed the council's endorsement in full as part of a news story. In it, the Building Trades Council decried the opposition of "certain interests imbued with selfish motives, who have on every occasion opposed housing schemes no matter in what form they were submitted. It would not be fair to mention names at this moment, but certain members of the city council are certainly past masters of the art of playing Dr. Jeckill [sic] and Mr. Hyde."[166]

Queen won the 1935 election handily, 32,013 to 21,070. And labour retained its nine seats on council. But the housing bylaw was defeated 11,312 to 4,459, with 1,154 votes rejected (it appears many voters marked their ballots with a cross when they should have written a numeric figure). As can be seen from these figures, of the 53,083 Winnipeggers who voted for mayor, only 16,925 owned enough property to be allowed to vote on the housing bylaw.[167] Writing in the *Tribune*, A. Vernon Thomas attributed the bylaw's defeat to a lack of voter confidence in the proposal. Not enough, he wrote, had been done to explain the housing plan: "Long lulls took place during which little progress was made. The consequence was that things had to be rushed as the election approached."[168] He may have been correct about the vigour of the campaign, but there is no ignoring the fact that if all Winnipeggers, as opposed to all property owners, had been allowed to vote on the bylaw, the result would have been different.

Queen continued to make the case for public housing throughout his second term in office.[169] In March 1936 council approved a motion that would have paved the way for spending bylaws to allow up to $1.5 million to be spent on new housing and renovations.[170] But the referendum defeat had clearly taken the wind out of labour's sails: there was no appetite for a second referendum and the proposal was dropped. In the 1936 election F.E. Warriner, a dentist and school board member, defeated Queen and the number of labour seats on council was reduced to six.[171] A pair of *Free Press* headlines, "Rightists secure control of city council" and "Control of Winnipeg Civic Administration Out of Labor's Hands," underscored the shift in the balance of power.[172]

1937: "FOOLING AROUND FOR FIVE YEARS, AND NOT ONE HOUSE BUILT"

J.W. Clarke, the minister at Knox United Church, fired the opening shots in a 1937 campaign for low-cost housing in a speech to the civics bureau of the Winnipeg Board of Trade. Clarke told the assembled businesspeople in one city district near his church that 960 houses originally built for single families were now housing 3.5 families each. In one instance twenty-six people were living in a house intended for a single family.[173] In a separate presentation to the city's housing committee, Clarke said that dogs were living in better conditions than many Winnipeggers.[174] In response to Clarke's call for government action, H.C. Morrison, a Citizen representative on council, said that private enterprise would soon take care of the housing shortage, and it would be able to do this more quickly if government stayed out of the housing field. All Clarke could do was inform Morrison that he was "living in a fool's paradise."[175]

The *Free Press* followed up on Clarke's speeches with a series of front-page articles on slum conditions in Point Douglas and the old Hudson's Bay Reserve land. The articles had a sensationalist tone, but they were all written by James Gray, who had finally gotten off relief and found himself a long-sought-after job at the *Winnipeg Free Press*. Following on Gray's exposés, which were laced with sensationalism, sentimentality, and passion, the *Free Press* turned to W.H. Carter, the chairman of the provincial advisory board to the National Employment Commission and the vice-chairman of the Winnipeg Housing Commission, for what it termed a "revolutionary new plan to rid the city of slums." Claiming that it was "impractical" for government to meet the housing needs of low-income people, Carter proposed the creation of a limited-dividend corporation. This was the panacea to which the business community would turn whenever the pressure for public housing grew strong. Limited dividend corporations had failed to deliver in the

A series of articles in the Free Press in 1937 drew attention to the crowded and unhealthy conditions in Winnipeg's rooming-house district. "220 Persons Cram These Terrace Homes," Winnipeg Free Press, March 15, 1937.

first two decades of the century and they would fail, dismally, in the 1930s.

Under Carter's proposal, the City would provide the corporation with free building lots, while the federal government would provide low-interest construction loans. Members of the private sector would invest $1,000 each in a non-profit corporation, which would pay them a "nominal interest." The first step was to "get a sufficient number of businessmen interested in getting the thing started." Carter's response to those in the business community who would oppose this state intervention in the market was that "the people we have to reach have not got enough money to make private enterprise interested in them."[176] He was one of the few Winnipeg business people prepared to recognize the obvious: in its 1937 report, the Winnipeg Housing Commission noted that there was no way to improve the housing conditions of low-income Winnipeggers without the introduction of some form of subsidy.[177]

Newly elected city councillor R.A. Sara took over the leadership of a campaign for the construction of homes that could be sold at a low cost to private owners. An engineer by training, Sara believed that rhetorical battles between the left and the right had blocked any progress on the creation of affordable housing. After listening to one heated exchange between Simpkin and Simonite, he could not hide his impatience, saying, "it was plain to see why the city was getting nowhere with its housing schemes. 'Fooling around for five years, and not one house built,' he said, accusingly." These were words he would live to regret since the campaign that he led would result in the construction of exactly one house.[178] Elected from the South End Ward 1, Sara, who ran with the Citizens' support, often found himself at odds with Simonite, who had returned to council in 1937 and sometimes sided with labour council members.[179] As the Winnipeg manager of Aladdin Homes, a Canadian branch of a U.S.-based company that specialized in the design and sale of mail-order housing construction kits, Sara believed he knew something about house building.[180]

He also had friends in high places: since 1935, in his role with Aladdin Homes Sara had been in correspondence with federal deputy minister of finance W.C. Clark about the prospects of federally funded housing in Winnipeg.[181] Clark was desperate to improve the *Dominion Housing Act*'s record on the prairies, fearing that if the Act did not succeed, the government would commit itself to "real low cost housing and slum clearance."[182] David Mansur, a senior executive with Sun Life Assurance (and the future head of the Central Mortgage and Housing Corporation) was also committed to seeing *Dominion Housing Act* money used to build low-cost private homes in Winnipeg.[183] The original plan, which was similar to one originally put forward by the HPOA, was to build $3,500 houses on 140 lots donated by the City. Purchasers would have to put up $300 in cash and get a twenty-year mortgage.[184] The federal government would fund 20 percent of these mortgages at 3.5 percent interest, while private lenders were expected to cover the remaining 80 percent of the mortgage. The return to the private investors would be limited to 6 percent, but the federal government was also prepared to cover 80 percent of their losses per house on loans of up to $3,000.[185]

The future of the plan hung on the willingness of private lenders to make the loans and accept the limits on their returns. In May 1937, Sara met with representatives of the Manitoba Mortgage Loans Association and the mortgage department of several large life insurance companies to beg for their support.[186] By the end of the month, he had been turned down by seventeen lenders: none were prepared to make loans if there was any risk, nor were they interested in funding the construction of low-cost homes. Sara and Margaret McWilliams, who had also emerged as a supporter of the plan, were highly critical of the local lenders. McWilliams said that all the local property industry would "ever do is oppose anything that the city suggests. They have never offered us any help or advice."[187]

Following this rejection by local lenders, Sara met with Clark and Mansur, and with their backing, he proposed the establishment of a limited dividend company. The scope of the project was far less ambitious than had been originally contemplated: instead of 140 houses, he was now talking about twenty-five houses, to be built on land donated by the City. He proposed the creation of the City of Winnipeg Housing Company, a limited dividend housing corporation that would be jointly owned by the City, which would receive $25,000 worth of common shares for providing twenty-five lots, and private investors, who would purchase a total of $50,000 in preferred shares. The money would be used to make up the difference between the down payment and what people could get from private lenders.[188] Sun Life had committed to advance 60 percent on twenty-five houses and an additional 20 percent when they were sold.[189]

Simonite and the real-estate industry fought the project tooth and nail.[190] The HPOA and the Winnipeg Board of Trade opposed the plan: slums, the Board argued, should be fought by enforcement of bylaws and single men should be forced to live in converted warehouses. In the opinion of the Dominion Mortgage and Investments Association, the creation of a limited dividend housing company was the first step toward public housing.[191] Even Sun Life's local staff resisted the plan: according to Mansur, the local staff did not want to see any new housing built in Winnipeg until every vacant house was sold.[192]

The labour councillors had been shunted to the sideline throughout this debate: they were not going to oppose any plan that might increase employment and house construction, nor were they interested in adding their voices to Simonite's opposition to the plan. But both Morris Gray and Jack Blumberg pointed out that the plan would do little for the people who could not afford a down payment or thirty dollars a month. Blumberg felt that over the year, the City had lost sight of its original goal. In the face of these criticisms, Sara had to acknowledge that "there was no anticipation of solving slum conditions with this plan but merely to alleviate them slightly while providing a great deal of employment."[193] While welcoming the Sara plan, the *Tribune* noted, "it will not meet another pressing need, which is for houses at low rental for many of our people who out of their meagre and uncertain earnings could not possibly pay $30 a month."[194]

City council approved the charter of the City of Winnipeg Housing Company in July 1937. By then it was projected that the houses would cost $3,500 and purchasers would have to put up 20 percent of the purchase price as a down payment and finance the houses over twenty years.[195] In September 1937, Sara was able to announce that the company's stock had been oversubscribed and the "last obstacle in the way to a low-cost housing project has been hurdled." With the assistance of W.H. Carter and Mayor Warriner, Sara had been able to convince the Winnipeg Electric Company, James Richardson, and the Timothy Eaton's Company to invest in the housing company.[196]

This success was short-lived. In the spring of 1938, the provincial legislature refused to amend the city charter to allow the City to own the company's common stock. Since the provision of City-owned land in exchange for the stock was the economic basis on which the company was conceived, this proved to be an insurmountable obstacle.[197] The Province's refusal to pass what amounted to enabling legislation that would cost it nothing was an example of the Bracken government's indifference to urban issues.

As this project fell apart, Sara proposed the construction of what he termed a "demonstration house," which he estimated would cost $4,000.[198] Bizarrely, the original plan was to build the house in River Heights, but the location was eventually shifted to 804 Ashburn Street in the West End.[199] In December 1937 Sara had to report that the City had received no bids on the house, which had come in $3,000 over budget. Returning to a point that he had made numerous times, ILP council member Morris Gray pointed out, "many people want the house, but can't pay the cash outright."[200] The demonstration home eventually was sold to the engineer of a local orphanage.[201] This, it would turn out, was the closest the City came to building any public housing during the Great Depression.

1938–1939: "THE LANDLORDS ... WANT THIS SCHEME KILLED AND THEY WILL SEE IT IS KILLED"

The 1937 election saw Queen returned to the mayor's office, defeating Warriner by a ten thousand-vote margin.[202] But labour failed to regain control of council, where eight labour councillors faced eleven Citizen councillors.[203] Following the collapse of the City of Winnipeg Housing Company, Queen and Sara, who were not natural political allies, were forced to make common cause on a proposal for a large-scale public-housing development in the city's West End.[204] Designed by Green, Blankstein, Russell, and Ham, the $1.4 million proposal contained many of the elements of the firm's 1934 proposal. It would house 474 low-income families in a mixture of low-rise apartments and rowhouses on twelve acres of land that would be landscaped with parks and be free of traffic.[205] Debate on the proposal dragged on into 1939, with C.E. Simonite and Frederick G. Thompson opposing it at every step. In one debate, Thompson alleged that "the sponsors of the measure were either communists or fascists."[206]

As in 1935, the major barrier was the requirement to hold a ratepayers' referendum. In early 1939, the Citizen majority on council rejected Queen's efforts to have council ask the provincial government to waive the requirement for such a referendum.[207] The vote led J.B. Graham, the head of the Building Trades Council, to question whether the members of council had "any sincere desire to build homes for low paid workers." R.B. McCutchan of the Winnipeg Trades and Labor Council observed, "The landlords who charged $15 and $25 per month for one and two room hovels want this scheme killed and will see it is killed."[208] Labour councillor Simpkin's 1938 proposal to hold a plebiscite as to whether Winnipeg should move to a system of adult suffrage was defeated by the Citizen members of council.[209]

Queen and Blumberg, working with Margaret McWilliams, succeeded in getting council to seek exemption from the referendum requirement for a scaled-down $300,000 proposal.[210] The real-estate industry was able to convince the Province not to grant the exemption and thereby ensured its collapse.[211] It was during the debate on this proposal that the *Tribune* ran what could have been the default housing-story headline for the decade: "Low-cost housing scheme again debated by council but no action taken."[212]

Housing had continued to deteriorate right through to the decade's end. Alexander Officer reported that on May 3, 1938, there were only fifty habitable vacant houses in the city. A 1938 survey of the congested areas had found nine houses of six rooms with thirty families living in them, nineteen houses of seven rooms with fifty-three families living in them and seventy-four houses of six to eleven rooms with 276 families living in them. In 1937, 848 infants had been born to families living in one to two rooms.[213]

In his 1938 annual survey of housing, a disheartened Officer wrote:

> There is little I can say that has not been said previously. I have been pointing out for years the deficiency in housing accommodation for our low-wage earners; that bad housing is unprofitable to the community; that our substandard housing is increasing in area and even invading some of our better class residential districts; and that we are finding more and more single family dwellings occupied as tenements, many families have only one room.

According to Officer, "The serious shortage of dwellings for the low-wage earning class becomes more acute every year."[214] There was, he estimated, a need for five thousand new housing units in Greater Winnipeg.[215] Two years later he wrote, "Slum conditions are rapidly developing in this city, becoming more acute in certain sections and beginning to show evidence in districts that only a few years ago were considered exclusive." He continued:

> In many sections of the city, there is an increasing number of houses, built for occupation by one family, filled by people of all ages to such an extent that every square foot of available space is in constant use day and night, often with reckless disregard to privacy and the elementary principles of hygiene.[216]

By then the country was at war. Money that could not be found to build homes was suddenly available to build munitions plants, tanks, bombers, and barracks. The need to house newly hired munitions workers would finally lead the federal government into making a major investment in the national housing market.

NOTES

1. John Kendle, *John Bracken: A Political Biography*, Toronto: University of Toronto Press, 1979, 109–113, 124, 127, 128, 130, 159, 160, 271; Gerald Friesen, *The Canadian Prairies: A History*, Toronto: University of Toronto Press, 1984, 401–403.
2. James Struthers, *No Fault of Their Own: Unemployment and the Canadian Welfare State, 1914-1941*, Toronto: University of Toronto Press, 1983, 208–209; John Kendle, *John Bracken: A Political Biography*, Toronto: University of Toronto Press, 1979, 109–113, 124, 127, 128, 130, 159, 160, 271; Gerald Friesen, *The Canadian Prairies: A History*, Toronto: University of Toronto Press, 1984, 401–403.
3. James Struthers, *No Fault of Their Own: Unemployment and the Canadian Welfare State, 1914-1941*, Toronto: University of Toronto Press, 1983, 208–209; John Kendle, *John Bracken: A Political Biography*, Toronto: University of Toronto Press, 1979, 109–113, 124, 127, 128, 130, 159, 160, 271; Gerald Friesen, *The Canadian Prairies: A History*, Toronto: University of Toronto Press, 1984, 401–403.
4. "City may again submit bylaw on housing plan," *Winnipeg Free Press*, March 10, 1936.
5. Michael Goeres, "Disorder, Dependency and Fiscal Responsibility: Unemployment Relief in Winnipeg, 1907-1942," Master of Arts thesis, University of Manitoba, 1981, 177.
6. Michael Goeres, "Disorder, Dependency and Fiscal Responsibility: Unemployment Relief in Winnipeg, 1907-1942," Master of Arts thesis, University of Manitoba, 1981, 229.
7. John Kendle, *John Bracken: A Political Biography*, Toronto: University of Toronto Press, 1979, 109–113, 124, 127, 128, 130, 159, 160, 271.
8. V.B. Anderson, "Ald. Anderson on the taxation subject," *Winnipeg Evening Tribune*, November 17, 1934.
9. Stefan Epp-Koop, *"We're Going to Run This City": Winnipeg's Political Left after the General Strike*, Winnipeg: University of Manitoba Press, 2015, 120.
10. "Huge arrears," *Winnipeg Free Press*, June 1, 1937.
11. "The housing problem," *Winnipeg Evening Tribune*, March 22, 1937.
12. "Rent paying policy of social welfare commission probed," *Winnipeg Free Press*, October 4, 1937.
13. "Committee to study housing of unemployed," *Winnipeg Tribune*, May 13, 1936. For national rents, see: Statistics Canada, *Canada Year Book*, Ottawa, 1937, 800.
14. "Immigration hall is likely to be used to shelter unemployed," *Manitoba Free Press*, December 32, 1929; Michael Goeres, "Disorder, Dependency and Fiscal Responsibility: Unemployment Relief in Winnipeg, 1907-1942," Master of Arts thesis, University of Manitoba, 1981, 181.
15. Robert Vineberg, "Welcoming immigrants at the gateway to Canada's west: Immigration halls in Winnipeg, 1872-1975," *Manitoba History*, 65 (Winter

2011): 12–22.

16. Michael Goeres, "Disorder, Dependency and Fiscal Responsibility: Unemployment Relief in Winnipeg, 1907–1942," Master of Arts thesis, University of Manitoba, 1981, 184.

17. Michael Goeres, "Disorder, Dependency and Fiscal Responsibility: Unemployment Relief in Winnipeg, 1907–1942," Master of Arts thesis, University of Manitoba, 1981, 186-190.

18. Michael Goeres, "Disorder, Dependency and Fiscal Responsibility: Unemployment Relief in Winnipeg, 1907–1942," Master of Arts thesis, University of Manitoba, 1981, 215.

19. Doug Smith, *Let Us Rise: An Illustrated History of the Manitoba Labour Movement*, Vancouver: New Star Books, 1985, 85–88.

20. "Single unemployed ask for voucher system of relief," *Winnipeg Free Press*, March 10, 1936.

21. "Plight of unemployed men in comparison with lions," *Winnipeg Free Press*, December 2, 1939.

22. "Would burn like rats," *Winnipeg Free Press*, March 25, 1937.

23. "Authority to be sought to borrow $1,500,000 for building of homes," *Winnipeg Free Press*, February 20, 1934.

24. "Authority to be sought to borrow $1,500,000 for building of homes," *Winnipeg Free Press*, February 20, 1934.

25. "Overcrowding in houses continues, officer reports," *Winnipeg Free Press*, February 1, 1934.

26. Dimitrios Styliaras, Arnold Koerte and William Hurst, *A Study of Apartment Housing in Winnipeg and Recommendations for Future Apartment Building in the Prairie Region*, The Planning Research Centre at the Faculty of Architecture, University of Manitoba, 1967, 59-60.

27. "Situation as to housing poor, so Officer reports," *Winnipeg Free Press*, February 14, 1936.

28. James Gray, *The Winter Years: The Depression on the Prairies*, Calgary: Fifth House, 2003, 11–23.

29. Ann Henry, *Laugh, Baby, Laugh*, Toronto: McClelland and Stewart, 1970, 92.

30. James Gray, *The Winter Years: The Depression on the Prairies*, Calgary: Fifth House, 2003, 75–80.

31. James Gray, *The Winter Years: The Depression on the Prairies*, Calgary: Fifth House, 2003, 75–80.

32. David G. Burley and Mike Maunder, *Living on Furby: Narratives of Home, Winnipeg, Manitoba, 1889-2005*, Winnipeg, Institute of Urban Studies, University of Winnipeg, 2008, 34-40.

33. James Gray, *The Winter Years: The Depression on the Prairies*, Calgary: Fifth House, 2003, 75–80.

34. Ann Henry, *Laugh, Baby, Laugh*, Toronto: McClelland and Stewart, 1970, 57.

35. Ann Henry, *Laugh, Baby, Laugh*, Toronto: McClelland and Stewart, 1970, 58.

36. Harry Gutkin with Mildred Gutkin, *The Worst of Times, the Best of Times: Growing up in Winnipeg's North End*, Markham: Fitzhenry and Whiteside, 1987, 199.

37. J.H. Gray, "Disgrace to city," *Winnipeg Free Press*, March 13, 1937.

38. J.H. Gray, "Slumduggery: No bath nor furnace for forty in one house," *Winnipeg Free Press*, March 16, 1937.

39. J.H. Gray, "Disgrace to city," *Winnipeg Free Press*, March 13, 1937.

40. J.H. Gray, "Downtown blocks are congested," *Winnipeg Free Press*, March 15, 1937.

41. "Mother kills two, suicides," *Winnipeg Free Press*, December 18, 1934; "Deaths," *Winnipeg Evening Tribune*, December 19, 1934; "Mother, crazed by poverty, kills two children, ends own life," *Winnipeg Free Press*, December 18, 1934; "Control urged on sale of all disinfectants," *Winnipeg Evening Tribune*, December 21, 1934.

42. "Police charge when stones begin to fly," "6,000 demonstrators mass in front of Parliament Building," *Winnipeg Evening Tribune*, April 16, 1931.

43. "Communists to pick against all evictions," *Winnipeg Evening Tribune*, May 19, 1933; "Picketing against all evictions and seizures planned," *Winnipeg Free Press*, May 19, 1933.

44. James Gray, *The Winter Years: The Depression on the Prairies*, Calgary: Fifth House, 2003, 90–91.

45. "Stormy council favors putting men off relief," *Winnipeg Tribune*, April 20, 1937.

46. Victor Howard, *"We Were the Salt of the Earth!" The On to Ottawa Trek and the Regina Riot*, Regina: University of Regina, 1985.

47. Doug Smith, *Let Us Rise: An Illustrated History of the Manitoba Labour Movement*, Vancouver: New Star Books, 1985, 89–91.

48. George Anderson, *Housing Policy in Canada: Lecture Series*, Canada Mortgage and Housing Corporation, 1992, 7.

49. John C. Bacher, *Keeping to the Market: The Evolution of Canadian Housing Policy*, Montreal and Kingston: McGill-Queen's University Press, 1993, 63.

50. Joan Selby, "Urban Rental Housing in Canada 1900–1985: A Critical Review of Problems and the Response of Government," Master's thesis, University of British Columbia, 1985, 46.

51. Toronto (Ont.), and Herbert A. Bruce, *Report of the Lieutenant-Governor's Committee on Housing Conditions in Toronto, 1934*, Toronto: Press of the Hunter-Rose Co., Ltd., 1934, 115–122.

52. John C. Bacher, *Keeping to the Market: The Evolution of Canadian Housing Policy*, Montreal and Kingston: McGill-Queen's University Press, 1993, 67–69.

53. Joan Selby, "Urban Rental Housing in Canada 1900–1985: A Critical Review of Problems and the Response of Government," Master's thesis, University of British Columbia, 1985, 62.

54. League for Social Reconstruction, *Social Planning for Canada*, Toronto: University of Toronto Press, 1975, 456–460.

55. Joan Selby, "Urban Rental Housing in Canada 1900–1985: A Critical Review of Problems and the Response of Government," Master's thesis, University of British Columbia, 1985, 61.

56. John C. Bacher, *Keeping to the Market: The Evolution of Canadian Housing Policy*, Montreal and Kingston: McGill-Queen's University Press, 1993, 83.

57. *Hansard*, June 24, 1935, 3930, quoted in J. David Hulchanski, "The 1935 Dominion Housing Act: Setting the stage for a permanent federal presence in Canada's housing sector," *Urban History Review/Revue d'histoire urbaine*, 15, 1 (1986): 23.

58. Parliamentary Committee on Housing, Minutes of Proceedings and Evidence of Special Committee on Housing, Ottawa: King's Printer, 1935, 170–181, 364,

quoted in John C. Bacher, "Keeping to the Private Market: The Evolution of Canadian Housing Policy, 1900–1949," Doctoral thesis, McMaster University, 1985, 138–139.

59. *Hansard*, June 24, 1935, 3930, quoted in J. David Hulchanski, "The 1935 Dominion Housing Act: Setting the stage for a permanent federal presence in Canada's housing sector," *Urban History Review/Revue d'histoire urbaine*, 15, 1 (1986): 23.

60. George Anderson, *Housing Policy in Canada: Lecture Series*, Canada Mortgage and Housing Corporation, 1992, 10.

61. John C. Bacher, *Keeping to the Market: The Evolution of Canadian Housing Policy*, Montreal and Kingston: McGill-Queen's University Press, 1993, 66.

62. Robert B. Bryce, *Maturing in Hard Times: Canada's Department of Finance During the Great Depression*, Kingston and Montreal: McGill–Queen's Press, 1986, 165–166.

63. John C. Bacher, *Keeping to the Market: The Evolution of Canadian Housing Policy*, Montreal and Kingston: McGill-Queen's University Press, 1993, 66.

64. Library and Archives Canada, R.G. 19, Vol. 711, 203-2-L, Department of Finance Papers, W.C. Clark to D.B. Mansur, August 10, 1936, quoted in J. David Hulchanski, "The 1935 Dominion Housing Act: Setting the stage for a permanent federal presence in Canada's housing sector," *Urban History Review/ Revue d'histoire urbaine*, 15, 1 (1986): 33.

65. John Belec, "The Dominion Housing Act," *Urban History Review/Revue d'histoire urbaine*, 25, 2 (March 1997): 53.

66. Robert B. Bryce, *Maturing in Hard Times: Canada's Department of Finance During the Great Depression*, Kingston and Montreal: McGill–Queen's Press, 1986, 165–166.

67. F.W. Nicolls, "Housing in Canada, 1938," in *National Housing Yearbook 1938*, Chicago: National Association of Housing Officials, 1938, republished by the Centre for Urban and Community Studies, University of Toronto, Urban Public Housing Archive. At <urbancentre.utoronto.ca/pdfs/policyarchives/1938FWNicolls.pdf>, accessed June 20, 2021.

68. J. David Hulchanski, "The 1935 Dominion Housing Act: Setting the stage for a permanent federal presence in Canada's housing sector," *Urban History Review/Revue d'histoire urbaine*, 15, 1 (1986): 30.

69. House of Commons, Debates, 1935, 3773.

70. J. David Hulchanski, "The 1935 Dominion Housing Act: Setting the stage for a permanent federal presence in Canada's housing sector," *Urban History Review/Revue d'histoire urbaine*, 15, 1 (1986): 29.

71. House of Commons Debates, 1935, 3929. In this Irvine anticipating J.M. Keynes, who, in 1943 wrote "Anything we can actually do we can afford." J.M Keynes, "How much does finance matter," *The Listener*, April 2, 1942.

72. H. Peter Oberlander and Arthur L. Fallick, *Housing a Nation: The Evolution of Canadian Housing Policy*, Canada Mortgage and Housing Corporation, 1992, 20.

73. Subcommittee on Housing and Community Planning, *Report of Advisory Committee on Reconstruction 4*, Ottawa: King's Printer, 1944, 28; John C. Bacher, *Keeping to the Market: The Evolution of Canadian Housing Policy*, Montreal and Kingston: McGill-Queen's University Press, 1993, 108; J. David Hulchanski, "The 1935 Dominion Housing Act: Setting the stage for a permanent federal

presence in Canada's housing sector," *Urban History Review/Revue d'histoire urbaine*, 15, 1 (1986): 18.

74. Humphrey Carver, *Compassionate Landscape: Places and People in a Man's Life*, Toronto: University of Toronto Press, 1975, 56.

75. "John Queen opens his campaign for chief magistracy," *Winnipeg Free Press*, November 15, 1932; "John Queen nominated as I.L.P. candidate for mayoralty of Winnipeg," *Winnipeg Free Press*, October 30, 1933.

76. "Veteran MLA, M.A. Gray dies," *Winnipeg Free Press*, January 13, 1966; Henry Trachtenberg, "Jews and left wing politics in Winnipeg's North End, 1919–1940," in Daniel Stone (ed.), *Jewish Radicalism in Winnipeg, 1905-1960, Jewish Life and Times, Volume VIII*, 2003, 138.

77. Manitoba Historical Society, "Matthew William Stobart" <mhs.mb.ca/docs/people/stobart_mw.shtml>, accessed July 17, 2021.

78. Roland Penner, *A Glowing Dream: A Memoir*, Winnipeg: J. Gordon Shillingford Publishing Limited, 2007, 16–17, 28–29, 38–39; Jim Mochoruk with Nancy Kardash, *The People's Co-op: The Life and Times of a North End Institution*, Halifax: Fernwood Books, 2000, 35; Rheinold Kramer and Tom Mitchell, *When the State Trembled: How A.J. Andrews and the Citizens' Committee Broke the Winnipeg General Strike*, Toronto: University of Toronto Press, 2010, 4; Brian McKillop, "Citizen and Socialist: The Ethos of Political Winnipeg, 1919-1935," Master of Arts thesis, University of Manitoba, 1970.

79. Errol Black, "Brandon's revolutionary forkins," in Errol Black and Tom Mitchell (eds.), *A Square Deal for All and No Railroading: Historical Essays on Labour in Brandon*, St. John's: Canadian Committee on Labour History, 2000, 125.

80. John H. Thompson, "The political career of Ralph H. Webb," *Red River Valley Historian* (Summer 1976): 1–7.

81. Brian McKillop, "Citizen and Socialist: The Ethos of Political Winnipeg, 1919–1935," Master of Arts thesis, University of Manitoba, 197–199.

82. For details on Gunn's career, see: Brian McKillop, "Citizen and Socialist: The Ethos of Political Winnipeg, 1919-1935," Master of Arts thesis, University of Manitoba, 194–195.

83. For details on Rice-Jones's career, see: Brian McKillop, "Citizen and Socialist: The Ethos of Political Winnipeg, 1919-1935," Master of Arts thesis, University of Manitoba, 194–195.

84. David J. Bercuson, *Confrontation at Winnipeg: Labour, Industrial Relations and the General Strike*, Montreal and London: McGill-Queen's Press, 1974, 147–149; Rheinold Kramer and Tom Mitchell, *When the State Trembled: How A.J. Andrews and the Citizens' Committee Broke the Winnipeg General Strike*, Toronto: University of Toronto Press, 2010, 124, 137–139.

85. "Housing scheme advanced," *Winnipeg Free Press*, April 21, 1938; Archives of Manitoba, Keystone Archives Descriptive Database, "Frederick George Thompson" <http://pam.minisisinc.com/scripts/mwimain.dll/125236122/1/0?SEARCH&ERRMSG=[PAM]descNo.htm>.

86. "Charles Edward Simonite," *Winnipeg Free Press*, December 10, 1973; Manitoba Historical Society, "Charles Edward Simonite" <mhs.mb.ca/docs/people/simonite_ce.shtml>, accessed November 10, 2020.

87. "Re-elect Charles E. Simonite," *Manitoba Free Press*, November 26, 1931.

88. Michael Goeres, "Disorder, Dependency and Fiscal Responsibility: Unem-

ployment Relief in Winnipeg, 1907–1942," Master of Arts thesis, University of Manitoba, 1981, 168.

89. "Committee to study housing of unemployed"; "City council approves plan for construction of $3,200 model home," *Winnipeg Evening Tribune*, August 10, 1937; "House plan passes," *Winnipeg Free Press*, August 10, 1937; "Rent paying policy of social welfare commission probed," *Winnipeg Free Press*, October 4, 1937; "Low-cost housing scheme again debated by council but no action taken," *Winnipeg Evening Tribune*, April 4, 1939.

90. "Revival of housing scheme is favored by civic committee," *Winnipeg Free Press*, March 7, 1935; "Two million civic housing scheme recommended," *Winnipeg Evening Tribune*, March 7, 1935. For McWilliams's election see: "Mayor Webb again returned to office by large majority, *Winnipeg Free Press*, November 25, 1933; "Gunn, Andrews and Mrs. McWilliams are elected in Ward One," *Winnipeg Free Press*, November 27, 1933.

91. Mary Kinnear, *Margaret McWilliams: An Interwar Feminist*, Montreal and Kingston: McGill-Queen's Press, 1991, 121.

92. "Scheme to help young married couples is urged," *Winnipeg Free Press*, January 10, 1936; "Speaker urges that public interest be aroused on housing question in the city," *Winnipeg Evening Tribune*, April 25, 1936; "Housing scheme to provide jobs favored by city," *Winnipeg Evening Tribune*, July 30, 1936; "Would exempt improved homes from tax raise," *Winnipeg Evening Tribune*, November 11, 1936; "Federal housing help is sought," *Winnipeg Evening Tribune*, April 29, 1938.

93. "'Honeymoon hotel' at low rent is Mrs. McWilliams' plant to aid newlyweds," *Winnipeg Evening Tribune*, March 7, 1936.

94. "More houses for city needed, says builders' letters," *Winnipeg Free Press*, August 27, 1934.

95. "More houses for city needed, says builders' letters," *Winnipeg Free Press*, August 27, 1934.

96. "Labor women seek housing improvement," *Winnipeg Free Press*, April 9, 1937.

97. "Mrs. Maclennan urges slum action," *Winnipeg Free Press*, March 8, 1939.

98. Jeffrey Thorsteinsson and Brennan Smith, *Green Blankstein Russell and Associates: An Architectural Legacy*, Winnipeg: Winnipeg Architectural Foundation, n.d., 1–3, 16, 26.

99. "Speaker urges that public interest be aroused on housing question in the city," *Winnipeg Evening Tribune*, April 25, 1936.

100. "Shocked by slums," *Winnipeg Free Press*, March 13, 1937; "Youth Council sees movies of slum districts," *Winnipeg Evening Tribune*, December 17, 1937.

101. "The housing problem," *Winnipeg Evening Tribune*, March 22, 1937.

102. A.V. Thomas, "Transformation of area in Elmwood into Minature [sic] Garden City is New Plan," *Winnipeg Evening Tribune*, November 17, 1934.

103. A.V. Thomas, "Systematic grants aiding councils called greatest advance in Great Britain," *Winnipeg Evening Tribune*, May 25, 1935.

104. Duncan Irvine, "Reform, war, and industrial crisis in Manitoba: F.J. Dixon and the framework of consensus, 1903–1920," Master of Arts thesis, University of Manitoba, 1981, 55, 98.

105. James Gray, *The Boy from Winnipeg*, Toronto: MacMillan of Canada, 1970, 93.

106. Robert E. Hawkins, "Lillian Beynon Thomas, woman's suffrage and the re-

turn of Dower to Manitoba," *Manitoba Law Journal*, 27, 45-113 (1999): 105.

107. G.H. Irwin, "Home and property owners' association," *Winnipeg Evening Tribune*, April 19, 1935.

108. "Home, property owners hit city wage increases," *Winnipeg Free Press*, February 15, 1935; G.H. Irwin, "Home and property owners' association," *Winnipeg Evening Tribune*, April 19, 1935; "W.J. Christie dies Thursday at age of 86," *Winnipeg Free Press*, May 15, 1942; "Advisory board appointed by Stevens party," *Winnipeg Evening Tribune*, August 19, 1935; "Manitoba citizens to receive Jubilee medals," *Winnipeg Evening Tribune*, May 6, 1935.

109. "Mass meeting of property owners," *Winnipeg Free Press*, March 19, 1934.

110. "Your home," *Winnipeg Evening Tribune*, January 24, 1933; G.H. Irwin, "Home and property owners' association," *Winnipeg Evening Tribune*, April 19, 1935.

111. G.H. Irwin, "Home and property owners' association," *Winnipeg Evening Tribune*, April 19, 1935; "Protest increase in allowance for food for jobless," *Winnipeg Free Press*, June 8, 1935; "Thinks economies could be made in three civic depts.," *Winnipeg Free Press*, April 18, 1935; J.F. Feilde, "Protests an increases in civic salaries," *Winnipeg Free Press*, August 10, 1935; "Home, property owners hit city wage increases," *Winnipeg Free Press*, February 15, 1935,

112. "Property owners prepare for battle on assessment," *Winnipeg Free Press*, March 26, 1934.

113. "Home, property owners hit city wage increases," *Winnipeg Free Press*, February 15, 1935,

114. "Property owners and building program," *Winnipeg Evening Tribune*, March 16, 1935.

115. "Says housing plan must be cautiously dealt with by city," *Winnipeg Free Press*, January 23, 1935.

116. J.F. Feilde, "City council's housing problem," *Winnipeg Evening Tribune*, October 30, 1935; "Feilde sees need of taxes being reduced to safeguard city," *Winnipeg Free Press*, November 22, 1935.

117. "Civic election count completed," *Winnipeg Free Press*, November 28, 1933.

118. "Authority to be sought to borrow $1,500,000 for building of homes," *Winnipeg Free Press*, February 20, 1934.

119. "New housing plan for city placed before committee," *Winnipeg Free Press*, March 23, 1934; "Architects say housing plan attack unfair," *Winnipeg Tribune*, May 7, 1934; "Architects reply to criticism of housing scheme," *Winnipeg Free Press*, May 7, 1934; "Proposed low-cost housing development for the city of Winnipeg," *Journal, Royal Architectural Institute of Canada*, XI, 7 and 8: 109–112.

120. "Proposed low-cost housing development for the city of Winnipeg," *Journal, Royal Architectural Institute of Canada*, XI, 7 and 8, 112; "Relief housing plan outlined," *Winnipeg Tribune*, April 18, 1934.

121. "Building notes," *Winnipeg Tribune*, April 14, 1934.

122. "Mass meeting" (Advertisement), *Winnipeg Free Press*, April 21, 1934.

123. "Architects say housing plan attack unfair," *Winnipeg Tribune*, May 7, 1934; "Architects reply to criticism of housing scheme," *Winnipeg Free Press*, May 7, 1934.

124. "Taxpayers of North End hear Ald. Rice-Jones," *Winnipeg Tribune*, June 16, 1934.

125. "Mayor Webb vigorously attacks city newspapers; says he was misquoted,"

Winnipeg Free Press, December 18, 1934.

126. "Mayor and Gunn to go to Ottawa on relief plans," *Winnipeg Free Press*, May 11, 1934.

127. "Builders' union urges low-cost housing plan," *Winnipeg Tribune*, August 25, 1934.

128. "Apathy killed housing plan, says Bennett," *Winnipeg Tribune*, June 21, 1934; "Council blamed for shelving of garden city plan," *Winnipeg Free Press*, June 22, 1934.

129. "Property owners and building program," *Winnipeg Evening Tribune*, March 16, 1935.

130. "Builders' union urges low-cost housing plan," *Winnipeg Tribune*, August 25, 1934.

131. *House of Commons Debates*, 1935, 1, 168–171, quoted in John C. Bacher, "Keeping to the Private Market: The Evolution of Canadian Housing Policy, 1900–1949," Doctoral thesis, McMaster University, 1985, 136–137.

132. "Webb urges province to force action in problem of housing," *Winnipeg Tribune*, March 19, 1937.

133. "Winnipeg tax system reviewed in report," *Winnipeg Free Press*, July 31, 1934; "Conclusions and recommendations of Bradshaw Commission report," *Winnipeg Free Press*, July 31, 1934; "Urges province share taxes," *Winnipeg Free Press*, July 31, 1934; G.H. Irwin, "Home and property owners' association," *Winnipeg Evening Tribune*, April 19, 1935.

134. Brian McKillop, "Citizen and Socialist: The Ethos of Political Winnipeg, 1919–1935," Master of Arts thesis, University of Manitoba, 1970.

135. "Queen fires his opening gun in civic election," *Winnipeg Evening Tribune*, November 10, 1934.

136. Brian McKillop, "Citizen and Socialist: The Ethos of Political Winnipeg, 1919–1935," Master of Arts thesis, University of Manitoba, 1970, 203–207. For examples of opposition to the Bradshaw recommendations, see: "Letters to the editor," *Winnipeg Evening Tribune*, September 1, 1934.

137. "The new city council," *Winnipeg Free Press*, November 28, 1934.

138. "Proposed city tax on businesses further attacked," *Winnipeg Free Press*, March 21, 1935.

139. "Tense drama punctuates business tax hearings when White, Scott clash," *Winnipeg Free Press*, March 23, 1935.

140. "Lawrence says 'Big interests' defeated tax," *Winnipeg Evening Tribune*, April 15, 1935.

141. Richard Harris, "Working-class home ownership and housing affordability across Canada in 1931," *Histoire sociale/Social History*, 19, 37 (May 1986): 127–128.

142. J.H. Gray, "Inside Winnipeg," *Winnipeg Free Press*, September 17, 1938.

143. "105,000 electors eligible to vote at civic elections," *Winnipeg Free Press*, October 9, 1935; "Work to start on city voters' list on Monday," *Winnipeg Evening Tribune*, May 1, 1936.

144. "Adult suffrage passed by civic legislation body," *Winnipeg Evening Tribune*, February 23, 1935; "Committee gives approval to adult suffrage in city," *Winnipeg Free Press*, February 23, 1935; Stefan Epp-Koop, *"We're Going to Run This City": Winnipeg's Political Left after the General Strike*, Winnipeg: University of Manitoba Press, 2015, 130–131.

145. "Proposed city tax on businesses further attacked," *Winnipeg Free Press*, March 21, 1935.

146. "Seven-week session of legislature is ended," *Winnipeg Free Press*, April 8, 1936; "Work to start on city voters' list on Monday," *Winnipeg Evening Tribune*, May 1, 1936.

147. A.V. Thomas, "City hall speaking," *Winnipeg Evening Tribune*, March 10, 1936.

148. "New council may advance housing plan," *Winnipeg Evening Tribune*, December 27, 1934.

149. "Housing plans advanced by city council," *Winnipeg Free Press*, March 19, 1935; "Council favors housing plan without vote," *Winnipeg Evening Tribune*, March 19, 1935.

150. "Revival of housing scheme is favored by civic committee," *Winnipeg Free Press*, March 7, 1935; "Two million civic housing scheme recommended," *Winnipeg Evening Tribune*, March 7, 1935. For McWilliams's election, see: "Mayor Webb again returned to office by large majority, *Winnipeg Free Press*, November 25, 1933; "Gunn, Andrews and Mrs. McWilliams are elected in Ward One," *Winnipeg Free Press*, November 27, 1933.

151. For the report on housing conditions, see: Stefan Epp-Koop, "Class, capitalism, and construction: Winnipeg's housing crisis and the debate over public housing, 1934-1939," *Histoire sociale/Social History*, 43, 86 (2010): 411. For concerns over lack of political will, see: "Speakers see lack of 'Will for housing,'" *Winnipeg Evening Tribune*, March 22, 1939.

152. "Legislators decry slum conditions," *Winnipeg Free Press*, March 19, 1937.

153. "Ward 2 I.L.P. candidates pledge selves to raise living standard if elected," *Winnipeg Evening Tribune*, November 14, 1935; "Aldermen favor spending of $500,000 on home building," *Winnipeg Free Press*, October 3, 1935; "Winnipeg may vote on $500,000 housing scheme in November," *Winnipeg Free Press*, October 3, 1935; "Stobart gives details of city housing plan," *Winnipeg Evening Tribune*, November 21, 1935.

154. "Truth about the housing by-law," Advertisement, *Winnipeg Tribune*, November 22, 1935.

155. "Stobart gives details of city housing plan," *Winnipeg Evening Tribune*, November 21, 1935.

156. A.V. Thomas, "Housing certain to be big civic election issue," *Winnipeg Evening Tribune*, October 19, 1935. For details on Gunn's career, see: Brian McKillop, "Citizen and Socialist: The Ethos of Political Winnipeg, 1919-1935," Master of Arts thesis, University of Manitoba, 1970, 194-195.

157. "Aldermen favor spending of $500,000 on home building," *Winnipeg Free Press*, October 3, 1935; "Winnipeg may vote on $500,000 housing scheme in November," *Winnipeg Free Press*, October 3, 1935; A.V. Thomas, "Housing certain to be big civic election issue," *Winnipeg Evening Tribune*, October 19, 1935.

158. "Council gives second reading to housing plan; goes to voters," *Winnipeg Evening Tribune*, October 22, 1935. For details on Victor B. Anderson's career, see: "Aldermanic, Victory B. Anderson," *Winnipeg Evening Tribune*, November 11, 1939.

159. "City of Winnipeg: Notice re submission of by-law to the vote of the electors," *Winnipeg Evening Tribune*, November 7, 1935; "Truth about the housing by-law," *Winnipeg Evening Tribune*, November 21, 1935.

160. "Board states house building scheme unsound," *Winnipeg Evening Tribune*,

November 20, 1935.

161. J.F. Feilde, "City council's housing problem," *Winnipeg Evening Tribune*, October 30, 1935; "Feilde sees need of taxes being reduced to safeguard city," *Winnipeg Free Press*, November 22, 1935.

162. "Women urged to support Gunn in mayoralty race," *Winnipeg Free Press*, November 18, 1935.

163. "Ald. Rice-Jones charges housing plan misrepresented," *Winnipeg Evening Tribune*, November 21, 1935.

164. "The housing scheme," *Winnipeg Free Press*, November 18, 1935.

165. "The housing bylaw," *Winnipeg Evening Tribune*, November 18, 1935.

166. "Building trades council backs housing bylaw," *Winnipeg Evening Tribune*, November 21, 1935.

167. "Queen re-elected: Bylaw beaten," *Winnipeg Free Press*, November 23, 1935.

168. A.V. Thomas, "Housing bylaw defeated because votes lacked confidence in proposal," *Winnipeg Evening Tribune*, December 14, 1935.

169. "Problems facing city in 1936 are cited by mayor," *Winnipeg Free Press*, January 15, 1936.

170. "City may gain submit bylaw on housing plan," *Winnipeg Evening Tribune*, March 10, 1936.

171. "Transfers sweep Warriner into mayoralty; Sara and Morrison Ward I aldermen," *Winnipeg Free Press*, November 30, 1936.

172. "Rightists secure control of city council," *Winnipeg Free Press*, December 1, 1936; "Control of Winnipeg civic administration out of labor's hands," *Winnipeg Free Press*, January 4, 1937.

173. "Slum conditions in city are decried by minister," *Winnipeg Free Press*, March 6, 1937.

174. "Citizens must be awakened to 'dreadful conditions' of city slums, minister says," *Winnipeg Evening Tribune*, March 11, 1937.

175. "See folk worse off than dogs," *Winnipeg Free Press*, March 11, 1937.

176. J.H. Gray, "Slum riddance: Carter sees terrace scheme as solution," *Winnipeg Free Press*, March 18, 1937; "Provincial committee on home improvements named," *Winnipeg Evening Tribune*, March 6, 1937.

177. "Subsidy needed for low-cost housing scheme," *Winnipeg Evening Tribune*, February 11, 1937.

178. "Council seeks Dominion aid for slum clearance," *Winnipeg Evening Tribune*, April 6, 1937.

179. See: "Work for taxes plan carried on by city council," *Winnipeg Evening Tribune*, June 1, 1937; "Huge arrears."

180. "Who's who in the civic election," *Winnipeg Tribune*, November 14, 1938; Les Henry, "Mail order houses," Canadian Museum of History. <historymuseum.ca/cmc/exhibitions/cpm/catalog/cat2104e.html#1222116>, accessed July 3, 2021.

181. For correspondence, see: Trevor Wideman, "Land Use, Planning, and Private Property: Waste and Improvement in Early 20th Century Winnipeg and Vancouver, Canada," Doctoral thesis, Simon Fraser University, 2020, 100; Roberts, B., Letter from B. Roberts, Assistant Deputy Minister of Finance (Canada) to R.A. Sara, Esq., Aladdin Homes, October 9, 1935, City of Winnipeg Archives Box A561 File 3; Clark, W., Letter from W. Clark, Deputy Minister of Finance (Canada) to R.A. Sara, Esq., Aladdin Homes, August 30, 1935, City of

Winnipeg Archives Box A561 File 3.

182. Library and Archives Canada, Record Group 19, Volume 3435, David Mansur to John A. Flanders, June 14, 1937, quoted in John C. Bacher, "Keeping to the Private Market: The Evolution of Canadian Housing Policy, 1900–1949," Doctoral thesis, McMaster University, 1985,241.

183. Library and Archives Canada, quoted in John C. Bacher, "Keeping to the Private Market: The Evolution of Canadian Housing Policy, 1900–1949," Doctoral thesis, McMaster University, 1985, 241.

184. "Aldermen working on low-cost housing on city-owned property," *Winnipeg Evening Tribune*, April 13, 1937; J.F. Parker, "Home Owners' Association viewpoint on housing," *Winnipeg Evening Tribune*, April 27, 1937.

185. "$500,000 house plan is in sight Sara declares," *Winnipeg Evening Tribune*, May 4, 1937; "Sara criticizes lending companies' aloof attitude," *Winnipeg Evening Tribune*, June 1, 1937; "Housing fight," *Winnipeg Free Press*, June 2, 1937.

186. "Debate housing loans," *Winnipeg Free Press*, May 20, 1937.

187. "Sara criticizes lending companies' aloof attitude," *Winnipeg Evening Tribune*, June 1, 1937; "Housing fight," *Winnipeg Free Press*, June 2, 1937.

188. "City-backed company urged as experiment in 'rent-by' houses," *Winnipeg Evening Tribune*, June 26, 1937.

189. "City-backed company urged as experiment in 'rent-by' houses," *Winnipeg Evening Tribune*, June 26, 1937.

190. "City will apply for incorporation of housing company," *Winnipeg Free Press*, July 14, 1937.

191. Copy of letter from Mansur to Flanders, op. cit.; Letter June 23, 1937, from D.B. Mansur to W.C. Clark, Letter R.A. Sara, Chairman Winnipeg City Council Special Committee on Housing, June 15, 1937 to W.C. Clark all in PAC, RG19, Vol. 3435. Quoted in Bacher, "Keeping to the Private Market," 243; "The cost of model houses," *Winnipeg Evening Tribune*, August 25, 1937; "Inconsistency of house planned denied by group," *Winnipeg Tribune*, September 3, 1937.

192. John C. Bacher, "Keeping to the Private Market: The Evolution of Canadian Housing Policy, 1900–1949," Doctoral thesis, McMaster University, 1985, 243–244.

193. "City-backed company urged as experiment in 'rent-by' houses," *Winnipeg Evening Tribune*, June 26, 1937; "City council approves plan for construction of $3,200 model home," *Winnipeg Evening Tribune*, August 10, 1937; "House plan passes," *Winnipeg Free Press*, August 10, 1937.

194. "Low-cost houses," *Winnipeg Evening Tribune*, September 11, 1937.

195. "Building contest planned," *Winnipeg Free Press*, July 7, 1937.

196. City of Winnipeg Archives, Housing Folder 6, "The City of Winnipeg Housing Company Limited Preferred Stock," November 4, 1937, cited in Stefan Epp-Koop, "Class, capitalism, and construction: Winnipeg's housing crisis and the debate over public housing, 1934–1939," *Histoire sociale/Social History*, 43, 86 (2010): 419; "Money ready for new homes," *Winnipeg Free Press*, September 9, 1937.

197. "Housing project collapses," *Winnipeg Free Press*, April 20, 1938.

198. "Finance body unable to get its work done," *Winnipeg Evening Tribune*, June 19, 1937; "Model house will be the kind housewives will like," *Winnipeg Evening Tribune*, September 23, 1937; "Winnipeg's newest demonstration home,"

Winnipeg Evening Tribune, November 1, 1937.

199. "City council approves plan for construction of $3,200 model home," *Winnipeg Evening Tribune*, August 10, 1937; "House plan passes," *Winnipeg Free Press*, August 10, 1937.

200. "City will seek profit on sale of model house," *Winnipeg Evening Tribune*, November 13, 1937; "City has no bids for model home when tenders close; offers it on instalment plan," *Winnipeg Evening Tribune*, December 11, 1937.

201. "Gilbert George Crook," *Winnipeg Free Press*, December 22, 1943; Stefan Epp-Koop, "Class, capitalism, and construction: Winnipeg's housing crisis and the debate over public housing, 1934–1939," *Histoire sociale/Social History*, 43, 86 (2010): 422.

202. "Re-check of votes complete," *Winnipeg Free Press*, November 29, 1937.

203. "Status quo undisturbed by civic elections," *Winnipeg Free Press*, December 1, 1937.

204. "City council studies new $1,250,000 housing project," *Winnipeg Free Press*, May 11, 1938.

205. "Housing project," *Winnipeg Free Press*, September 23, 1938; "Suite argument," *Winnipeg Free Press*, November 3, 1938.

206. "Council asks Dominion to finance big housing project," *Winnipeg Free Press*, May 18, 1938.

207. "Queen elected by 3,255 votes," *Winnipeg Tribune*, November 28, 1939; "$1,500,000 quandary," *Winnipeg Free Press*, February 14, 1939.

208. "Taxpayers get say in housing," *Winnipeg Tribune*, February 21, 1939; "Building trades delegation scores housing committee," *Winnipeg Free Press*, February 28, 1939.

209. "Adult suffrage killed; Pritchard Baths open for winter months; School board criticized," *Winnipeg Tribune*, October 18, 1938.

210. "Low-cost housing scheme"; "Pastor pleads," *Winnipeg Free Press*, April 4, 1939; "Compromise on housing plan," *Winnipeg Evening Tribune*, April 5, 1939; "$300,000 Job," *Winnipeg Free Press*, April 5, 1939.

211. Stefan Epp-Koop, "Class, capitalism, and construction: Winnipeg's housing crisis and the debate over public housing, 1934–1939," *Histoire sociale/Social History*, 43, 86 (2010): 426.

212. "Low-cost housing scheme again debated by council but no action taken," *Winnipeg Evening Tribune*, April 4, 1939.

213. "City council studies new $1,250,000 housing project," *Winnipeg Free Press*, May 11, 1938.

214. "Acute shortage of houses for low-wage class," *Winnipeg Free Press*, January 27, 1938.

215. "Expert says 5,000 new houses needed in Greater Winnipeg," *Winnipeg Free Press*, February 12, 1938.

216. "Housing in Winnipeg," *Winnipeg Free Press*, January 23, 1940.

Chapter 5

WARTIME HOUSING AND EMERGENCY HOUSING: 1940–1953

At the start of World War II in 1939, there was, according to one government estimate, a need for ten thousand homes in Canada. "Doubling up"—two families occupying one household—was increasingly common. Throughout the Great Depression little had been spent on maintaining housing, particularly rental housing, which had become increasingly dilapidated.[1] The outbreak of war only exacerbated the country's housing shortage. While the war brought an end to mass unemployment, cities dramatically increased in population while housing construction remained static. Roughly 300,000 people moved from rural Canada to cities during the war, about equal to the rise in the number of households that lacked their own dwelling unit by the war's end.[2] Federal finance department officials initially hoped that the civilian population would just double up and carry on.[3] Since the major thrust of the *National Housing Act* had been to stimulate employment, and the war had all but eliminated unemployment, in 1940, the government ended its involvement in the housing marking by ceasing to issue *National Housing Act* construction loans.[4]

But the federal government soon found it could not operate a wartime economy without intervening in the housing market. At first, it restricted itself to regulatory matters: in the fall of 1940, it introduced rent controls and began to regulate evictions to prevent the increase in demand from leading to a dramatic increase in housing costs.[5] Two years later, the federal government prohibited what was termed "winter evictions" by restricting them to the period from May 1 to September 30.[6] Reasons of national security led to a far more dramatic departure from past policy. In February 1941, the government established Wartime Housing, a Crown corporation mandated to build housing that was intended for people who worked in war-production industries. The story of Wartime Housing Limited was one of the great might-have-beens in the history of Canadian housing. By the war's end in August 1945, it had built 16,869 units of housing. (Confusingly, the distinctive housing that Wartime Housing built has come to be termed "wartime housing"—meaning the housing had the same name as the corporation. Further confusion arises from the fact that Wartime Housing continued to build wartime housing after the war ended. All of Winnipeg's wartime housing, for example, was built after the end of the war.)[7]

At the war's end, military personnel returning to civilian live in the tens of thousands meant that the housing shortage continued on into the post-war period, forcing the federal government to establish a makeshift "Emergency Housing" program. In response to opposition from the construction and real-estate industries, it wound down the operations of Wartime Housing Limited at the war's end and sold off its housing stock. While the market had once more prevailed, there was now a clear example of how government could enter the housing market, rapidly increase production, and meet a need that the market was failing to address.

WARTIME HOUSING LIMITED

With the outbreak of war, the Canadian government invested dramatically in munitions plants, shipbuilding, and aircraft construction. For example, by February 1941, munitions plants in Hamilton, Ontario employed 13,500 people and it was expected that the workforce would swell to 20,000 by the end of the year. The workforce in Valcartier, Quebec was expected to go from 2,700 to 11,000 in the same period.[8] But already by late 1940, munitions workers were quitting their jobs because they could not find homes for their families while plants in remote communities were having trouble recruiting workers.[9] If the government wanted to continue to build bombs and bombers, it had to build housing for the war workers.

In February 1941, C.D. Howe, the federal minister of Munitions and Supply (a man more commonly referred to as the "minister of everything" in Prime Minister Mackenzie King's wartime cabinet), overcame Finance Department opposition to any form of government-built housing and created Wartime Housing Limited. He recruited Hamilton construction executive Joseph Piggott to run the corporation for a dollar a year and mandated the corporation to build temporary housing for workers in war-related industries.[10] Wartime Housing got off to a quick start. One month after its establishment in February 1941, the corporation was assembling prefabricated demonstration homes in Ottawa in nine hours, at a cost of $1,500. By the summer, contracts had been let for the construction of two thousand houses in ten Canadian cities.[11]

Wartime Housing built on land that it bought, land it received from municipalities, and land already owned by the federal government. Local builders and architects developed the projects according to national designs with construction being carried out on a semi-prefabricated basis. A typical storey-and-a-half, 957-square-foot wartime house had three bedrooms, a living room, and a kitchen.[12] They rented for $20 to $30 a month based on the size of the house. The rents covered the federal government's costs and were within reach of the war industry workers for whom the houses were being built. To meet the needs of low-income people, however, housing would have had to be priced between $12 and $20 a month.[13]

Wartime Housing was not without its critics. The Department of Finance, which believed that the construction of permanent housing should be left to the private sector, insisted that wartime houses be "temporary" in nature. To ensure this, Finance required that the houses be built without basements and be heated with stoves as opposed to furnaces.[14] After the war, owners added basements and furnaces, and many of these "temporary" houses have now been occupied for decades. The construction industry objected to the fact that Wartime Housing was given privileged access to scarce building materials and worried that the corporation might continue to dominate house building in the post-war era.[15]

There was also criticism from the left. The Co-operative

Commonwealth Federation (CCF—the forerunner to today's New Democratic Party) commended the government for initiating the wartime housing program but objected to the low-cost and temporary nature of the housing.[16] The CCF would have preferred to see the *National Housing Act* amended to provide 90 percent mortgages on houses valued at $3,500 or less. Up until then the benefits of the *National Housing Act* had been reserved for the purchasers of more expensive housing.[17] In his first speech as national leader of the CCF, M.J. Coldwell accused Wartime Housing of building "so-called homes, the unit cost of which is atrocious, and which will become slum areas."[18] As late as November 1945, Winnipeg CCF MP Alistair Stewart was condemning wartime housing as potential slums.[19] The CCF's criticism of the cost of the construction of Wartime Housing appears to have been off the mark since it did not take into account additional development costs that Wartime Housing assumed.[20]

WARTIME HOUSING IN WINNIPEG

It was not until December 1945 that construction was completed on the first of nearly two thousand units of wartime housing that were to be built in Winnipeg. In addition, wartime housing was built in this period in most of the surrounding municipalities, including East Kildonan, Fort Garry, St. Boniface, St. James, and Transcona.[21] Every expansion of the number of Wartime Housing homes in Winnipeg was the subject of heated debate and all the houses were built over the increasingly predictable opposition of the local property development industry.[22] The industry had good reason to oppose Wartime Housing: the reality of state-built and administered low-cost housing would inspire a fifteen-year campaign to have the City build and operate its own public-housing projects.

At the start of the war, Winnipeg had a severe housing shortage: 15 percent of the city's households were doubled up, 19 percent were living in what was described as overcrowded conditions, and 36 percent were living in substandard buildings.[23] At the beginning of 1941, the vacancy rate for the city was .43 percent.[24] CCF city council member Jack Blumberg said that in early 1941 landlords were evicting long-term tenants so they could charge new tenants higher rents. Blumberg spoke of:

> One case where a tenant who had been in a house for eight years and not been late with a single rent payment was ordered out, of another where an airman with a wife and two children was turned out although he had not been able to obtain another house.[25]

Since the city's housing shortage was not attributable to war-related industry, Winnipeg did not initially qualify for wartime housing.[26] John Queen, who was mayor during the early war years, was initially resistant to building wartime housing in the city, largely because of its supposedly temporary nature. "Why," he asked, "in the face of the great housing shortage should we sanction construction of houses to be pulled down in a couple of years?"[27] Instead, Queen worked with the Winnipeg Trades and Labor Council, and W.H. Carter and W.B. Simpson, two former members of the Winnipeg Housing Commission, on a plan to have the federal government support the construction of permanent low-cost housing in the city.[28] It was only when the federal government rejected this plan that Queen was prepared to countenance the construction of wartime housing in the city.

The housing shortage intensified every spring when the federally imposed wintertime ban on evictions ended. As the May 1, 1941 deadline approached, Winnipeg's social agencies were besieged by families in search of housing. In what was described as the most serious housing crisis in the city's history, between 300 and 400 households were facing eviction. Enforcement of the city's public-health laws would likely have led to the eviction of at least 6,000 families.[29] In May the city converted its former relief building on Elgin Street into sixteen units of housing. In addition to these sixteen families, at least four families were living in what were termed "shacks" at the back of the city property.[30] By mid-June, the city council was besieged by families facing eviction.[31] A year later the housing situation was even tighter. A.W. Johnson, a regional rental officer with the Wartime Prices and Trade Board, told the *Tribune* that scores of people were being evicted with no place to go. "Many are staying on where they are under terrible conditions. I know of eight persons living in a three-room suite because they can't find any place to move." Dr. Morley Lougheed, the city's medical health officer, called local housing conditions disgraceful, adding "We could fill the paper with incidents of families living under conditions which are against the law."[32]

Depression-era defaults on property taxes meant that the City had unintentionally become a slum landlord. In 1943, for example, the City moved to demolish the tenement that it owned on Market Street. Badly damaged by fire, the building had thirteen-two-room suites, one of which was home to a family of nine. Each room was heated by a small tin stove. According to a newspaper report, "Entrance to one suite was through a narrow tunnel underneath the stairs. You had to duck your head to enter."[33] By April 1944, there were 2.6 families living in each house in the city.[34] By the end of June, Percy Pickering, the city's housing inspector, said there were no suites for rent or vacant houses in the city.[35]

Possibly emboldened by the fact that he was a year away from retirement, Pickering told Winnipeg's Board of Trade (the equivalent of today's Chamber of Commerce) that the city faced a looming housing disaster. "If you could see, as I have, women with husbands overseas, crying because they could not find a home, and hear the expressions of men on leave from active service—you would realize that action is past due." There was, he said, nothing being done to prepare for the inevitable post-war housing crisis. Not only was low-cost housing in short supply, but the houses that did exist were often dilapidated and unfit for occupancy.

> Overcrowding is rife, the plumbing fixtures are inadequate. There are gas ranges in practically every room and the odors, especially in winter, due to the lack of ventilation, are often nauseating. We provide these children with milk and facilities at school for their well-being and then allow them to reside in what one may term, without exaggeration, a hovel.[36]

City council member James Black, head of the city's housing committee, feared that when the wintertime freeze on evictions was lifted in the spring of 1944, the city would be overwhelmed. He told the council, "People have been phoning me while holding eviction papers in their hands. What are we going to do with them?" There was, he said, one family with seven children that would soon be on the street.[37]

POST-WAR WARTIME HOUSING WINNIPEG

In 1942, C.D. Howe announced that Wartime Housing was going to shift from building housing for war workers to addressing the larger urban housing shortage. In light of the federal government's unwillingness to fund the permanent housing plan that he had proposed, Winnipeg mayor John Queen had little choice but to commence negotiations with the federal government for the construction of 500 wartime homes.[38] After visiting Winnipeg, Wartime Housing staff recommended that 600 houses be built in Winnipeg and St. Boniface.[39] But the federal government never finalized the deal, and the housing was never built.[40] What happened? Federal finance department officials, ever zealous in their protection of the private construction sector, were horrified at Howe and Piggott's plans to build wartime housing for anyone other than people involved in war-related work, in part because it might prove too popular. One federal official characterized Piggott's approach as "dangerous" and warned that it could be the beginning of "the socialization of all our housing."[41] Finance Minister J.L. Isley worried that Wartime Housing Limited might supplant the private sector and serve as a model for a type of post-war housing that he opposed.[42] Lending institutions, private developers, and building supply firms all lined up to oppose any extension of Wartime Housing into the production of permanent homes.[43] By late 1942 the Finance Department had won the battle, and Wartime Housing Limited was told to limit construction to meet the housing needs of workers employed in war-related production. Piggott privately told the Wartime Housing board of directors that his approach had been blocked by "loan companies, builders, lumber companies, and others."[44] The plan to build 600 houses in Winnipeg was quietly shelved.

Piggott did live to fight another day. In 1943, the federal government was talking about winding down Wartime Housing. But the national housing shortage remained unaddressed. In May 1944, left without any real options, the federal government expanded

Wartime Housing's mandate to allow it to build housing for the families of people serving in the armed forces and returned service personnel.[45] Piggott recommended in the spring of 1945 that Wartime Housing build 30,000 more homes over the next three years.[46] Howe, for whom, as journalist Blair Fraser once wrote, "No abstract principle was as important as Getting Things Done," supported the plan.[47]

In 1945 Winnipeg council and Wartime Housing had reached an agreement for the construction of at least 100 of these new houses in the working-class community of Elmwood. The houses were to be leased to service personnel or their dependants, cost approximately $3,000 to build, and would be rented for between $22 and $30. The *Free Press* estimated that similar private-sector housing would cost $40 a month or more. Wartime Housing would build and maintain the houses on serviced land provided by the City and pay the City between $24 and $30 in place of property taxes.[48] Winnipeg city council approved the agreement by an 11-to-6 vote that laid bare the divisions that would emerge every time wartime housing came up for debate at council. Except for Jack Blumberg, the CCF councillors voted for the measure, the communist councillors were unanimous in their support of the project, while the Citizens on council were split on the issue.[49]

While ideological differences played a significant role in the debate over Wartime Housing, the conflict was often framed as a battle royale between C.E. Simonite, the chair of the finance committee, and H.B. Scott, Black's successor as chair of the housing committee. Not surprisingly, Simonite viewed Wartime Housing as an unneeded and potentially distorting intrusion in the private real-estate market, rarely missing an opportunity to speak against it. When Black worried at a council meeting about the fate of a family of seven that was facing eviction, Simonite responded that this was not the city's problem: "There are too many citizens who would love to weep on the shoulder of a kind-hearted alderman like Ald. Black or camp on the mayor's doorstep and let the city handle their problems for nothing."[50]

Scott, who took over from James Black as the chair of the housing committee in 1945, served on council for sixteen years, being defeated in 1958. From 1953 to 1958 he was also a Conservative mem-

ber of the provincial legislature.[51] He was no shrinking
violet. An advertisement for
his 1943 campaign for council proclaimed that he was
"independent, represent-
ing all the people and is under no compulsion to flatter
any group." He said he was
"fearless," having spent the
years between election campaigns denouncing "things
which appeared wrong to
him and championed the
cause of the sufferers from
and the victims thereof."[52]
The operator of a bakery on
Sargent Avenue, a few blocks
from his home on Sherbrook
Street, he had run for council four times without suc-

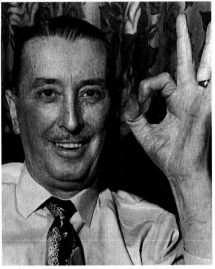

Councillor Henry Scott led the fight on city
council for wartime housing in Winnipeg.
University of Manitoba Archives & Special
Collections. Winnipeg Tribune fonds,
PC 18 (A1981-12), item, UM_pc018_A81-
012_015_0546_009_0002.

cess before finally being elected in 1942.[53] Initially, Scott ran as an
independent and did not receive the backing of the Civic Election
Committee until 1950.[54]

In his role as the chair of the housing committee, he emerged
as a dogged advocate of Wartime Housing and as C.E. Simonite's
nemesis. In describing one debate, a *Free Press* editorialist wrote,
"Alderman Scott, sniffing suspiciously at each cloud of rhetoric
as it drifted past his nose, smelt a dark plot against his wartime
housing babies in all this. He snarled like a she-wolf defending
her young." Mayor Garnet Coulter once felt obliged to admonish
both Scott and Simonite for the use of what a *Tribune* reporter described as "fighting words" in a debate over Wartime Housing.[55]
Scott claimed that at one point, Simonite's vocal opposition led
Wartime Housing to cancel the development of an additional three
hundred homes in Winnipeg, while the *Winnipeg Tribune* hailed
Scott as the "man of the hour" when he had the federal commitment reinstated.[56]

Scott scandalized his opponents when he warned that returning service personnel might take to the streets if they felt the City
was ignoring their housing needs. He reminded his critics that
Canadian soldiers and sailors had rioted in Aldershot in Britain
and in Halifax out of frustration with years of military discipline
and the slow return to civilian life.[57] Councillors were also well
aware that veterans had occupied the old Hotel Vancouver in 1946
to protest the lack of post-war housing in that city.[58] This was not
the last time Scott traded on the fear of public disorder to prod his
more conservative colleagues into supporting public housing.

While the CCF councillors tended to vote in favour of the construction of wartime housing, Jack Blumberg, one of the most re-
spected members of their caucus, was, at best, tepid in his support. Blumberg acknowledged that wartime housing was better
than nothing, but he would have preferred to see the government
build larger, more permanent housing. As he put it, "I don't care
how you paint it, a shack is still a shack."[59] Jacob Penner, the leading Communist member on the council, was a steadfast supporter of Wartime Housing, and paradoxically often sounded much
more "pragmatic" (and less "communist") than Blumberg. Penner
worried that if faced with demands for larger houses with basements, Wartime Housing would simply forego building houses in
Winnipeg altogether.[60] "We are not," he said, "in a position to say
to the Dominion government 'Give us ideal houses or none at all.'"[61]

Perhaps the most vocal and successful proponents of Wartime
Housing were the representatives of the people who would benefit from them: the veterans' organizations. The local chapter of
the British Empire Service League and the local veterans' welfare committee supported the City's initial request for Wartime
Housing.[62] Major-General C.B. Price, the national president of the
Canadian Legion, applauded the construction of wartime housing
in Winnipeg saying: "These houses are wonderful accommodation
for people in the lower income bracket." He also made the case
for the knock-on social benefits of housing. "Through more and
more of these homes, we can lower the population in hospitals and
jails. Children do not have to be cramped in small quarters and are
brought up in a healthier way in the new homes."[63]

The returned veterans were seen as members of the "deserving poor"—who were quite clearly being failed by the current housing market. The *Tribune* editorialized, "For a young veteran to saddle himself with the payments needed to purchase a very average bungalow, selling in Winnipeg today at $7,500, would be most unwise, even if he could raise the $2,500 or $3,000 cash payment required."[64] While Simonite claimed that veterans with large incomes were living in wartime housing, 75 percent of the 217 households allocated wartime housing in early 1947 earned less than $150 a month.[65] The *Free Press* profiled three of the households on the waiting list at that time.

> Case No. 1—One child. Three people living in two rooms in a lodging house. The rooms are separated from each other. Meals are cooked on a community stove in a hallway. All tenants in the house share a common bathtub and toilet. The man was overseas three years, six months. He earns $125 per month. He pays $25 per month for the two rooms.

> Case No. 2—Two children, a third expected. The family is living in one room on the ground floor of an old terrace in the centre of the city. They share a bathroom and toilet on the second floor with other tenants in the house. Meals are cooked on a gas stove in their room. Rental is $15 per month. The veteran, who was three years overseas service, earns $140 per month.

> Case No. 3—Two children. The family occupies three-roomed housing in a heavy industrial area, next door to a coal yard and a gas works. The house has been condemned by the city health department, which has advised the family to leave as the landlord refuses to repair the house. There is no bath, only a toilet. Rental is S10 per month. The veteran earns $35 per week, is a pensioner, was wounded overseas.[66]

The demand for housing intensified as troops began to return home. Army representatives told a regional conference on social work in Winnipeg in October 1945 that the housing conditions in Winnipeg were "worse than inadequate," with every second returning serviceman "facing a difficult housing problem."[67] In November 1945 the armed forces were discharging 1,200 men a month for Winnipeg.[68]

If veterans favoured building wartime housing in Winnipeg, the local construction industry was firm in its opposition. In reflecting on his years as the chairperson of the housing committee, Citizens councillor James Black commented that every time someone attempted to do something about housing in Winnipeg, "the Lumber Dealers' association sends a communication to Ottawa objecting."[69] In July 1945 the Western Retail Lumberman's Association lobbied the federal government to discontinue Wartime Housing, claiming the private sector could build housing as quickly and efficiently.[70] The breadth of the business community's opposition to Wartime Housing was captured by the claim of A.H. Brett, the manager of the Greater Winnipeg Lumber Dealers Association, to speak on behalf of the Greater Winnipeg Lumber Dealers' Association, the Building Materials Association, the National Home Builder's Association, the Greater Winnipeg House Dealers' Association, the Winnipeg Home Builders' Association, the Winnipeg Home-owners' Association, and somewhat surprisingly, the Building Trades Council and the Winnipeg Trades and Labor Council, when he opposed Wartime Housing at a council meeting. (A *Free Press* columnist later facetiously wrote that he appeared to be representing "Everyone but the Sons and Daughters of 'I Will Arise'"—a non-existent social club popularized by the novelist Octavus Roy Cohen.)[71] In response to the private homebuilders' allegation that wartime housing did not conform to the city building code, city engineer W.D. Hurst said they "were reasonably adequate considering the emergency purpose for which they are designed."[72] Scott, having pointed out wartime houses were built to national building code standards, suggested that the builders' real complaint arose from the fact that the houses threatened their profit. "Too many builders built too many four-roomed bungalows and charged far too high a price for them. Now, when we are trying to give the veteran a house with a reasonable rent to live in—they are feeling the pinch."[73] The private sector was having trouble selling the houses it did build. In 1947 Fred C. Austin, the city's chief housing inspector, noted that there were 400 newly constructed buildings that the owners could not sell at the prices they were asking. "It has always been a wonder to me," he told a *Free Press* reporter, "that some of those unfortunate persons, living three and four in a room with their beds next to a greasy, smelling oil stove, haven't taken possession of these unoccupied houses and defied the authorities to throw them out."[74]

The Manitoba government provided no support for Wartime Housing projects, a policy that irked the Manitoba and Northwestern Ontario Branch of the Canadian Legion, which could point to the Ontario government's decision to fund the cost of lots and servicing.[75] Certainly, council member Scott kept the Province apprised of the demand for low-cost housing. In 1946, he told a legislative committee that there were 2,000 applications for wartime housing and that a minimum of 10,000 new homes was needed in the city.[76]

Talk to the effect that wartime houses would deteriorate into shacks and shantytowns helped legitimize the complaints of Winnipeggers who wanted to keep wartime housing out of their neighbourhoods. The Elmwood Home and School Association objected to the building of the first 100 units of wartime housing in that neighbourhood.[77] Three north-end city councillors and two CCF members of parliament supported the residents in their opposition to the housing. At a public meeting, Stanley Knowles told residents they were "fighting for the principle of public housing— good public housing." Scott and Penner, the strangest of political bedfellows, stood together on this issue, with Scott accusing the critics of jeopardizing the entire project, and Penner urging them to offer the federal government words of encouragement for what it was doing.[78]

On December 22, 1945, eight families moved into the first wartime houses to be occupied in Winnipeg. W.H. Durnin and his wife had been living in a tent on his parents' lawn until the cold weather hit. From then on, they had been living in his parents' house. Looking at the snow and slush that the movers had tracked in that moving day led one woman to comment, "I'm glad to have some floors to clean."[79] On moving into her house in Elmwood, Edith Phillips told the *Free Press*, "It's a shame there has been so much thoughtless talk about these houses. I am simply tickled with our

Councillor Henry Scott turns over the keys to the 1,000th wartime housing unit to be built in Winnipeg. These houses, which were often condemned as slums in the making, are still standing. "1,00th War House Opens for Public," Winnipeg Free Press, September 9, 1947.

house." By the time all the Elmwood houses were completed in the spring of 1946, there were 1,700 applications on file for wartime housing in Winnipeg.[80] A year later there were more than 4,000 former servicemen on the waiting list for wartime housing in Winnipeg and its surrounding suburbs.[81] Not surprisingly that fall, the Canadian Legion called on municipalities to ask for 1,600 more wartime houses for the Winnipeg area.[82] In September 1947, a family that had been living in the city's former relief building at 981 Elgin Street moved into 702 Rosedale Avenue, the one-thousandth wartime house to be built in the city.[83] By July 1949, there were 1,900 wartime houses in the city.[84]

The proposed sites for wartime housing were reshuffled on several occasions in response to concerns that the lots being proposed were too valuable.[85] In 1947 residents of Ward 2, an area dominated by modest housing in the city's inner core, were able to block the placement of fifty-eight wartime houses in the ward.[86] Residents of River Heights succeeded in blocking a proposal to build wartime housing in their exclusive south Winnipeg community. C.D. Heseltine told a public meeting, "I think you will agree that homeowners make the best citizens and, and in our district, we are 90 percent homeowners, who have little enough security."[87] This opposition was met with a stinging rebuke from a returned serviceman.

> Do these people, who already have a home, not care a bit if the servicemen who are not so fortunate as themselves, ever have a proper home for their wife and children, or is it a case of "the war is over. Our side won. Now let's get back to the old days and forget about the sacrifices these boys made."
>
> In my case, as many others, my wife, our child and myself live in one room. The Wartime Housing people have deemed fit to put me on the list for a house, but, there are people with two or more children in similar circumstances which must be looked after first. If they stop building these houses, what is to happen to people as in my case?[88]

Municipal opposition to Wartime Housing was aggravated by the federal government's boast that it was providing little if any subsidization to Wartime Housing since the buildings were inexpensive to build and the rents would, over time, cover the government costs.[89] The City of Winnipeg, was, however, making a substantial contribution to the cost of Wartime Housing by donating, servicing, and preparing the lots. By 1947, it was estimated that the servicing cost was half-a-million dollars, while the federal grant in lieu of taxes was only a quarter of the taxes the City would have received from privately owned homes.[90] When the *Winnipeg Tribune* provided editorial support for Wartime Housing, it also accused the federal government of failing "to recognize the housing shortage as a national crisis" and trying "to pass the buck to local governments by not fully covering taxes."[91]

THE PRIVATIZATION OF WARTIME HOUSING

From 1941 to 1948 Wartime Housing built 40,100 units of low-cost rental housing across Canada. It could have served as the basis of a national low-cost housing program. Wartime Housing Limited president Joe Piggott recommended as much in May 1945 when he wrote:

> If the Federal Government has to go on building houses for soldiers' families; if they have to enter the field of low cost housing which it is my opinion they will undoubtedly have to do, then there is a great deal to be said in favour of using the well-established and smoothly operating facilities of Wartime Housing to continue to plan and construct these projects and afterwards to manage and maintain them.[92]

The 1944 report of the federal Advisory Committee on Reconstruction (often referred to as the Curtis Committee) called for "a comprehensive low-rental housing program" that would see the government work with municipal housing authorities and limited dividend corporations to develop 92,000 units of low-cost housing in the immediate post-war period.[93] While the houses were small, there had been constant improvements in design throughout the war and the potential existed for further improvements to the houses.[94]

But as housing advocate Humphrey Carver has written, the veterans housing program had proven to be too successful. "The prospect of the federal government becoming a landlord to even more than 40,000 families horrified a Liberal government that was dedicated to private enterprise and would do almost anything to avoid getting into a policy of public housing."[95] Just as the 1935 *Dominion Housing Act* ignored the major recommendations of the Ganong Committee report, the *National Housing Act* of 1944 did not incorporate the Curtis Committee recommendations relating to housing for low-income people. The government continued to view housing not as a matter of social policy, but as an instrument of economic stimulus. At the same time, the Central Mortgage and Housing Corporation was established with a mandate to oversee the development of a national housing market by increasing the assistance available to homebuyers.[96]

As early as 1946 the government began the process of selling wartime houses to existing tenants. Six years later half of them had been sold.[97] The Canadian Legion opposed the sale of houses in Winnipeg, while some of the tenants favoured it since they could not otherwise afford to buy houses.[98] The residents of the Elmwood homes, which had been originally disparaged as slums in the making, appear to have been receptive to the idea, while concerns over the quality of the construction left the residents of wartime houses in Weston reluctant to buy. Some were suspicious of the terms, which they thought were too good to be true, while others said that they could not afford the proposed prices.[99] Politicians took, what appears in retrospect, to be surprising positions on the privatization of this housing. Both CCF councillor E.A. Brotman and Communist councillor Joseph Forkin supported the sale of the housing.[100] Under the leadership of Duff Roblin and James Cowan, one a future premier, the other a future city councillor and member of the legislative assembly, Manitoba's Young Conservatives opposed the sale of wartime houses.[101]

The initial contract with the City placed limits on the federal government's ability to sell wartime housing without municipal consent. In 1949 and 1950, the City withheld this consent. By then, the labour members of council were united in their opposition to the sale of wartime housing, while the Citizens were split, with Simonite serving as the prime advocate of privatization. The Canadian Legion maintained strong opposition to the sale of wartime housing. James Cowan, who was the chairman of the Legion's housing committee, proposed that the City purchase the houses to ensure that they were available for rent to low-income veterans. Veterans who wanted to buy their own homes would buy houses on the private market and leave wartime housing for their "less fortunate comrades."[102]

The government's decision to sell off its stock of wartime housing actually exacerbated the nation's post-war housing problems. The sale of wartime housing and the lifting of federal rent controls reduced the supply of rental housing in the city while increasing its cost.[103] Starting in November 1948, a rental unit (be it an apartment or a house) was taken out of rent controls once the current tenant moved out.[104] The following year the federal government allowed for rent increases of up to 22 percent, a measure that affected Winnipeg's 11,000 apartment tenants and 14,000 house tenants.[105] Rent controls were set to end in Manitoba at the end of September 1951, unless a municipality asked the Province to continue to have controls in place.[106] Lifting rent controls was delayed by a Canadian Congress of Labour (CCL) legal challenge, which argued that the housing shortage constituted a national menace that justified the retention of rent controls.[107] But in September 1953 rent controls were ended in Winnipeg—with reports of some tenants being hit with 100 percent increases in their rents.[108] The severity of the problem is best captured in the name of the resulting government housing program: "Emergency Housing."

THE ORIGIN OF EMERGENCY HOUSING: "THERE'S NO PLACE TO GO"

The return of tens of thousands of soldiers to civilian life at the end of the Second World War brought the country's housing shortage to a boiling point. The crisis was underscored by a page-wide headline in the July 11, 1945 *Winnipeg Tribune* that screamed: "Service man and family evicted." An RCAF corporal, his wife, and four daughters had been evicted by a bailiff and two policemen from the St. Boniface home they had been renting for a year and a half. As the husband explained, "We had a proper eviction notice and everything. The trouble is, we can find no place to go. They just laugh at you when you go to rental agents. As for buying a house, they all want at least $1,000 down. I can make only a small down payment." The owners of the house did not fit the stereotype of the hard-hearted landlord. For the previous two years, they had been living with in-laws in a home that housed fourteen people: they simply wished to move into their own home.[109] A *Winnipeg Tribune* report noted on April 30, the day before the winter-long freeze on evictions was to lapse: "There's no place to go, yet people must go. In desperation, citizens bought houses at fancy prices but present tenants refuse to budge."[110]

On January 18, 1946, city council members received a report warning that if the housing shortage was not addressed, the returned soldiers "might develop a resentment of constituted order."

Should this happen, "repercussions of the gravest order might be the aftermath." The spectre of another 1919 haunted the city's elite, and the ghosts were active. As the heroes returned, meat-packing workers in St. Boniface prepared to join a strike wave that would sweep the nation that year. According to the housing report prepared by Fred C. Austin, the city's chief inspector, there were only eleven vacant houses and two vacant suites in the entire city: none were fit for habitation without repair. The housing conditions that low-income people endured were, he wrote, a "festering sore." Many Winnipeggers were living in emergency housing, 161 families were housed in garages, sheds, and immigration halls.[111] Austin wrote:

> Whereas the city formerly possessed to a limited degree what might definitely be termed "slum areas," it is now becoming difficult to differentiate between actual and potential slum areas. There have been a number of efforts made to improve conditions. but these efforts met with the active disapproval of certain interests and apathy on the part of others.

The marriage statistics painted a grim picture: there had been 22,604 marriages during the war: over the same period, only 3,592 dwelling units had been created.[112] As the winter ban on evictions drew to an end in spring 1945, over 800 Winnipeg families had been served with court orders to leave their rented lodgings. When civic officials sent out 65,000 cards to Winnipeggers asking them to take in people on an emergency basis, only 163 people responded, mostly with offers of single rooms.[113] A similar campaign, launched by the city's Council of Social Agencies, found little in the way of housing for families.[114]

The eviction ban ended on May 1, 1945. The day before Mrs. J. Dorian of 562 McGee Street saw people walking up and down the street watching her home and telling her to move out. "I'm a widow. I've lived here four years. My son is in the navy. And I won't get out. I keep my door locked." Another evictee expressed sympathy for his landlord, who was "a returned man and wants to move in. But where am I to go with my five children?"[115] One woman seeking to evict a family from a house she had purchased was living in a basement on Herbert Street in Elmwood. Few of these evictions were because people were behind in their rent, indeed many of those who refused to leave continued to pay rent.[116]

Parents with children were desperate for decent housing. One frantic woman who the *Tribune* interviewed at the city's housing office lamented, "The only landlords who will accept children have cockroaches and bed bugs in their houses. I have been living in such a place and I have to get out." Another woman said, "You'd think

This mother and her children were among the many evictees who crowded municipal offices in the spring of 1945. "Evictees Say They Won't Move Out," Winnipeg Tribune, April 30, 1945.

children had smallpox. My children and I are living with my mother. My husband lives downtown."[117] Eviction day, May 1, 1945, was chaotic: two landlords found themselves facing court charges. One had thrown a tenant's belongings on the street and attempted to choke her, while another had broken a front door to force an eviction.[118]

The need for emergency housing continued: in 1946 only 1,317 of the 16,482 families on the city's housing registry had been accommodated.[119] Predictably, Scott and Simonite clashed once more. Simonite chastised Scott for advising families facing eviction notices not to move, fulminating that Scott was creating a legal liability for the City, but Scott said, "What else could I do? We cannot have these people on the street."[120]

Housing shortages continued well into the 1950s. The number of houses built in Winnipeg declined from 3,000 in 1950 to 2,100 in 1951.[121] This reflected a national trend, as the number of housing starts in 1951 nationally was down by 40 percent from the previous year. This decline could be traced back to the federal government's preference for investing in bombs over basements.[122] O.J. Firestone, an economic advisor to CMHC, attributed the failure to meet housing needs to the "creation of an industrial defence structure." The lack of investment in housing would, he said, lead to a housing shortage that was even more extreme than the country had experienced at the end of the Second World War.[123]

George Kelly, Fred Austin's successor as the city's inspector of sanitation and housing, wrote in January 1950 that there were 129 people living in housing that was unfit for occupancy. These people were housed in garages, attics, cellars, sheds, shacks, and unfinished buildings. There was little the City could do since "the people have no other place to go." The dwelling unit vacancy rate was .08 percent.[124] The city's medical health officer Morley Lougheed said the housing situation was worse than it had been at the end of the war.[125]

In the spring of 1950, the city was nearly washed away by rising floodwaters as the Red River overflowed its banks. The headline on the May 10, 1950 *Free Press* read, "Evacuation is advised" after Brigadier R.E.A. Morton, the director of flood relief, recommended that women and children be evacuated from the city.[126] Over two thousand people were displaced by flooding, many of them came from substandard housing that would never be rendered habitable.[127] In what was termed the "Notre Dame East-Water Avenue District" (a residential district east of Main Street) it was felt that 60 percent of the flooded housing could not be rehabilitated.[128] Once more, city officials said that the City could not enforce its sanitation and building bylaws "without causing hardships, because of the lack of alternative accommodation."[129]

EMERGENCY HOUSING

The housing shortage problem was national in scope and gave rise in 1946 to the federal Emergency Housing program.[130] Under this program, Central Mortgage and Housing Corporation converted military barracks to what were termed Emergency Shelters. The federal government placed a strict limit on what it would contribute to the conversion of the barracks. To make life as uncomfortable as possible, severe restrictions were placed on the amenities that would be allowed in the shelters.[131] Some municipalities had simply turned vacant buildings over to the homeless and left them to fend for themselves. Federal politicians could, however, rest comfortably, secure in the knowledge that no one living in an emergency shelter was being coddled.[132]

Councillor Scott worked with federal officials to have two former immigration halls (one on Water Street and one on Maple Street), two air training centres (one in the municipality of Tuxedo, formerly the Manitoba School for the Deaf, and one in St. James, known as Jameswood), one equipment depot (on Notre Dame and Empress), and one former naval barracks (583 Ellice Avenue) converted into Emergency Housing.[133] The fact that two of the former military bases were located in municipalities that bordered the city gave rise to the unusual situation of the City paying to house residents outside the city limits. Tuxedo mayor David Finkelstein, ever protective of his community's elite status, was reluctant to see the Tuxedo air training school used for emergency family housing and suggested the buildings be moved into Winnipeg.[134]

Having acquired the right to use the buildings for emergency housing, Scott had to struggle with Simonite to have the City spend money renovating them for family use, warning at one point, "If we don't get on with work at the airport, we may have the veterans taking over the buildings as they have done elsewhere." Simonite opposed spending money on temporary accommodation when local builders could build homes that would last for decades if only the City would give them the money they needed. Scott admonished him, "When you talk of finishing homes, the type of men we are looking after, including returned men accommodated at the airport, are [in] no position to buy homes."[135] By 1947, the City and the federal government had spent $137,497 on emergency housing; the tenants were charged a rent that was expected to cover operating costs.[136]

LIFE IN EMERGENCY HOUSING:
"HOPELESSNESS, FRUSTRATION, AND REJECTION"

Life in emergency housing was cramped, bleak, and unhealthy. The one hundred children living in the Water Street immigration hall were at risk of outbreaks of diseases and were distant from any city schools.[137] Seventeen families living on one floor of the building shared

Ann Henry and her young children lived surreptitiously in the Emergency Housing in the Dominion Immigration Hall in the 1940s. She later wrote, "It was anarchy and chaos." Archives of Manitoba, Archives of Manitoba photo collection, Architectural Survey - Winnipeg - Maple Street. 83 Maple. Canada Dept. of Immigration [196-], P1114, N21668.

a single toilet. Not surprisingly, diphtheria, chickenpox, and measles were prevalent in both halls.[138]

William Courage, the city's supervisor of Emergency Housing, was not shy in drawing attention to the "overcrowding, communal use of washrooms and toilet facilities, insufficient privacy because of flimsy walls" that characterized life in these facilities. The Tuxedo units were "unsuitable for the large families housed there," while the housing at Jameswood was sub-standard housing and expensive to operate.[139] In 1948 the fifty-eight families living at Jameswood complained that the heating was inadequate, dangerous, and dirty, the halls unclean, the roofs leaky, the sanitary facilities insanitary, and the windows drafty.[140]

By the late 1940s, Ann Henry, once more trying to eke out a living as a single mother, found herself homeless. A good friend living in the immigration shelters agreed to let Henry and her children sneak in and live with her. In her memoirs, Henry left a vivid picture of shelter life.

The building itself, intended for the reception of immigrants, had that lofty government impersonality that suggests the omnipotence of law and order, with just a hint of the threat that infractions could result in imprisonment, even hanging by one's neck until dead. It had authority— outside that is. Inside, rows of small rooms, more officelike than homelike, served as bedroom-living space for whole families, and centre rows of large storerooms-type spaces, with no windows and walls only three-quarters of the way to the ceiling, let out all the sounds. It was anarchy and chaos.[141]

After five weeks of living surreptitiously in the shelter Henry took her youngest child in hand and marched down to city hall, where, more by chance than anything else, she cornered councillor Scott. She pointed out that her husband was an ex-serviceman, and she had a right to live in a wartime house. When Scott said he did not have time to talk, Henry said, "I didn't come to talk. I came to fight." Soon a knot of councillors and city hall staff had gathered around.[142]

I told of my efforts to get a house, of the stupid rules which, I said, defeated their own purpose. And then I went on about the entire welfare system, denouncing it in all directions. I don't think my father in his finest hour, could have done much better. I was flinging words about like "idiot" and "nincompoop" and "inane" and "damnable" and I hadn't even started.

Indeed, she only stopped when Scott told her she could have a house. Moving into the small wartime house on Carter Avenue in Fort Rouge, was, she later wrote, "one of the greatest moments of my life."[143]

Getting out of the shelter also reduced her children's risk of infection. There was an outbreak of more than sixty cases of dysentery at the Number 4 Wireless Station in June 1950. Thirteen people, including a two-month-old baby, were hospitalized. Rats and mice were omnipresent, and it was recognized that the barracks did not meet provincial or municipal housing and sanitation standards. Courage noted that some families had been living at the station since 1946 and were being overwhelmed by feelings of "hopelessness, frustration, and rejection." He said that conditions were even worse at the Number 5 Emergency Station.[144] One young woman reported that she had difficulty getting a job once employers discovered that she lived at the station.[145]

FLORA PLACE:
"THE COMMUNITY'S RESPONSIBILITY"

Under Courage's leadership, the City built new Emergency Housing on City-owned land in the North End. Courage initially proposed the construction of several three-storey brick-and-concrete apartment blocks on the site of the former Exhibition Grounds that would provide low-cost housing for 750 households.[146] This would have created long-term housing and was reminiscent of the projects that had been designed by Green, Blankstein, Russell, and Ham in the previous decade. Instead, in the summer of 1947, the council agreed to build one hundred units of tiny, prefabricated housing on the site. The cost per unit was $2,500, with the Central Mortgage and Housing Corporation providing a grant of $1,000 a unit.[147] As with Wartime Housing, this development, which was known as Flora Place, was meant to be temporary.[148] The rents at Flora Place were set at $22 a month, which amounted to a three-dollar-a-month subsidy.[149] In December 1947, less than half a year after the project was approved, the first units were ready for occupancy.[150] Courage had concerns about the quality of construction at Flora Place, warning that "low construction costs inevitably result in a rapid rate of deterioration of buildings and ultimately high operation and maintenance costs."[151] But, he said, "the real significance of these homes is that they stand as a concrete example of public recognition of the community's responsibility for the maintenance of the integrity of the family."[152]

The consequences of the decision to skimp on size and quality were inescapable. The houses had been built to accommodate two adults and two children, as long as the children were of the same sex. In 1952 there were reports of two adults and eight children living in a three-bedroom unit at Flora Place; while in 1959, fifteen of the families living at Flora Place had an average of seven children.

The City wanted to evict these families because they were living in overcrowded conditions, but there was nowhere in Winnipeg they could get better housing at the same price. The families facing evictions had incomes of between $150 a month for a family of eight and $270 a month for a family of ten. None were paying more than $50 a month in rent.[153] One father said that if his family was forced to move back into what he termed the "slums," he would turn over his seven children to the Children's Aid Society. He said the only homes that he could afford were in dilapidated houses on Jarvis Street. He recognized that his family was too large for the tiny Flora Place houses but said, "I won't live among bootleggers and prostitution. That sort of place has done me enough harm."[154] In the end, the families were moved into the housing that city officials found for them.[155] In other cases, the City evicted families from Flora Place when their incomes rose.[156] Flora Place proved to be far from temporary: most of the houses were occupied until 2000 when seventy of them were demolished. The remaining units were knocked down in 2006, to make way for the construction of twenty-eight units of low-cost housing that opened in the following year.[157]

DEMONIZING THE HOMELESS: "SHIRKING THEIR RESPONSIBILITIES AS CITIZENS"

Simonite never missed an opportunity to criticize the shelters and sought to have them closed as quickly as possible.[158] In November 1952 the City imposed a 15 percent rent increase on the shelters in part to drive out families who were seen to have turned temporary housing into full-time housing.[159] The campaign to close the shelters was accompanied by the demonization of the people who lived in them. When Maude McCreery, the head of the city's housing committee, accused families that had sufficient resources to live elsewhere of "shirking their responsibilities as citizens," CCF council member H.V. McKelvey came to their defence, saying "Those people are no more a disgrace than you or I. They're not committing a crime."[160] Courage also found himself obliged to defend the shelter residents, reminding the media "These people are a carefully selected group who have done a fine job of creating a good community spirit under adverse physical conditions."[161]

Courage said that thirty-two families living at the Tuxedo site in 1953 felt as though they were being held in a concentration camp. Young people living in the shelter "have been denied the social environment of ordinary neighbourhoods" and "a strong feeling of rejection is felt by the whole group."[162] Shelter residents also spoke out on their own behalf: Margaret Cowtan, a resident of one of the shelters made it clear that it was only lack of economic opportunity that stopped her from leaving. "I don't like it there and I want to get out. But I was stupid enough to have four children. It costs me $120 a month in feed and I defy anyone here to do better than that."[163]

In January 1952, there were 1,100 people living in the city's emergency shelters. Turnover in the shelters had declined by 50 percent, meaning that the tenants were becoming permanent residents.[164] Courage told a council meeting in April 1952 that families were not able to leave the shelter because of lack of supply, high rents, and landlord objections to children. "The need now met by city shelters will continue to exist until the city, province and dominion governments proceed with a low-rental housing project."[165] As late as the spring of 1953 there were still 140 families living at the Tuxedo and Jameswood sites.[166] While twenty families had been served with eviction notices in Tuxedo, Courage noted that there was no affordable housing available for them.[167] The strict enforcement of building and health bylaws would, he predicted, result in further hardship as people would be evicted with a "lack of alternative accommodation." In 1953 the City had been able to place only 320 of 4,234 families that had applied for shelter.[168] It is not surprising that in that year, Winnipeg property owners were once more asked to vote on a proposal to build public housing.

NOTES

1. John C. Bacher, "Keeping to the Private Market: The Evolution of Canadian Housing Policy, 1900–1949," Master of Arts thesis, University of Toronto, 1985, 293–295, 303.
2. Joan Selby, "Urban Rental Housing in Canada 1900–1985: A Critical Review of Problems and the Response of Government," Master of Arts thesis, University of British Columbia, 1985, 71–74.
3. Jill Wade, "Wartime Housing Limited, 1941–1947: Canadian housing policy at

the crossroads," *Urban History Review/Revue d'histoire urbaine*, 15, 1 (1986): 44, 47.

4. John C. Bacher, "Keeping to the Private Market: The Evolution of Canadian Housing Policy, 1900-1949," Master of Arts thesis, University of Toronto, 1985, 5, 273-279.

5. John C. Bacher, "Keeping to the Private Market: The Evolution of Canadian Housing Policy, 1900-1949," Master of Arts thesis, University of Toronto, 1985, 291.

6. Jeff Keshen, *Saints, Sinners, and Soldiers: Canada's Second World War*, Vancouver: UBC Press, 2004, 85.

7. Jill Wade, "Wartime Housing Limited, 1941-1947: Canadian housing policy at the crossroads," *Urban History Review/Revue d'histoire urbaine*, 15, 1 (1986): 46.

8. John C. Bacher, "Keeping to the Private Market: The Evolution of Canadian Housing Policy, 1900-1949," Master of Arts thesis, University of Toronto, 1985, 5, 293-295, 303.

9. John C. Bacher, "Keeping to the Private Market: The Evolution of Canadian Housing Policy, 1900-1949," Master of Arts thesis, University of Toronto, 1985, 293-295, 303.

10. Jill Wade, "Wartime Housing Limited, 1941-1947: Canadian housing policy at the crossroads," *Urban History Review/Revue d'histoire urbaine*, 15, 1 (1986): 44, 47.

11. "No house building near cordite plant," *Winnipeg Tribune*, April 22, 1941; "Wartime Housing being hindered by supply shortages," *Winnipeg Tribune*, July 11, 1941.

12. Jill Wade, "Wartime Housing Limited, 1941-1947: Canadian housing policy at the crossroads," *Urban History Review/Revue d'histoire urbaine*, 15, 1 (1986): 46; Jill Wade, "Wartime Housing Limited, 1941-1947: Canadian Housing Policy at the Crossroads," University of British Columbia, Master of Arts Thesis, 1984, 113.

13. Jill Wade, "Wartime Housing Limited, 1941-1947: Canadian housing policy at the crossroads," *Urban History Review/Revue d'histoire urbaine*, 15, 1 (1986): 49.

14. John C. Bacher, "Keeping to the Private Market: The Evolution of Canadian Housing Policy, 1900-1949," Master of Arts thesis, University of Toronto, 1985, 306-307, 310-317.

15. *Wade, "Wartime Housing Limited," 128-129.

16. Jill Wade, "Wartime Housing Limited, 1941-1947: Canadian housing policy at the crossroads," *Urban History Review/Revue d'histoire urbaine*, 15, 1 (1986): 46, 49, 53; "Mayor Queen raps temporary homes," *Winnipeg Tribune*, May 29, 1942.

17. "Conscription call heard in Commons," *Winnipeg Free Press*, November 11, 1941; "Member backs housing plan," *Winnipeg Tribune*, March 25, 1942; "M.P. asks why wartime houses cost so much," *Winnipeg Tribune*, May 20, 1942.

18. "Coldwell urges postwar plans be made now," *Winnipeg Free Press*, August 5, 1942.

19. "Wartime Housing hit in Commons," *Winnipeg Free Press*, November 21, 1945.

20. Jill Wade, "Wartime Housing Limited, 1941-1947: Canadian housing policy at the crossroads," *Urban History Review/Revue d'histoire urbaine*, 15, 1 (1986): 49.

21. "1,625 vets seek city homes," *Winnipeg Tribune*, February 5, 1948.

22. For reports on the debate over expansion of Wartime Housing in Winnipeg,

see: "Winnipeg will enter agreement to construct 100 Wartime Homes," *Winnipeg Free Press*, January 30, 1945; "Council approves 100-house plan," *Winnipeg Tribune*, January 30, 1945; "Housing sites passed," *Winnipeg Tribune*, July 30, 1946; "New wartime housing sites draw strong protests," *Winnipeg Free Press*, July 19, 1946; "St. Boniface council rejects war houses," *Winnipeg Free Press*, July 10, 1945; "Contract let for Transcona wartime homes," *Winnipeg Tribune*, October 3, 1945; "City will apply for another 400," *Winnipeg Tribune*, October 10, 1945; "Basements in homes still delay building," *Winnipeg Free Press*, July 31, 1945.

23. Jill Wade, "Wartime Housing Limited, 1941–1947: Canadian housing policy at the crossroads," *Urban History Review/Revue d'histoire urbaine*, 15, 1 (1986): 43.

24. "Rent control," *Winnipeg Tribune*, August 8, 1941.

25. "Evictions reported at 'all-time high,'" *Winnipeg Daily Tribune*, May 27, 1941.

26. "Gourley reports on city survey," *Winnipeg Free Press*, December 5, 1941.

27. "May use warehouses as temporary homes," *Winnipeg Tribune*, April 28, 1942; "Mayor Queen raps temporary homes."

28. "Campaign for housing plan," *Winnipeg Tribune*, May 15, 1942.

29. Dick Sanburn, "400 facing moving day without homes," *Winnipeg Tribune*, April 23, 1941.

30. "Relief building will be home to fifth family," *Winnipeg Free Press*, May 6, 1942; "More families homeless June 1," *Winnipeg Tribune*, May 29, 1942.

31. "20 families face eviction," *Winnipeg Tribune*, June 16, 1942.

32. "Moving day brings new housing jam," *Winnipeg Tribune*, April 30, 1943.

33. "City to demolish dilapidated block," *Winnipeg Tribune*, June 12, 1943.

34. "City housing squeeze forces doubling up," *Winnipeg Tribune*, April 20, 1944; "Housing crisis action planned by Coulter," *Winnipeg Free Press*, April 28, 1944.

35. "Housing woes," *Winnipeg Tribune*, June 28, 1944.

36. "City housing situation termed 'disgrace,'" *Winnipeg Tribune*, November 18, 1944. For Pickering's appointment, see: "Free care urged for tuberculosis," *Winnipeg Free Press*, July 30, 1942. For Pickering's retirement see: Margaret May, "Retires—with worries," *Winnipeg Tribune*, July 5, 1945.

37. "But what to do about families out on the street at the end of month," *Winnipeg Tribune*, May 23, 1944.

38. "Wartime Housing to build homes here, says mayor," *Winnipeg Tribune*, August 17, 1942; "Queen says houses to be permanent," *Winnipeg Free Press*, August 27, 1942; Jill Wade, "Wartime Housing Limited, 1941–1947: Canadian housing policy at the crossroads," *Urban History Review/Revue d'histoire urbaine*, 15, 1 (1986): 51.

39. "Approve request for 600 hundred houses," *Winnipeg Free Press*, September 16, 1942.

40. "Queen regrets Ottawa delay over housing," *Winnipeg Free Press*, October 5, 1942.

41. Quote from Library and Archives Canada, RG19, Vol. 3980, File H-1-15 Cyril R. DeMara, Rentals Administrator, to R.C. Carr, Assistant Secretary, WPTB, November 2, 1942, cited in Jill Wade, "Wartime Housing Limited, 1941–1947: Canadian housing policy at the crossroads," *Urban History Review/Revue d'histoire urbaine*, 15, 1 (1986): 51.

42. Library and Archives Canada, RG19, Vol. 3980, File H-1- 15, J.L. lsley to C.D.

Howe, October 21, 1942, in Jill Wade, "Wartime Housing Limited, 1941-1947: Canadian housing policy at the crossroads," *Urban History Review/Revue d'histoire urbaine*, 15, 1 (1986): 51.

43. Jill Wade, "Wartime Housing Limited, 1941-1947: Canadian housing policy at the crossroads," *Urban History Review/Revue d'histoire urbaine*, 15, 1 (1986): 51

44. John C. Bacher, "Keeping to the Private Market: The Evolution of Canadian Housing Policy, 1900-1949," Master of Arts thesis, University of Toronto, 1985, 310-317. Piggott quote from Minutes of Wartime Housing Board of Directors, PAC RG83, Vol. 70, Book One, cited in John C. Bacher, "Keeping to the Private Market: The Evolution of Canadian Housing Policy, 1900-1949," Master of Arts thesis, University of Toronto, 1985, 315.

45. John C. Bacher, "Keeping to the Private Market: The Evolution of Canadian Housing Policy, 1900-1949," Master of Arts thesis, University of Toronto, 1985, 357, 433-444, 457, 460; "Mayor urges indemnities for war plants," *Winnipeg Tribune*, May 28, 1943; Jill Wade, "Wartime Housing Limited, 1941-1947: Canadian housing policy at the crossroads," *Urban History Review/Revue d'histoire urbaine*, 15, 1 (1986): 46-47.

46. John C. Bacher, "Keeping to the Private Market: The Evolution of Canadian Housing Policy, 1900-1949," Master of Arts thesis, University of Toronto, 1985, 442.

47. Blair Fraser, "Howe at the controls," *Maclean's*, February 1, 1948, 10, 43-44; John C. Bacher, "Keeping to the Private Market: The Evolution of Canadian Housing Policy, 1900-1949," Master of Arts thesis, University of Toronto, 1985, 442, 457, 460.

48. "Home for veterans' project seeks Council's approval," *Winnipeg Tribune*, January 26, 1945; "Wartime homes ready before winter comes," *Winnipeg Free Press*, August 24, 1945. For the estimate on the comparative cost of private sector housing, see: "Wartime housing accomplishments," *Winnipeg Free Press*, February 13, 1947.

49. "Winnipeg will enter agreement to construct 100 Wartime Homes," *Winnipeg Free Press*, January 30, 1945; "Council approves 100-house plan," *Winnipeg Tribune*, January 30, 1945.

50. But what to do about families out on the street at the end of month," *Winnipeg Tribune*, May 23, 1944.

51. "H.B. Scott dies at 73," *Winnipeg Free Press*, October 6, 1972.

52. Election ad, *Winnipeg Free Press*, November 14, 1942.

53. "Aldermanic candidates—Ward Two," *Winnipeg Free Press*, November 17, 1942; Election results, *Winnipeg Free Press*, November 30, 1942. For Scott's address, see: "Ald. Scott fined $15 for speeding," *Winnipeg Tribune*, July 5, 1944.

54. "5 seek council seats in Winnipeg," *Winnipeg Free Press*, October 7, 1950.

55. "Star performance," *Winnipeg Tribune*, June 28, 1949. For more on the conflicts between Simonite and Scott, see: "Site revelations rock city hall," *Winnipeg Free Press*, June 22, 1946; "Housing hits another snag," *Winnipeg Tribune*, July 12, 1946; "City's bid for homes refused," *Winnipeg Tribune*, June 25, 1946; "Charge of civic inefficiency rouses vigorous protest," *Winnipeg Free Press*, August 16, 1946; "City to investigate Scott charges of inefficiency," *Winnipeg Free Press*, August 27, 1946; "Civic committee drops 'Inefficiency' question," *Winnipeg Free Press*, October 25, 1946; "Alderman Scott obtains revision," *Winnipeg Tribune*, July 12, 1946; "Monday night club," *Winnipeg Free*

Press, February 26, 1947.

56. "City's bid for homes refused," *Winnipeg Tribune*, June 25, 1946; "'Alderman Scott obtains revision," *Winnipeg Tribune*, July 12, 1946.

57. "Aldermen's failure to discuss wage report disappoints gallery," *Winnipeg Free Press*, October 10, 1945. For more on the Halifax riot, see: Stephen Kimber, *Sailors, Slackers and Blind Pigs: Halifax at War*, Toronto: Anchor Canada, 2002. For the Adershot riot, see: "Canadian troops riot in Aldershot," *New York Times*, July 5, 1945.

58. Jill Wade, "'A palace for the public': Housing reform and the 1946 occupation of the Old Hotel Vancouver," *BC Studies*, 69–70 (Spring-Summer 1986): 288–310 <https://doi.org/10.14288/bcs.v0i69/70.1235>.

59. "100 Wartime Houses for Elmwood," *Winnipeg Tribune*, June 19, 1945.

60. "Housing scheme again attacked," *Winnipeg Tribune*, June 5, 1945.

61. "100 Wartime Houses for Elmwood," *Winnipeg Tribune*, June 19, 1945.

62. "100 Wartime Houses for Elmwood," *Winnipeg Tribune*, June 19, 1945.

63. "Gen. Price has high praise for Wartime Housing role," *Winnipeg Free Press*, January 17, 1947.

64. "The Legion's stand on housing," *Winnipeg Tribune*, July 12, 1947.

65. "Simonite says whole Wartime Housing scheme rotten," *Winnipeg Free Press*, June 14, 1946; B.M., "The need is great," *Winnipeg Free Press*, February 15, 1947.

66. B.M., "The need is great."

67. "Housing: 'Worse than inadequate,'" *Winnipeg Tribune*, October 23, 1945.

68. "Central volunteer bureau," *Winnipeg Free Press*, November 24, 1945.

69. "Winnipeg will enter agreement to construct 100 Wartime Homes," *Winnipeg Free Press*, January 30, 1945. C.T. Lount of the Winnipeg Homebuilders Association opposed the construction of Wartime Housing claiming that local contractors could do a better job at a lower price, "City news request for congested area," *Winnipeg Free Press*, April 10, 1945.

70. "Want Wartime Housing to quit," *Winnipeg Tribune*, July 6, 1945.

71. "Citizens protest further wartime home building," *Winnipeg Tribune*, January 28, 1947; "Monday night club."

72. "100 Wartime Houses for Elmwood," *Winnipeg Tribune*, June 19, 1945.

73. "Ald. Scott claims building code not violated by Wartime Housing," *Winnipeg Free Press*, February 1, 1947.

74. "City short 10,000 housing units, yet 400 stand empty says official," *Winnipeg Free Press*, September 29, 1947.

75. "Legion parley passes resolution requesting liquor act amendment," *Winnipeg Free Press*, June 8, 1949.

76. "City needs more than 10,000 homes," *Winnipeg Tribune*, March 28, 1946.

77. "Elmwood protests Wartime Housing," *Winnipeg Tribune*, June 20, 1945.

78. "100 Wartime Houses for Elmwood"; "Resolution asks better war homes," *Winnipeg Tribune*, June 29, 1945.

79. "Vets' families in Wartime homes," *Winnipeg Free Press*, December 24, 1945.

80. "Veterans Now Occupy 117 Homes in Elmwood," *Winnipeg Free Press*, February 28, 1946.

81. "4,000 local veterans seek wartime houses," *Winnipeg Free Press*, May 9, 1947.

82. "Legion urges 1,600 more homes here," *Winnipeg Tribune*, November 8, 1946.

83. "1,000[th] war house opens for public," *Winnipeg Free Press*, September 9, 1947.

84. "Housing group rejects debate on vets' rent," *Winnipeg Tribune*, July 7, 1949.

Winnipeg's Wartime Housing allotment expanded incrementally. See: "City to get 400 more homes," *Winnipeg Tribune*, November 1, 1945; "City to ask for 500 more wartime homes," *Winnipeg Tribune*, June 4, 1946; "'1,000ᵗʰ war house opens for public," *Winnipeg Free Press*, September 9, 1947; "City's bid for homes refused," *Winnipeg Tribune*, June 25, 1946; "Those additional wartime houses," *Winnipeg Tribune*, January 10, 1947; "City to get 1,000 new homes," *Winnipeg Free Press*, January 24, 1947.

85. "Housing sites passed," *Winnipeg Tribune*, July 30, 1946; "'New wartime housing sites draw strong protests," *Winnipeg Free Press*, July 19, 1946.

86. "Approves 518 lots for war houses," *Winnipeg Free Press*, April 15, 1947.

87. "City starts work on Howe's rental collection offer," *Winnipeg Free Press*, July 26, 1946; "Builders seek council committee to probe wartime houses set-up," *Winnipeg Free Press*, January 31, 1947.

88. "Houses for veterans," *Winnipeg Tribune*, February 7, 1947.

89. "Mr. Isley on housing subsidies," *Winnipeg Tribune*, April 4, 1947.

90. "Lots for 100 wartime houses," *Winnipeg Free Press*, May 10, 1945; "Those additional wartime houses," *Winnipeg Tribune*, January 10, 1947.

91. "Those additional wartime houses," *Winnipeg Tribune*, January 10, 1947; "Mr. Isley on housing subsidies," *Winnipeg Tribune*, April 4, 1947.

92. Minutes, Annual Meeting of WHL Shareholders, May 29, 1945, 6, Public Archives of Canada [hereafter PAC], Defence Construction Ltd. Papers, RG 83, Vol. 70, Minutes, Vol. 2, quoted in Jill Wade, "Wartime Housing Limited, 1941–1947: Canadian housing policy at the crossroads," *Urban History Review/Revue d'histoire urbaine*, 15, 1 (1986): 42.

93. Humphrey Carver, *Compassionate Landscape: Places and People in a Man's Life*, Toronto: University of Toronto Press, 1975, 107.

94. John C. Bacher, *Keeping to the Market: The Evolution of Canadian Housing Policy*, Montreal and Kingston: McGill-Queen's University Press, 1993, 182; Jill Wade, "Wartime Housing Limited, 1941–1947: Canadian housing policy at the crossroads," *Urban History Review/Revue d'histoire urbaine*, 15, 1 (1986): 40–59.

95. Humphrey Carver, *Compassionate Landscape: Places and People in a Man's Life*, Toronto: University of Toronto Press, 1975, 110.

96. John C. Bacher, *Keeping to the Market: The Evolution of Canadian Housing Policy*, Montreal and Kingston: McGill-Queen's University Press, 1993, 172; Albert Rose, *Canadian Housing Policies (1935-1980)*, Toronto: Butterworths, 1980, 27–28; George Anderson, *Housing Policy in Canada: Lecture Series*, Canada Mortgage and Housing Corporation, 1992, 14; H. Peter Oberlander and Arthur L. Fallick, *Housing a Nation: The Evolution of Canadian Housing Policy*, Canada Mortgage and Housing Corporation, 1992, 35.

97. John C. Bacher, "Keeping to the Private Market: The Evolution of Canadian Housing Policy, 1900-1949," Master of Arts thesis, University of Toronto, 1985, 520–521; Jill Wade, "Wartime Housing Limited, 1941–1947: Canadian housing policy at the crossroads," *Urban History Review/Revue d'histoire urbaine*, 15, 1 (1986): 49.

98. "City to get 1,000 new homes," *Winnipeg Free Press*, January 24, 1947; "Sale of wartime houses," *Winnipeg Tribune*, November 30, 1949.

99. "Vets undecided on buying homes," *Winnipeg Tribune*, January 25, 1947.

100. "Aldermen back Ottawa scheme," *Winnipeg Free Press*, January 25, 1947.

101. "Prog. Cons. study housing," *Winnipeg Tribune*, February 7, 1947.

102. "Veterans to request sales of basementless homes," *Winnipeg Free Press*, November 23, 1950; "Committee approves sale of 1,600 wartime homes," *Winnipeg Free Press*, December 2, 1950; "City council votes down sale of wartime houses," *Winnipeg Free Press*, December 12, 1950; "Legion branch urges draft for training," *Winnipeg Free Press*, January 24, 1951; "Legion urges city action to keep homes for rent," *Winnipeg Free Press*, February 23, 1951.

103. "High rents held forcing out poor," *Winnipeg Free Press*, February 22, 1951.

104. Michael Best, "Rents zooming all around," *Winnipeg Free Press*, August 30, 1951.

105. "Coulter names rent delegation," *Winnipeg Tribune*, January 11, 1950; "Mayor to meet premier on rent," *Winnipeg Free Press*, January 25, 1950; "Premier hears city on rents; stands pat," *Winnipeg Free Press*, February 1, 1950; Best, "Michael Best, "Rents zooming all around," *Winnipeg Free Press*, August 30, 1951.

106. "Rent control change due September 30," *Winnipeg Free Press*, August 10, 1951.

107. "Housing shortage 'national menace,'" *Winnipeg Tribune*, January 26, 1950.

108. "City rents soar as controls go," *Winnipeg Free Press*, September 1, 1953.

109. "Service man and family evicted," *Winnipeg Tribune*, July 11, 1945.

110. "Evictees say they won't move out," *Winnipeg Tribune*, April 30, 1945.

111. "City housing survey reveals shortage as desperate stage," *Winnipeg Free Press*, January 18, 1946.

112. "City housing survey reveals shortage as desperate stage," *Winnipeg Free Press*, January 18, 1946; "Local Swift workers authorize strike vote," *Winnipeg Free Press*, January 18, 1946.

113. "City news request for congested area," *Winnipeg Free Press*, April 10, 1945.

114. "Share-the-home appeal planned in Winnipeg," *Winnipeg Tribune/Winnipeg Free Press*, January 4, 1946; "The crisis in housing," *Winnipeg Free Press*, January 16, 1946.

115. "Evictees say they won't move out," *Winnipeg Tribune*, April 30, 1945.

116. "Tenants stand firm in moving day spats," *Winnipeg Free Press*, May 1, 1945.

117. "Evictees say they won't move out," *Winnipeg Tribune*, April 30, 1945.

118. "Two landlords charged with using force," *Winnipeg Tribune*, May 3, 1945.

119. "Housing shortage in Winnipeg," *Winnipeg Tribune*, February 6, 1947.

120. "Stay put, says Alderman Scott," *Winnipeg Free Press*, April 10, 1945.

121. "City construction tops last year's high level," *Winnipeg Free Press*, March 2, 1950; "Hignett sees big drop in housing; top factor: cost," *Winnipeg Free Press*, January 28, 1952.

122. "Housing drop may prompt Govt. action," *Winnipeg Free Press*, September 25, 1951.

123. "Critical lack of homes predicted," *Winnipeg Free Press*, September 18, 1951.

124. "Little home seen of moving 129 from unfit housing here," *Winnipeg Free Press*, January 28, 1950.

125. "54 live in city cellars; housing problem worse," *Winnipeg Tribune*, January 28, 1950.

126. "Evacuation is advised," *Winnipeg Free Press*, May 10, 1950.

127. "New homes opened for flood victims," *Winnipeg Tribune*, May 10, 1950; "Volunteers help keep registry costs down," *Winnipeg Free Press*, May 23, 1950; "Flood loss boosts city housing need," *Winnipeg Tribune*, June 24, 1950.

128. "Need for housing authority," *Winnipeg Tribune*, July 27, 1950.

129. "4,234 apply for housing; 320 placed," *Winnipeg Free Press*, January 14, 1950.

130. Library and Archives Canada, RG19, Volume 3961, Department of Finance Papers, J.F. Parkinson, "Notes on Discussions with Rentals' Officials in Western Canada," May 11, 1946, quoted in John C. Bacher, "Keeping to the Private Market: The Evolution of Canadian Housing Policy, 1900–1949," Master of Arts thesis, University of Toronto, 1985, 492.

131. John C. Bacher, "Keeping to the Private Market: The Evolution of Canadian Housing Policy, 1900–1949," Master of Arts thesis, University of Toronto, 1985, 493–494.

132. Library and Archives Canada, RG19, Volume 728, File 203 CMHC-1, Memo for C.D. Howe from David Mansur re: Emergency Shelter, May 23, 1947; John C. Bacher, "Keeping to the Private Market: The Evolution of Canadian Housing Policy, 1900–1949," Master of Arts thesis, University of Toronto, 1985, 494.

133. "No shelter relief, says committee," *Winnipeg Tribune*, September 6, 1945; "Ottawa hears from Ald. Scott," *Winnipeg Tribune*, October 30, 1945; "600 to get homes in Immigration Hall," *Winnipeg Tribune*, October 31, 1945; "City sees grim housing picture," *Winnipeg Tribune*, July 23, 1946; "Repair depot units available to city," *Winnipeg Tribune/Winnipeg Free Press*, March 6, 1946; "Alderman Scott obtains revision," *Winnipeg Tribune*, July 12, 1946; "Families to move into Flora Place," *Winnipeg Tribune*, December 6, 1947; "City gets $135,000 aid for emergency shelters," *Winnipeg Tribune*, March 7, 1947; "Emergency shelter costs city $48,547," *Winnipeg Tribune*, July 3, 1947; "Fires brightly burning in Flora Place homes," *Winnipeg Free Press*, December 15, 1947. For information on Jameswood, see: Manitoba Historical Society, "Historic Sites of Manitoba: No. 8 Repair Depot/Jameswood Place (Winnipeg), <mhs.mb.ca/docs/sites/repairdepot8.shtml>, accessed December 9, 2020. This site was also known as the No. 5 Release Centre.

134. "Use of the no. 3 wireless huts up to city and Tuxedo firm," *Winnipeg Free Press*, July 26, 1946.

135. "City may break even on emergency housing costs," *Winnipeg Tribune*, September 24, 1946.

136. "Emergency shelter costs city $48,547," *Winnipeg Tribune*, July 3, 1947; ""Fires brightly burning in Flora Place homes," *Winnipeg Free Press*, December 15, 1947.

137. "Aim to safeguard shelter dwellers," *Winnipeg Tribune*, November 7, 1945.

138. "City housing 'bad as ever': Courage," *Winnipeg Tribune*, April 8, 1947; "Housing project vote by ratepayers urged," *Winnipeg Free Press*, July 3, 1947.

139. "Courage report urges cheap, public housing," *Winnipeg Free Press*, December 22, 1948.

140. "Emergency shelter residents condemn living conditions," *Winnipeg Free Press*, February 27, 1948.

141. Ann Henry, *Laugh, Baby, Laugh*, Toronto: McClelland and Stewart, 1970, 154.

142. Ann Henry, *Laugh, Baby, Laugh*, Toronto: McClelland and Stewart, 1970, 164–165.

143. Ann Henry, *Laugh, Baby, Laugh*, Toronto: McClelland and Stewart, 1970, 165–166.

144. "45 stricken in shelter; city launches clean-up," *Winnipeg Tribune*, June 29, 1950; "Disease outbreak may spur province-city housing plan," *Winnipeg Tribune*, July 8, 1950; "Outbreak ends at city housing says Lougheed," *Winnipeg Tribune*, July 24, 1950.

145. "Housing publicity spoils job luck says irate girl," *Winnipeg Free Press*, September 28, 1950.

146. "Courage report urges cheap, public housing," *Winnipeg Free Press*, December 22, 1948.

147. "City council votes to build 100 new emergency houses," *Winnipeg Free Press*, August 26, 1947.

148. "Central Mortgage agrees to emergency shelter grant," *Winnipeg Free Press*, August 1, 1947; "Flora Place project going ahead rapidly," *Winnipeg Free Press*, September 29, 1947.

149. "Flora Place rents set at $22 a month," *Winnipeg Free Press*, November 4, 1947.

150. "Fires brightly burning in Flora Place homes," *Winnipeg Free Press*, December 15, 1947.

151. "Courage report urges cheap, public housing," *Winnipeg Free Press*, December 22, 1948.

152. "Courage urges slum clearing plan," *Winnipeg Free Press*, December 17, 1947.

153. "Flora Place probe on housing ordered," *Winnipeg Tribune*, August 26, 1952; "14 families must find new homes," *Winnipeg Free Press*, January 22, 1959; "Tenant fights eviction; 'What about others?'" *Winnipeg Free Press*, February 3, 1959; "Eviction hangs over their heads," *Winnipeg Free Press*, August 18, 1959.

154. Pat Benham, "Says he'd give up family rather than live in slum," *Winnipeg Free Press*, July 4, 1959.

155. "Flora Place: Just 2 to go," *Winnipeg Free Press*, October 31, 1959.

156. "City orders family from Flora shelter," *Winnipeg Free Press*, August 20, 1953.

157. Kari Schulz in collaboration with David Dessen, *Flora Place, Winnipeg: Integrating the Public and Community Sectors in a Place-based Approach to Affordable Housing, Case in Point 2007*, University of Manitoba, Department of City Planning, 2007.

158. "Close shelter by mid-year, aldermen ask," *Winnipeg Free Press*, February 14, 1952.

159. "Aldermen OK higher rents for shelters," *Winnipeg Free Press*, November 13, 1952.

160. "'Quit shelter' five families may be told," *Winnipeg Free Press*, November 18, 1952.

161. "City inspectors deny risk of fire at shelter, *Winnipeg Free Press*, January 12, 1952.

162. "Vandalism worries Tuxedo," *Winnipeg Free Press*, January 8, 1953; "Housing lack acute, city warned," *Winnipeg Free Press*, January 28, 1953.

163. "City won't oust tenants at emergency shelter," *Winnipeg Free Press*, May 27, 1952.

164. "City gets grim report—housing far behind need," *Winnipeg Free Press*, January 11, 1952.

165. "Airport housing shelter families face eviction," *Winnipeg Free Press*, April 24, 1952.

166. "Flora Place housing plan given city," *Winnipeg Free Press*, May 22, 1953; "Quit-shelter notices sent by city," *Winnipeg Free Press*, November 4, 1953.

167. "20 families get notices," *Winnipeg Free Press*, May 14, 1953.

168. "4,234 apply for housing; 320 placed," *Winnipeg Free Press*, January 14, 1950.

Chapter 6

THE ROAD TO THE 1953
REFERENDUM: 1946–1953

As it wound down Wartime Housing Limited, the federal government could not fully escape its responsibilities for low-cost housing. In 1947, senior federal cabinet Louis St. Laurent had, famously, told the nation, "No government of which I am a part will ever pass legislation for subsidized housing."[1] What St. Laurent meant was the federal government would not subsidize the rents of people living in public housing. The government was, however, already in the business of subsidizing middle-class homebuyers. Amendments made to the *National Housing Act* in 1944 provided homebuyers with 25 percent of a mortgage at a lower-than-the-market rate, a provision that amounted to a direct loan to privileged families at a reduced rate.[2]

Despite St. Laurent's reservations, C.D. Howe committed the government to working with the provinces and the municipalities to address "the long-term housing problem, which includes slum clearance."[3] In keeping with this approach, the *National Housing Act* was amended in 1949 to allow for federal funding of low-cost housing, but only on the condition that provincial governments contribute 25 percent of the cost. To veteran housing analyst Humphrey Carver, this was a "shabby trick." Provincial governments were dominated by rural electorates, had shown almost no interest in housing for low-income people in the past, and "were most unlikely to show any leadership in solving the very real problems of low-income people in the centre of the big cities."[4] The 1949 amendment avoided embarrassing St. Laurent, who by then was prime minister, by making no mention of subsidies. Instead, it committed the federal government to funding three-quarters of any operating losses. St. Laurent could also take comfort from the

fact that the phrase "public housing" did not appear in the amended Act.[5]

The 1949 amendments to the *National Housing Act* opened the
door to the creation of low-cost housing in Canada by committing
the federal government to provide 75 percent of capital funding for
low-cost housing projects if the provincial government arranged
the remaining 25 percent. The federal government was also prepared to cost-share operating losses on a similar basis, a provision
that would allow for subsidizing rents. While provinces could, if
they chose, provide the full 25 percent, it was expected that most
would require the municipality in which a project was to be located to fund some of the provincial portion. Skeptics believed that
the difficulties in negotiating multiple agreements between three
levels of government, coupled with provincial government disinterest in public housing, would prove to be a nearly insurmountable barrier to the development of low-cost housing. They were
correct: across Canada, only eleven thousand units of public housing were created over the next fourteen years.[6] In Manitoba, not
a single unit of housing was funded under these provisions from
1949 to 1963, when the Act underwent amendment.

Led throughout the 1950s by Douglas Campbell, a farmer who
had first been elected in the Manitoba legislature in 1921 as part of
a rural revolt against the reformist government of Liberal Premier
Tobias Norris, the Manitoba government never embraced the
National Housing Act amendments. By the time Campbell became
premier in 1948, he was nominally a Liberal, the head of a coalition
government that, like the Citizens group on Winnipeg city council, argued that it was non-partisan but invariably implemented
conservative policies. It was also a government that could afford
to ignore the concerns of urban voters, who continued to be under-represented in the legislature. In 1952 Manitoba had 228,280
urban voters and 224,083 rural voters. But urban areas had only
seventeen seats in the legislature compared to forty rural seats. In
1953 the Campbell government was able to win a majority while
capturing only three seats in Winnipeg. Even after the system
was reformed in 1957, there were still thirty-six rural seats in the
fifty-seven-seat legislature.[7] Throughout the 1950s the Campbell
government ran substantial surpluses, which it was unwilling

to spend on services, an example of what political commentator Paul Barber described as "a tight-fisted approach extending to all government programs." Earl Levin, who served in various city planning capacities in Winnipeg in the 1960s, described the Campbell administration as a "do-nothing government, paralyzed by its obsession with government economy and holding down taxes."[8] When it came to housing, the government approach was not so much tight-fisted as non-existent. It declined to commit itself to fund public housing and insisted that any municipality that wished to construct public housing hold a referendum on the project in which voting would be restricted to property owners.

Not all provinces took this approach. Regent Park North in Toronto, Canada's first large-scale public housing project, was approved in a 1947 municipal plebiscite and had the support of both a community-led housing coalition and mayor Robert M. Saunders. Federal and provincial support for the project was provided following the 1949 amendment of the *National Housing Act*.[9] While most provinces insisted that municipalities pay half of the provincial costs, Ontario required that municipalities only contribute a quarter of the costs.[10] In 1951, Saskatchewan's CCF government became the first prairie government to seek federal funding for a low-cost housing project under the Act.[11] Nor did the Saskatchewan government wait to receive municipal proposals. In 1952 it developed a plan for a one-thousand-unit project in Regina and was prepared to fund two-thirds of the provincial costs.[12]

In February 1949, CCF MLA Lloyd Stinson, who a *Free Press* columnist described as "one of the legislature's most attractive performers," called on Manitoba's government to develop "public housing projects in conjunction with the Dominion Government and the municipalities."[13] When the Campbell government failed to make any mention of housing in its 1950 speech from the throne, the CCF returned to the issue.[14] In calling on the Province to support a proposed thousand-unit public-housing project in Winnipeg, Stinson recommended that government members be given a tour of the city's slums so that they could experience the depth of the city's housing needs. This proposal, which was never realized, won the support of Mayor Garnet Coulter.[15] Winnipeg city council organized a lobbying delegation in support of provincial funding of public housing that included civic officials from Brandon, St. Boniface, East and West Kildonan, Selkirk, Transcona, and Brooklands, along with representatives of the National Council of Women, the Canadian Legion, the Council of Social Agencies, the Community Planning Association, the One Big Union, the Federation of Civic Employees, and the Winnipeg and District Labour Council.[16]

In the early 1950s, the provincial government called on the City to close the emergency housing at the site of the Number 3 Wireless School, arguing that the conditions at the site were creating problems for the students studying at the nearby teacher training school.[17] Council member H.B. Scott called the Province's bluff, saying that the City would close the shelters if the Province "agrees to a housing scheme under section 35 of the *National Housing Act*."[18]

The Campbell government, however, was far more interested in closing low-cost housing than building new housing. All it was prepared to do was pass a *Manitoba Housing Act*, which gave the Province the right to enter into a housing agreement with the federal government but did not commit the Province to spend money on either the construction or operation of public housing.[19] Campbell told the legislature that the legislation was "not to be construed as committing the government to financial participation. On the other hand, it does not indicate that we will not participate." Commentators of the day noted that this sort of equivocation was reminiscent of Mackenzie King's famous commitment to "conscription, if necessary, but not necessarily conscription."[20] The *Manitoba Housing Act* also prohibited municipalities from borrowing to fund a housing project under the NHA unless the borrowing had been approved by 60 percent in a ratepayers' (in other words, a property owners') vote.[21]

Speaking on behalf of the Winnipeg Suburban Municipal Association, St. Boniface mayor George MacLean said rather than enabling its construction, the *Manitoba Housing Act* was "killing low-rent housing." MacLean said, "In Greater Winnipeg there is no such thing as low rental housing. Our standard of living is slipping [and] as a result people are living in shacks." East Kildonan councillor O.A. Earle described the provincial position as laughable.[22]

Appearing before the legislature as a private citizen, Communist council member Jacob Penner predicted that the legislation would not result in the construction of any low rental housing. Penner pointed to the 1935 ratepayers vote, saying that the requirement for a ratepayers vote would constitute a permanent barrier to any such development.[23] *Tribune* columnist Fred Johnson noted, "It is not unnatural that the majority of rural members evinced little interest in the housing bill for the problem of providing low rental housing [that] is chiefly confined to Greater Winnipeg and the other large centres in the province."[24]

GROWING SUPPORT FOR PUBLIC HOUSING: "NOW IS THE TIME FOR ACTION"

Jacob Penner emerged as the leading voice for the establishment of a municipal low-cost housing program. In 1946, for example, he won council support for a resolution asking the federal government to build ten thousand rent-subsidized homes in Winnipeg. The measure was opposed, in a rare moment of agreement, by both Hank Scott and C.E. Simonite, who dismissed the idea because it "was conceived by one political group." CCF council member Jack Blumberg, who supported the motion, pointed out that the proposal should also involve the provincial government, adding "We've never had a peep out of Premier Garson yet in connection with this housing."[25] Given that the federal government had told the City it would not support low-cost housing unless the Province also provided funding, the Province's silence was more than deafening: it was immobilizing.[26] Despite council's initial vote of support, the proposal went nowhere. Later that year, council rejected a proposal from Penner that the City request that the Province approve borrowing $10 million to finance the construction of ten thousand low-cost housing units. Penner said, "Private enterprise can't and won't do the job of low-cost housing." He also recognized that the ratepayers would never approve a money bylaw to finance the construction of low-cost housing. "Having homes of their own, they are not concerned with others' housing problems." He was supported by fellow Communist Joseph Forkin and CCFers E.A. Brotman, Jack Blumberg, and Victor Anderson.[27]

Constant criticism from the property-development industry led Winnipeg mayor Garnet Coulter to appoint a fact-finding board to investigate the economic and social impact of Wartime Housing in 1947.[28] The board's final report proved to be a disappointment to the development industry. It not only defended the honour of wartime housing, categorizing allegations that they were slum housing as a slur on the people who inhabited them, but it also legitimized the prospect of municipal development of public housing. Perhaps its most prominent conclusion was: "The housing of a large number of citizens who have not or may never have the ability or opportunity to earn sufficient to pay a competitive rent is a civic responsibility."[29] It proposed the creation of a Winnipeg Housing Administration to build and manage a "permanent low rental scheme" to house low-income families at a rate of no more than 20 percent of the family income. It was estimated (optimistically, according to a *Free Press* editorialist) that a four-room house could be built for $4,600 and a six-room house for $5,400. The mortgage payments on such houses would be between $29.42 and $33.89 a month, well beyond a quarter of the income of someone making $90 a month. The report said that this gap would have to be filled by government subsidy, which it said should come from the federal government as it did in Great Britain and the United States. As a first step towards

For nearly thirty years, Communist Party member of Winnipeg city council Jacob Penner was a tireless advocate for public housing on Winnipeg City Council. Archives of Manitoba, Archives of Manitoba Photo Collection, Penner-Norman Collection #3, c1933, P1200, N8915.

developing such housing, it recommended that council "submit a money-bylaw to the ratepayers this year for the purpose of constructing 500 houses as soon as possible for rental to low income families." (Of course, a money bylaw would have to be submitted to a referendum in which only property owners could vote.) It recommended that an additional 500 houses be built in the following year.[30] Council did not act on the proposal on the grounds that a project of that magnitude needed federal support, which at that time was not available.[31]

In 1949, council rejected—by one vote—Penner's proposed $7-million 1,000-unit low-cost housing program. The communist city councillor had the rare support of the Canadian Legion, which pointed out that there were still over 1,000 people in emergency shelters.[32] At that time the City was receiving 300 applications a month for emergency shelter and was finding placements for about 30 a month.[33]

In January 1950, the council's housing committee approved an $8 million plan to build 1,000 houses. As the vice-chair of the housing committee, Penner proposed that the City provide half of the 25 percent of the funding required from the Province under the NHA.[34] The committee proposed that the City contribute the land, the streets, the sidewalks, the boulevards, and lanes. The City would also assume half of the Province's portion of rent subsidy by reducing taxes on the properties. Tenants should be charged no more than 20 percent of their income.[35] The council rejected the housing committee proposal, calling, instead, on the Province to establish a Winnipeg Housing Authority.[36] At a time when 6,000 families were looking for low-cost homes, an infuriated Penner said, "We've been studying this city's housing situation for the last five years. I'm sick and tired of reading reports on housing. The situation is so urgent it can't be delayed for another year."[37]

While some calls for further study were made in good faith, others appear to have been part of a campaign to use procedural measures to block the development of public housing. In a 1951 election campaign advertisement, Citizens council member Charles Simonite spoke of how he had "consistently opposed the free spending faction of the city council and the hair-brained [sic] scheme sponsored by certain political parties, mainly disguised as commendable and worthy projects, that are in reality formulated solely to upset the sound economy of our city, and, if possible, to destroy our way of life."[38] The headline on one story about Simonite's procedural battle with public housing proposals observed, "Aldermen slow down housing plan."[39]

In November 1950, a frustrated Penner moved that the City put forward a housing plan to the Province. Instead, council called on the Province to create an investigating committee to report on housing needs and how such needs could be met. Penner responded: "Reports, reports. We are absolutely drowning in reports. Now is the time for action." His proposal received the support of the CCF members of council.[40] By the end of February of the following year, the City had yet to receive a response to its request to the Province.[41]

Labour members of city council were not the only ones calling for public housing. In a 1947 interview with a *Free Press* reporter, a clearly frustrated Fred Austin, then the city's chief housing inspector, pulled an earlier report from his desk, titled *The Crying Needs of Housing Today*. He pointed to the report's recommendation "That dwelling units be constructed out of adequate grants from the federal government, and that they pass to municipal control and be made available only to those families who need more space than they can pay for at a rental of about one fifth their salary or wages." The need for such an initiative was, he said, greater than ever.[42]

In his role as the head of Emergency Housing, William Courage was a passionate advocate of public housing. A profile in the *Tribune* likened him to a physician who over the preceding five years had "dealt with 33,000 cases caused by Canada's chief social disease, housing shortage." Born in Scotland, Courage had come to Canada in 1928, where he eventually found work in the City of Winnipeg's welfare department. He did not go to university until 1944, when he took a degree in social work. In his role as the head of emergency housing, he had met with every one of the households that were seeking housing. According to journalist Percy Rowe, Courage maintained that "one of the most important features of his work is to interpret the picture of the housing problem to council and show how limited has been the remedy."[43]

In his 1948 annual report, William Courage said that a public housing program was required to bring housing costs within the means of low-income earners. The private sector, he concluded, could not build enough housing units at an affordable price. He identified the large social cost associated with poor and inadequate housing, noting that the bulk of the workload of family, childcare, and protection agencies came from areas with the worst housing conditions. Courage said Wartime Housing and Flora Place had demonstrated how effectively public intervention could meet low-income housing needs.[44] The housing shortage presented a real threat to the community from increases in infant mortality, juvenile and adult delinquency, and communicable diseases. While the number of people applying for emergency housing had decreased from 17,320 in 1946 to 7,925 in 1947, the percentage of families with two or more children who were applying for emergency housing had doubled. Courage said, "This constitutes the challenge of the future.[45] Following the amendment of the *National Housing Act* in 1949 to allow for federal support for the construction of low-cost public housing, Courage wrote, "It is now necessary to demonstrate to the provincial government the degree of need for low-rent housing in the city which would justify the province in immediately enacting housing legislation so that the terms and conditions of the *National Housing Act* would become operative."[46] It was a call he was to repeat in 1950 and 1951.[47]

Social activists and social organizations continued to call for public housing. Feminist and labour activist Beatrice Brigden told a housing rally sponsored by the Manitoba Division of the Community Planning Association in 1950, "older people in Winnipeg were being forced to live in basements and attics because no other accommodation was available." She also called for the construction of bachelor apartments for "business girls."[48] Monica McQueen, the executive director of the Welfare Council of Greater Winnipeg, said, "Winnipeg and Manitoba are letting their low-income families down" by failing to take advantage of NHA funding to build housing for low-income people. She pointed out that there was always "organized opposition" to low-cost housing. Leadership on council was required to overcome such opposition.[49] Mrs. W.J. Shepherd, the national councillor of the Community

Planning Association of Canada and the executive secretary of the Association's Manitoba division, was another supporter of public housing.[50] The Manitoba division of the Community Planning Association of Canada endorsed the public-housing proposal in January 1952.[51] The Winnipeg Number 1 Branch of the Legion called on the provincial government to support the NHA and help provide low-rental housing.[52]

A PLAN EMERGES: "I CAN'T TAKE IT ANYMORE"

It was not until February 1951 that council approved a CCF resolution to create a civic housing authority to build public housing.[53] Ten months later, in December 1951, the Metropolitan Planning Commission, a planning body with representatives from Winnipeg and its surrounding suburbs, proposed the development of a $7-million, 848-unit low-rent housing project that would be located in either East Elmwood (an area bounded by Talbot Avenue on the north, Nairn Avenue on the south, Bird's Hill Road [now Lagimodiere Boulevard] on the east, and Keenleyside Street on the west) or Northwest Winnipeg (Inkster Boulevard on the north, Atlantic Avenue on the south, Airlies Street on the east, and McPhillips on the west), or split between the two locations.[54] In the end, the City agreed upon a proposal that split the project between the two locations. Council member Slaw Rebchuk said he thought the housing would reduce the attractiveness of the North End, to which north-end CCF councillor David Orlikow opined that if the housing was "good enough for Elmwood, it's good enough for other parts of the city."[55]

The plan was opposed by the Winnipeg Chamber of Commerce, which worried that public housing would "create a permanent renting class, whereas the long term interest of the city are bound up in developing a home owning group of citizens."[56] This position ignored the fact that the continued failure of the housing market to provide affordable housing had meant that the city had had a "permanent renting class" from the year of its incorporation. The plan was not submitted to the province until June 1952, which in turn decided to defer action until it had conducted a review of low-rent housing projects in other provinces.[57] Canadian Legion official J.H. Stafford poured scorn on the province, noting that the delay would likely push the start of construction into 1954.[58] That was overly optimistic.

Throughout this period of delay, housing conditions worsened. In a report issued at the beginning of 1953, Courage warned that the city "was faced with the chronic hard core of Winnipeg's basic housing problems." He noted that many of the city's emergency shelters had "all the elements of

Poor quality housing continued into the 1950s. In a report issued at the beginning of 1953, William Courage warned that the city "was faced with the chronic hard core of Winnipeg's basic housing problems." University of Manitoba Archives & Special Collections. Winnipeg Tribune fonds, PC 18 (A1981-12), items # UM_pc018_A81-012_045_3585_034_0001 and # UM_pc018_A81-012_045_3585_036_001.

substandard slum dwellings." 80 percent of the 1,427 applications for emergency housing came from households with two or more children, 50 percent from households with more than four children. Once more, he said that the only solution lay in the development of low-cost housing.[59] In January 1953, the city's housing committee members visited a home in Flora Place. There, according to the *Winnipeg Free Press*, they met with "a nerve-wracked mother of eight children, including twins and triplets, all crowded into a damp, two-bedroom house—her husband bedridden with arthritis and one of the children stricken with asthma." The city health department recognized the conditions were inappropriate, but there was no place for the family to move. As the councillors fidgeted, the woman asked, "I can't take it anymore. What am I to do?" The visit was held just before councillors were to meet with provincial officials to seek a response to its 1952 proposal for provincial sponsorship of the public-housing project in Winnipeg. According to the *Free Press*, the councillors recognized that the project would have to go to the ratepayers, and they were doubtful that it would be approved, but "they agreed they had to make the attempt."[60]

Jacob Penner tried to get city council to call on the provincial government to exempt the housing proposal from a ratepayers' vote, while David Orlikow proposed a motion that would allow tenants as well as property owners to vote on the proposal. In presenting the motion, Orlikow said the restrictions were particularly discriminatory towards women and young people who were still living with their parents. The Citizens, however, held the majority on council and rejected both requests. To them, the need to defend property rights from the mob was as urgent in 1952 as it has been in 1873.[61] The requirement for a ratepayers' vote meant that a minority of Winnipeg voters would determine the future of public housing. Just over 27,000 people cast ballots in the eventual ratepayers' vote, which was held in conjunction with the 1953 municipal election. In the same election, nearly 56,000 people voted in the mayoral contest, which was open to all eligible voters. In other words, nearly 29,000 Winnipeggers who were eligible voters could not have a say on the public housing proposal. And the people who could vote on the proposal were almost exclusively property owners.[62]

THE REFERENDUM

Council member Frank Wagner, as the newly appointed chair of the city's housing committee, was the chief proponent of the housing proposal that was put before voters in the fall of 1953.[63] The owner of a small taxi company, Wagner was first elected to represent the North End in 1950. Running as an independent, he had campaigned on a platform of City-owned hydro, an increase in education grants from the province, and lower taxes.[64] He argued that the City would make $141,000 a year on the public housing project since the municipal operating subsidy would be $74 a year, but the property tax would be $240 a year.[65] Council approved the housing plan in principle on August 4, 1953, after hearing Wagner describe city housing conditions as being "worse than ever."[66] The plan put before the ratepayers would build 848 units on two sites. The $8.7-million capital costs were to be split three ways, with the federal government paying 75 percent, and the provincial and municipal governments each paying 12.5 percent. The federal government would contribute 75 percent of the rent subsidy while the City would pay the remainder. As had been long predicted, the Province was not prepared to subsidize rents for low-income people.[67]

Winnipeg's longstanding political divide was reflected throughout the referendum campaign. The Winnipeg and District Trades and Labor Council distributed twenty thousand copies of a leaflet written by CCF member of the legislature Donovan Swailes.[68] The national Community Planning Association also backed the plan, saying it would likely lead to a reduction in civic spending on social welfare.[69] In the continuance of a rather unusual alliance with the left, the Canadian Legion supported the housing bylaw.[70]

The Winnipeg Chamber of Commerce doggedly opposed the housing bylaw. According to the *Free Press*, it was "against providing housing for one small group of about 850 families at the expense of the other ratepayers."[71] The Winnipeg Real Estate Board chose to focus on the fact that the housing, while intended for low-income people, included support for people who might be described as the "working poor." "This is not housing for indigents, social welfare cases, or other needy persons. This housing is planned for those where family income is under $3,500. Why should you as homeowners be the only group to be charged for such housing."[72] This argument conveniently ignored the fact tenants paid property tax indirectly, since landlords included the cost of the tax in the rents they charged.

The civic government officially backed the bylaw, taking out advertisements reminding Winnipeggers that ten thousand families were "sharing accommodation in Winnipeg because they are unable to pay rent for a suitable place of their own. This leads to heavy welfare costs when families break down under the pressure of adverse living conditions."[73] Winnipeg mayor Garnet Coulter had gone on the record in favour of public housing in the past: he was, however, seventy-one years old in 1953 and there is little evidence that he actively campaigned in favour of the proposal.[74]

One cannot help but get the impression that the supporters of the plan knew that the ratepayers' vote was a lost cause. If so, they were right. Property owners were asked to cast ballots on two housing bylaws: one that would grant approval in principle for the project, the other that would authorize the funding. [75] The vote on approval in principle was 16,921 against and 10,227 in favour, while the vote on the funding was 16,873 against and 10,314 in favour.[76] The project was dead. The 1953 defeat left the supporters of public housing in disarray. Even though a growing number of Winnipeggers, including most city councillors, now recognized the need for public housing, the dead hand of laws that favoured the narrow interests of property owners had strangled their efforts for a second time. To salvage its legitimacy, the business community turned to a tried-and-failed standby, limited-dividend housing.

NOTES

1. "St. Laurent gives jolt to central mortgage," *Winnipeg Free Press*, October 28, 1947.
2. Albert Rose, *Canadian Housing Policies (1935-1980)*, Toronto: Butterworths, 1980, 19.
3. "Government in business," *Winnipeg Free Press*, February 2, 1948.
4. Humphrey Carver, *Compassionate Landscape: Places and People in a Man's Life*, Toronto: University of Toronto Press, 1975, 110.
5. George Anderson, *Housing Policy in Canada: Lecture Series*, Canada Mortgage and Housing Corporation, 1992, 21.
6. John Bacher, *Keeping to the Market: The Evolution of Canadian Housing Policy*, Montreal and Kingston: McGill-Queen's University Press, 1993, 183.
7. Christopher Adams, *Politics in Manitoba: Parties, Leaders and Voters*, Winnipeg: University of Manitoba Press, 2008, 36, 80, 111; Christopher Adams, "Realigning Elections in Manitoba," in Paul Thomas and Curtis Brown (eds.), *Manitoba Politics and Government: Issues, Institutions, Traditions*, Winnipeg: University of Manitoba, 2010, 176; James Muir, "Douglas L. Campbell, 1948-1958" in Barry Ferguson and Robert Wardhaugh (eds.), *Manitoba Premiers of the 19th and 20th Centuries*, Regina: Canadian Plains Research Centre, 2010, 228.

8. Paul Barber, "Manitoba's Liberals: Sliding into third," in Paul Thomas and Curtis Brown (eds.), *Manitoba Politics and Government: Issues, Institutions, Traditions*, Winnipeg: University of Manitoba, 2010, 136; Earl Levin, "City History and City Planning: The Local Historical Roots of the City Planning Function in Three Cities of the Canadian Prairies," PhD thesis, University of Manitoba, 1993, 257.

9. Humphrey Carver, *Compassionate Landscape: Places and People in a Man's Life*, Toronto: University of Toronto Press, 1975, 83; Albert Rose, *Canadian Housing Policies (1935–1980)*, Toronto: Butterworths, 1980; Gregory Suttor, "Canadian Social Housing: Policy Evolution and Impacts on the Housing System and Urban Space," PhD dissertation, University of Toronto, 2014, 101.

10. Gregory Suttor, "Canadian Social Housing: Policy Evolution and Impacts on the Housing System and Urban Space," PhD dissertation, University of Toronto, 2014, 101.

11. "Sask. first province on prairies seeking housing project aid," *Winnipeg Free Press*, May 25, 1951.

12. "Sask. house gives housing costs bill second reading," *Winnipeg Free Press*, April 3, 1952.

13. F.B.W., "Under the Dome," *Winnipeg Free Press*, February 25, 1949.

14. "Manitoba coalition wins second vote of confidence," *Winnipeg Free Press*, March 3, 1950; "Winnipeg slum survey suggested by Stinson," *Winnipeg Free Press*, March 1, 1950; "Housing project urged by Gray," *Winnipeg Tribune*, March 9, 1950; "Roblin charges coalition govt. shares blame in market loss," *Winnipeg Free Press*, February 24, 1950.

15. "Coulter backs Stinson's plan on city slums," *Winnipeg Free Press*, March 2, 1950.

16. "Housing head says Manitoba still may help," *Winnipeg Free Press*, March 27, 1950; "City groups to press for low-rent housing," *Winnipeg Tribune*, January 31, 1950; "Join housing plea, urban groups asked," *Winnipeg Tribune*, February 22, 1950.

17. "Province demands city action in movement of Tuxedo huts," *Winnipeg Free Press*, October 6, 1950.

18. "Housing crisis threatens two emergency shelters," *Winnipeg Free Press*, December 4, 1950.

19. "City Council seeks housing authority," *Winnipeg Tribune*, May 2, 1950; "Legislature to get low-cost housing bill," *Winnipeg Free Press*, March 14, 1950.

20. Fred Johnson, "Pussyfooting on housing," *Winnipeg Tribune*, April 12, 1950.

21. "Housing aid bill wins 2nd reading," *Winnipeg Tribune*, April 20, 1950.

22. "Province 'kills' low rent housing, MacLean charges," *Winnipeg Tribune*, March 25, 1950; "Suburbs rap province for 'killing' housing," *Winnipeg Free Press*, March 24, 1950.

23. "Opposition sees housing bill discouraging municipalities," *Winnipeg Free Press*, April 21, 1950.

24. Fred Johnson, "Needless rush creates confusion," *Winnipeg Tribune*, April 24, 1950.

25. "10,000 rent-subsidized homes plan approved by city council," *Winnipeg Tribune/Winnipeg Free Press*, February 12, 1946.

26. "Sell wartime homes, city aldermen urge," *Winnipeg Tribune*, June 24, 1949.

27. "Council rejects $10,000,000 low-cost housing scheme," *Winnipeg Free Press*, November 5, 1946.

28. "Housing probe scheme for city defeated," *Winnipeg Tribune*, February 25, 1947; "Fact-finding board on housing hears Brown report on taxes," *Winnipeg Free Press*, May 13, 1947; "Low-cost city housing asked," *Winnipeg Tribune*, July 3, 1947.

29. "Low-cost city housing asked," *Winnipeg Tribune*, July 3, 1947; "City urged to purchase war homes," *Winnipeg Tribune*, July 3, 1947.

30. "Winnipeg's housing," *Winnipeg Free Press*, July 7, 1947.

31. "Housing plans," *Winnipeg Free Press*, July 17, 1947.

32. "Council delays decision on $7,000,000 housing plan," *Winnipeg Free Press*, September 20, 1949.

33. "It's now up to the Province," *Winnipeg Tribune*, December 17, 1949.

34. "Ald. Blumberg nominated ccf candidate for mayor," *Winnipeg Free Press*, January 21, 1950; "Committee approves 1,000-house plan," *Winnipeg Free Press*, January 14, 1950.

35. "City urged to build 1,000 low-rent homes," *Winnipeg Free Press*, April 29, 1950; "$8 million housing plan goes to council," *Winnipeg Tribune*, April 29, 1950; "1,000 homes is project of Winnipeg," *Winnipeg Free Press*, March 7, 1950.

36. "City to open negotiations with province on housing," *Winnipeg Free Press*, May 2, 1950; "City Council seeks housing authority," *Winnipeg Tribune*, May 2, 1950; "Housing authority," *Winnipeg Tribune*, May 3, 1950.

37. "City Council seeks housing authority," *Winnipeg Tribune*, May 2, 1950.

38. "Alderman Charles E. Simonite," *Winnipeg Free Press*, October 22, 1951.

39. "Aldermen slow down housing plan," *Winnipeg Free Press*, July 31, 1953.

40. "Aldermen agree to study low-rent housing scheme," *Winnipeg Free Press*, November 14, 1950; "Housing crisis threatens two emergency shelters," *Winnipeg Free Press*, December 4, 1950.

41. "City delegation to ask province about housing," *Winnipeg Free Press*, February 23, 1951.

42. "City short 10,000 housing units, yet 400 stand empty says official," *Winnipeg Free Press*, September 29, 1947.

43. Percy Rowe, "It's your business," *Winnipeg Tribune*, February 11, 1950.

44. "Courage report urges cheap, public housing," *Winnipeg Free Press*, December 22, 1948.

45. "Courage report urges civic housing scheme," *Winnipeg Free Press*, January 24, 1948.

46. "Home shortage worse, says Courage," *Winnipeg Tribune*, January 14, 1950.

47. "Home shortage worse, says Courage," *Winnipeg Tribune*, January 14, 1950; "High rents held forcing out poor," *Winnipeg Free Press*, February 22, 1951.

48. "Manitoba needs law to obtain new house aid," *Winnipeg Tribune*, January 6, 1950.

49. "Council panned for housing delay," *Winnipeg Free Press*, February 26, 1951.

50. Verena Garrioch, "Presenting twelve Winnipeg women of the year," *Winnipeg Tribune*, January 2, 1950.

51. "Community planning group endorses 850-family housing plan for city," *Winnipeg Free Press*, January 26, 1952.

52. "Allan elected a legion head of No. 1 Branch," *Winnipeg Free Press*, January 18, 1953.

53. "City council approves new housing authority," *Winnipeg Tribune*, February 20, 1951; "Aldermen move to start new civic housing project," *Winnipeg Free*

Press, May 15, 1951.

54. "City studies $7 million plan for 848 low-rental houses," *Winnipeg Free Press*, December 11, 1951; "Province pledges aid for housing," *Winnipeg Free Press*, July 16, 1953; "City of Winnipeg: Notice re submission of by-law to the vote of the electors," *Winnipeg Free Press*, October 22, 1953. For the Metropolitan Town Planning Committee, see: Randolph Patton, "Community planning is civic prudence," *Winnipeg Tribune*, March 8, 1952; Levin, "City History and City Planning," 251.

55. "Council okays plan for low-rent homes," *Winnipeg Free Press*, August 5, 1953.

56. "City won't oust tenants at emergency shelter," *Winnipeg Free Press*, May 27, 1952.

57. "Province eyes other plans for housing," *Winnipeg Free Press*, September 5, 1952.

58. "Housing data right here, sniffs Legion," *Winnipeg Free Press*, September 8, 1952.

59. "Housing lack acute, city warned," *Winnipeg Free Press*, January 28, 1953.

60. Art Robson, "Weeping mother begs city's help," *Winnipeg Free Press*, January 29, 1953.

61. "Council rejects wider money bylaw vote," *Winnipeg Free Press*, December 11, 1951; "Stadium bonds OK'd," *Winnipeg Tribune*, March 4, 1952.

62. "Civic election results are listed poll by poll," *Winnipeg Free Press*, October 29, 1953; "Some liked the idea but that's all," *Winnipeg Free Press*, October 29, 1953.

63. "3 likely to head same committees," *Winnipeg Free Press*, December 29, 1952; "City council may act soon on housing," *Winnipeg Free Press*, June 23, 1953.

64. "Close battle threatens in Ward 3 as eight seek three council seats," *Winnipeg Free Press*, October 10, 1950.

65. "Housing plan outlined," *Winnipeg Free Press*, August 18, 1953.

66. "Council okays plan for low-rent homes," *Winnipeg Free Press*, August 5, 1953.

67. "Meet to scan costs of civic housing scheme," *Winnipeg Free Press*, February 5, 1953; "Vote for the housing by-laws," *Winnipeg Free Press*, October 26, 1953.

68. "Unionists plan leaflet drive in support of housing bylaw," *Winnipeg Free Press*, October 7, 1953.

69. "National planning group backs city housing plan," *Winnipeg Free Press*, October 23, 1953.

70. "Legion votes support for housing bylaws," *Winnipeg Free Press*, October 23, 1953.

71. "Chamber thumbs down housing for 'one group,'" *Winnipeg Free Press*, October 23, 1953.

72. "Attention ratepayers: We are OPPOSING the housing by-law because," *Winnipeg Free Press*, October 26, 1953.

73. "Vote for the housing by-laws," *Winnipeg Free Press*, October 26, 1953.

74. "Coulter pledges low rental plan," *Winnipeg Free Press*, October 19, 1950.

75. Civic election results are listed poll by poll," *Winnipeg Free Press*, October 29, 1953; "Some liked the idea but that's all," *Winnipeg Free Press*, October 29, 1953.

76. "Civic election results are listed poll by poll," *Winnipeg Free Press*, October 29, 1953; "Some liked the idea but that's all," *Winnipeg Free Press*, October 29, 1953.

Chapter 7

FALSE STARTS, RE-ALIGNMENTS, AND "URBAN RENEWAL": 1953–1960

T he defeat of the 1953 referendum on public housing marked the beginning of seven years of false starts and political re-alignments, ending with the city's final embrace of "urban renewal" and "slum clearance." It would not be until 1961 that Winnipeg city council gave its approval to the Burrows-Keewatin Project and Lord Selkirk Park, the first two public-housing projects to be built in Manitoba. And it was not until the end of 1963 that families began to move into the Burrows-Keewatin Project (now known as Gilbert Park). By the end of the 1950s, the failure to develop low-cost housing had become a civic embarrassment. In 1961, *Winnipeg Tribune* reporter Bob Preston noted that in the dozen years since the 1949 amendment of the *National Housing Act* that allowed for federal support of the construction of public housing, 9,000 units of such housing had been built in Canada, but not one of these units had been built in Manitoba. The only two other provinces that had failed to take advantage of the program were Quebec and Alberta. By contrast, Hamilton, a much smaller city than Winnipeg, had built 1,100 units. It was a provincial as well as a civic embarrassment: the Saskatchewan government had stimulated the construction of public housing by shouldering 80 percent of the costs that were not covered by the federal government, leaving the municipalities to take on 20 percent of the cost. Manitoba was still insisting the Province and the City contribute on a fifty-fifty basis.[1]

The failure had not escaped public notice. In 1961, Stephen Sweeney—who in 1954 had been given a crest by the City in recog-

nition of his faithful volunteer attendance at Winnipeg city council meetings—argued that the majority on council was spending
"millions of dollars on a new city hall, new police station, libraries,
bridges, more up-to-date and better housing for the animals at the
zoo, etc. etc., while slum clearance and low-rental housing projects have been ignored." Given this indifference to the plight of the
poor, it was no surprise, he wrote, that Communists were doing so
well in municipal elections.[2] That same year, G. McMullen wrote
a letter to the editor proposing that instead of running a special
Christmas-season bus that toured the streets with holiday lights,
the city transit company should run a tour of the slums. This, he
thought, would stimulate people to "want to know why so much
talk and no action."[3] *Winnipeg Tribune* reporter Nick Hills wrote
that when it came to low-cost housing, "Winnipeg has done little
in the past eight years except to set up committees, make surveys
and argue about the cost of who should pay for redevelopment."[4]

The two most significant barriers to be overcome before any
project could be developed were: the hostility of the business community and its political representatives to public housing, and the
legislative requirement that the City hold a ratepayers' vote on
largescale capital expenditures such as public housing. Over the
decades the housing issue had come to be identified as the defining issue of the left on council. As a result, the Citizens group on
council (known as the Citizens' Election Committee or CEC during this period), was reflexively opposed to public housing. To
move from this position would, it feared, confer legitimacy on Co-
operative Commonwealth Federation politicians (who the Citizens
preferred to paint as the voices of special interests). The Citizens
also feared that public housing could provide the CCF with a permanent electoral base—although the size of the proposed developments was always so small that this prospect was remote.[5] The
election of Stephen Juba as mayor in 1956 disrupted the political
stand-off. A political independent, he told the right there would
be no North End redevelopment without public housing for the
people who would be relocated; and he told the left there would be
no public housing without urban renewal projects.[6]

The business community's opposition to public housing was
also blunted by the 1956 amendment of the *National Housing Act,*

which provided federal funding for the purchase of land to be used for urban renewal projects that included a public-housing component. The amendment allowed for land to be redeveloped to its best use, thereby opening the door to creating high-rent as well as low-rent housing. It also meant that a project could demolish bad housing without creating good housing.[7]

Many local business leaders were increasingly concerned about the general deterioration of the city's downtown. If the city could get federal funding to rebuild business and industrial areas, conservative councillors were prepared to hold their noses and support a limited amount of public housing. In the case of the Lord Selkirk Park development, for example, far more attention would be paid to the urban renewal and business elements of the project than to meeting the housing needs of low-income people. The extent of this change in attitudes is best captured by the fact that under the leadership of former Winnipeg mayor George Sharpe, the Winnipeg Chamber of Commerce had come out in favour of public housing.[8]

Change was also taking place at the provincial level. In 1958, Duff Roblin led the Progressive Conservative Party to victory. Roblin succeeded by moving the Conservatives to the political centre, presenting them as the party of modernity and progress. With a focus on education and health care, the Roblin government dramatically expanded social-sector spending. While housing was not a government priority, unlike his predecessor Douglas Campbell, Roblin was prepared to work with the City to address urban problems.[9] In February 1959, just six months after being elected premier, Roblin proposed to Mayor Juba that a three-person committee be established with a mandate to survey urban redevelopment in the city. Roblin told the *Free Press*, "I saw the centre of the city rotting and I thought I should do something about it."[10] That spring, Roblin's health minister George Johnson complained that the Province was losing millions in illness, unemployment, and health and welfare costs by failing to avail itself of federal and provincial housing funds.[11] While the Roblin government was slow to fulfill these commitments, it did, in the end, make an important break from the policies of its predecessor.

This break was necessitated by the fact that throughout the late

1950s, housing conditions continued to decline and private-sector initiatives, particularly the Triangle Gardens limited dividend housing project, proved ineffective at meeting low-income housing needs.

TRIANGLE GARDENS: RENT "TOO HIGH FOR MOST OF THE FAMILIES IN THE DEVELOPMENT"

In the wake of the 1953 referendum defeat, city council asked the Greater Winnipeg Welfare Council, the forerunner of the Social Planning Council of Winnipeg, to study housing needs.[12] Under the leadership of Bernie Wolfe, the Welfare Council's housing committee provided overall direction for housing reform in the coming years.[13] Wolfe had grown up in a working-class family in Transcona and would go on to serve as Winnipeg's deputy mayor. A life-insurance executive, Wolfe ran unsuccessfully for provincial office as a Liberal, and successfully for municipal office as a Citizens' candidate. In writing of Wolfe's role in Winnipeg civic life, city planner Earl Levin observed that while Wolfe was not a socialist, "his views were somewhat more socially sensitive than the councillors' from the south and west... Perhaps his years as a YMCA Secretary and Vice-President of the Community Welfare Planning Council influenced his social attitudes."[14] Progress on the development of public housing was complicated by the fact that Wolfe and Juba were bitter opponents in the 1950s and remained so until they both retired from political office in 1977.[15]

The Welfare Council worked in collaboration with the University of Manitoba Planning Research Centre and Alex Robertson, the head of both the Winnipeg Supply Company (a construction supply firm) and the Winnipeg Chamber of Commerce, to build support for Triangle Gardens, private-sector low-cost housing to be built on land in Elmwood next to the Canadian Pacific rail line that would be donated by the City.[16] The project was developed and owned by a newly created limited dividend corporation called Housing Developments of Winnipeg, a group of investors assembled by Alex Robertson.[17]

Since 1938, the *National Housing Act* had authorized the federal government to loan money to limited dividend corporations that would engage in the creation of low-income housing. The loans were generous: initially, the companies would receive a loan for 80 percent of the construction costs at a 1.75 percent interest rate and a thirty-five-year repayment period. In exchange, the company had to agree to pay its investors a dividend of no more than 5 percent on their investment—hence the name "limited dividend."[18] Despite these generous terms, almost no housing was built under these provisions, and much of what was built was undertaken by not-for-profit service clubs.[19] To entice more private-sector firms into the field, the terms were made even more generous. By the 1950s the government was offering to loan 90 percent of the capital costs at discount rates with an extended payback period.[20] The take-up on this remained limited: in 1950 only four loans were made to limited dividend corporations, in 1951 the number increased by two. Nationally, limited dividend corporations were producing less than one hundred units of housing a year.[21] But with the defeat of the 1953 public-housing proposal, limited-dividend housing was the only game in town in Winnipeg.

Triangle Gardens was billed as a demonstration project that would show how the private sector could effectively address the city's low-income housing problems. When the project was first announced, its supporters indicated that it would target "the most needy persons known to social welfare agencies in Winnipeg."[22] 90 percent of its funding came in the form of a low-interest forty-year loan from the federal government. The rest came from the Housing Developments of Winnipeg investors. Designed by Wolfgang Gerson, a professor at the University of Manitoba School of Architecture, Triangle Gardens was, in the words of the Royal Architectural Institute of Canada, "simple and uniform." The Gardens part of the title was at best aspirational, since the budget allowed for only "a bare minimum of landscaping." Construction costs were also kept to a minimum.[23]

Triangle Gardens was ready for occupancy in early 1957. The Welfare Council selected the tenants on a point system that considered family size, current living conditions, and economic situation. Families had to have a monthly income of five times the monthly rent, which varied from $55 to $76 a month.[24] In interviews with the newspapers of the day, residents spoke highly of the project and described the rents as affordable.[25] Despite this, in 1957, Elizabeth Lord, an architect and the chair of the town planning committee of the Women's Council of Winnipeg, noted that the Triangle Gardens rents were higher than the neediest Winnipeggers could afford, even though the project provided "the minimum decent accommodation that any family should have to take."[26] In 1958, Alex Robertson acknowledged that the development "would not solve the problems of people on extremely low incomes," while *Free Press* reporter Jim Hayes wrote in 1959 that the rents were "beyond the means of those people living in Winnipeg's worst housing."[27] In July 1959, Welfare Council officials concluded that the Triangle Gardens rents were "proving too high for most of the families in the development." A Welfare Council official observed that Triangle Gardens had demonstrated that if the City depended on the private sector, "The housing will be there, but it will not help the low-income families that need quarters in the city."[28]

As a pilot project, Triangle Gardens was a failure. In 1959, the City offered ten acres of land in North Winnipeg to any developer willing to develop low-cost housing on the site. It could not find any takers. Mayor Juba acknowledged that the City might have to go into the housing business.[29] In 1960, the City turned down three private-sector development proposals. *Winnipeg Tribune* reporter Bob Preston noted that the decision amounted to a repudiation of Mayor Juba's contention that, "private enterprise might provide a solution to the city's need for low-rental housing for hard-pressed low-income families. It reaffirms its previous stand that if the city wants to get low-income families out of blighted housing, then it must enter the subsidized housing field itself."[30]

However, Triangle Gardens continued with the residents paying their rents monthly and slowly paying off the project's mortgage. In 1998, forty-one years after it opened, Housing Developments of Winnipeg sold the development for $455,000. The property changed hands at least two more times in the next five years with the price reaching $735,000 in 2003. During this period, it continued to operate as rental housing. In February 2005, Triangle Gardens residents, one of whom had been living there for forty years, were served with eviction notices.[31] The latest owners had decided to convert Triangle Gardens, 90 percent of which had been financed by low-cost government loans that were largely paid for by low-income renters and constructed on land that had been donated by the City, into privately owned condominiums. In 2020, the units were selling for between $92,000 and $112,000, well beyond the reach of "the most needy."[32]

WORSENING HOUSING SUPPLY: "THIS IS A CITY BUILT TO BURN"

The housing needs of the "most needy" remained desperate throughout the mid to late 1950s. A series of fires demonstrated that the existing low-cost housing was in fact high-risk housing. In May 1956, a landlord was charged with setting two different fires at the rooming house he operated at 2 Broadway Place.[33] In June of the same year, two policemen on their way to work noticed smoke coming out of a rooming house on Smith Street. They were able to rouse the residents and the fire was extinguished before anyone was harmed.[34] In July a rooming house on Alfred Street in the North End caught fire.[35] In August, two men had to jump to safety from the second floor of a rooming house at 196 Higgins Avenue.[36] On the same day, a fire drove residents from a fourteen-room house at 659 William Avenue.[37] Following an October rooming-house fire at 361 McDermott Avenue, which took the lives of a forty-five-year-old woman and a five-year-old girl, Winnipeg fire chief David Clawson told the *Free Press*, "This is a city built to burn." The McDermott Avenue house had, according to observers, "gone up like matchwood." Clawson made his remarks as he took reporters on a tour of local rooming houses. "Dozens of people lived in each house visited. One—a rooming house offering a bed at 45 cents a night—has accommodation for more than 40 men. Beds are lined in rows, in dark musty rooms. Hallways are narrow and winding."[38] An inquest was told that the McDermott Avenue fire was likely the result of defective wiring.[39] In December 1956 a gas leak at a rooming house on Carlton Street led to a resident being rendered unconscious.[40]

The inadequacy of Canada's pension provisions meant that elderly Winnipeggers made up a significant portion of the rooming-house population. The Age and Opportunity Bureau reported that in 1959 there were 4,200 "poorly-housed aged persons" living in the rooming house district that extended from Main Street to Sherbrook and Assiniboine to Notre Dame. The once exclusive Hudson's Bay Reserve had, as C.H. Enderton had predicted at the beginning of the century, become the preserve of "third-rate boarding houses."[41] The downtown rooming-house district was expanding into the city's West End in violation of zoning laws. One West End homeowner had been fined three times in twelve months for housing six families in a single-family dwelling. His wife had also been fined for the same offence during that period.[42] A sign of this expansion to the west was a 1958 fire at a 226 Walnut Street rooming house that left twelve people homeless.[43]

These fires underscored the fact that rooming houses were largely unregulated, even though since 1913, Winnipeg city officials had been calling for their licensing.[44] In 1956 councillor Peter Taraska proposed that rooming houses be licensed so that they could be inspected and required to comply with fire and building code requirements. CCF councillor David Orlikow pointed out that licensing would not work if it was not accompanied by the construction of public housing. If the City wanted to end the unsafe overcrowding of rooming houses it would have "to put these people somewhere."[45] Following a 1957 fire at 453 Sherbrook Street, which claimed two lives, fire chief David Dunnett recommended that the City adopt a fire prevention code of its own, saying the provincial *Fire Protection Act* was "abstruse and vague." He also recommended that all rooming houses be inspected.[46] Four months later, two people died in separate rooming house fires in the space of one week. An elderly blind woman was trapped on the third floor of a rooming house on Sargent Avenue and Balmoral Street in an early morning fire. Dunnett pointed out that because rooming houses were treated as private residences, fire inspectors had no right to inspect them. The chief argued that mandatory fire alarms could have prevented the death and recommended that third-storey exits should be mandatory in rooming houses.[47] The few rules that did exist had little impact. In April 1957 a rooming house operator was fined $50 for housing fourteen people in a rooming house at 47–49 Martha Street. It was the third time he had been fined for this sort of violation.[48] In 1959, the city's welfare director, C.A.

Patrick, said that the fines for violating housing sanitation laws often ranged between five and ten dollars: rates so low that landlords simply looked at them as part of the cost of doing business.[49]

In April 1960 two pairs of sisters died in a rooming house fire in a fifty-five-year-old building at Smith and Assiniboine. Firefighters found that the landlord had bolted shut the exit doors between suites.[50] At the time of this fire, there was still no policy on rooming house licensing or inspections.[51] The coroner's jury that investigated the girls' deaths called for the implementation of a fire code that would give the fire department authority to inspect and order improvements in public buildings.[52]

Winnipeg Tribune reporter Val Werier described how, under what he termed "remote landlord control," the property in which the girls died had been designed to house six families when it was constructed in 1905 but had housed seventy-five people at the time of the fire. "The landlord rents each of the six [three-storey] sections to caretaker-landlords for $150 a month. They in turn sublet them to tenants for $200 a month. Tenant shares bathroom and toilet facilities. They do their cooking on hot plates. Or they may have a kitchen of their own, separated by a hall from their bedroom. As many as six live in a two-room suite."[53]

The dangers were not limited to rooming houses. Older apartment buildings were also unsafe: in April 1956 an apartment fire on Wardlaw Avenue sent people fleeing into the streets for safety.[54] In February 1959, twelve families had to evacuate an apartment block on Euclid Avenue and Barber Street in Point Douglas when the building caught fire.[55] In March 1959, three firefighters were treated in hospital for injuries sustained while battling a fire at an apartment building on College Avenue in the North End.[56] And in August of that year, forty people had to flee the Alloway Court Apartments on Maryland Street when the building caught fire.[57] The risk from poor maintenance in low-rent tenements was underscored when, in August 1959, a three-year-old girl fell through the slats on the railing of a third-floor exterior landing on a concrete lane thirty feet below. Miraculously the girl survived the fall. Interviewed later, other residents in the building at 365 Mountain Avenue said the landing, fire escape, and railings were all in poor shape and should have been condemned.[58]

The housing that low-income people inhabited was not only poorly maintained and dangerous—it was also publicly subsidized. By seizing on this point, public-housing advocates were able to move popular opinion in their favour in coming years.

SUBSIDIZING SLUMS:
"FAMILIES HAVE NO HOPE FOR ESCAPE"

In a 1956 speech Bernie Wolfe, then the chair of the Winnipeg Welfare Council's housing committee, told Kiwanis Club members that before they objected to the adoption of a program of public housing, they should remember that the City was already paying the rent of people on welfare. "Low-cost housing," he said, "might be a distasteful subject but it won't go away because you close your eyes."[59] Three years later, the point was driven home by a series of stories in the *Winnipeg Tribune*. The headline ran from one side of the front page of the paper's October 14, 1959 edition to the oth-

A series of articles in the Winnipeg newspapers in 1959 drew attention to the fact that civic welfare payments were subsidizing slum landlords. "Probe Bares City Slum Profits," Winnipeg Tribune, October 14, 1959.

er: "Probe bares city slum profit." The subhead underscored the message: "Taxes subsidize big landlords." The stories were based on a report prepared by the city's health and welfare department showing that four landlords who regularly violated health regulations were collecting thousands of dollars from the city's welfare department. In 1959, 187 city welfare cases were living in these properties. Over the previous three years, the City had identified 1,457 violations in the 94 premises owned by these four landlords. These included:

- 38 violations for insufficient heat
- 66 violations for insufficient plumbing
- 86 violations for bedbugs
- 54 violations for cockroaches
- 10 violations for rats
- 57 violations for dirty walls and floors
- 117 violations for defective floors, ceilings, and walls.

Providing inadequate housing to welfare recipients was also a very profitable business: one landlord collected 33 percent of his property's assessed value in rent in a single year, while a second landlord collected 47.7 percent of the assessed value. Property taxes to the city in one case amounted to 10 percent of revenue.[60]

It was big news, but the story was far from new. In 1956 councillor Lillian Hallonquist said that as long as the City continued to pay landlords to house welfare recipients without demanding improvements to the property, people would be housed in "shacks and hovels."[61] At least once a month in the late 1950s, tenants would refuse to vacate rented premises that the City had declared unfit for habitation because they had nowhere else to go. The tenants were usually welfare recipients and the City found itself forced to continue to pay rent to the landlord.[62]

The caption on the photograph of a dark two-storey brick housing unit that illustrated one story in the series read, "In a year— $7,600 revenue, $600 taxes, 10 health violations." The address was a six-unit terrace building at 716-726 Henry Street, one block south of the sprawling, noisy, and dirty Canadian Pacific Railway marshalling yards. In 1958 the building's owner had been cited for ten violations of provincial sanitation laws; in the previous four

"Life In The Slums," Winnipeg Free Press, October 17, 1959.

years, there had been thirty-six previous violations. *Tribune* reporter Jim Hayes wrote:

> A host of men, women and children—along with a liberal sprinkling of cats and dogs—are jammed into the Henry Ave. terrace. Occupancy figures are never static as families come and go but the buildings are always badly overcrowded.
>
> They squeeze up and down the three-feet wide stairways to the common bathroom on the second floor of each unit. A third storey room in one of the units is jammed with kindling and cardboard cartons. Naked stovepipes run through a wall.

Hayes's report concluded with the observation, "Some of the city's welfare cases live in the terrace. Through no fault of their own, some of these helpless families have no hope for escape unless the city acts."[63]

Welfare rates, which had not been increased since 1954, provided no more than fifty dollars a month to rent an unheated premise, and to receive that level of assistance, there had to be six people in the household. Provincial health regulations could hardly be described as stringent: they allowed six people and any number of infants to live in as little as 430 square feet.[64]

The *Free Press* followed the *Tribune's* lead and ran its own series on slum landlords with reporter Erik Watt providing the following description of a visit to one of the properties in question.

> There were 10 children, the oldest 16, the youngest a year-old baby. Nearly all had festering bedbug bites on their hands, their feet, their faces. So had their parents.
>
> The furniture was dilapidated except for the television set. In these filthy crowded rooms, it stood out like a beacon.
>
> The stench was indescribable. You stood there trying to breathe without betraying the nausea which filled you; trying not to stare too obviously at the grimy, unpainted plywood walls, the rotting linoleum, the gloomy cubbyhole with its ancient toilet; the rusting wood stove in the

kitchen which served as a heater as well as for cooking.

You tried to imagine what it is like for five children, sleeping in a room with crumbling plaster walls, barely large enough to accommodate the double bed and single bed which they share.

A workplace injury had rendered the husband unemployable. The family had moved into their current home after their previous dwelling had been condemned. An unnamed city inspector said he was well aware of the condition of the family's current dwelling, but asked: "If I condemned that place, where would they have gone?"[65] As in 1909, and every year since, city officials were reluctant to condemn housing, since it would place people on the street with no options.[66] This did not mean that such evictions did not take place. In 1959, for example, a family of eight was evicted from their home on Magnus after the City had condemned it. The father was unable to work due to illness and the family was on relief.[67]

While there was general agreement that welfare rates were too low to allow people to rent decent housing, council was reluctant to raise them. A 1959 proposal by Communist city councillor Jacob Penner to increase the rate from $50 to $75, easily justified by the cost of housing, could not find a seconder.[68] The city's welfare director, C.A. Patrick, said that families on welfare had to cover their rent by cutting down on their food budget. As he had in the past, Patrick warned that raising the housing allowance might well be followed by an increase in rents. "We have advised the committee in the past of our view that the housing problem cannot be solved simply by adjusting the rental scale. The real problem is the shortage of suitable accommodations. If you increased the allowance by much more than we propose, some people might still be living in the place they now occupy. They just could not find anything more suitable even at a higher rent."[69]

In commenting on some council members' opposition to the idea of the City getting into the provision of subsidized housing, one unnamed city official said, "Winnipeg is in subsidized housing now—the worst housing in the city."[70] The *Tribune* editorialized that the revelation "that certain slum property-owners were profiteering at the expense of taxpayers and trafficking in the misery of helpless tenants" underscored the need for the City "to provide decent alternative low-rental housing." Councillors were urged to have the City "sponsor one or more low-rental housing projects with the aid of the senior governments."[71]

When asked for a solution, welfare director Patrick said that limited dividend companies did not constitute a meaningful option. Speaking of Triangle Gardens, he said, "The units were built as cheaply as possible. All frills were eliminated. Yet the rental was beyond the schedule we work with. Our people could not afford to live there." Instead, he said, "Subsidized housing appears to be the best solution found in other cities in North America and Europe."[72]

THE YEARS OF STUDY: "QUIETLY SHELVED, AND NEVER HEARD FROM AGAIN"

Although there had already been numerous reports on the poor quality of the housing available to low-income people, Winnipeg's social service professionals and volunteers had few options but to conduct a near-endless series of studies in hopes of forcing the City into action. A 1955 survey, for example, demonstrated what everyone knew: housing conditions in the area bounded by Main Street and Sherbrook Street and Notre Dame and the Canadian Pacific tracks were in a state of serious deterioration.[73] The following year, at city council's request, the Greater Winnipeg Welfare Council established a twenty-eight-member advisory committee on urban redevelopment. The committee worked with the University of Manitoba School of Architecture on a plan for what was referred to as the Notre Dame-CPR area. Much of the pressure for doing this development came from local architect Elizabeth Lord, who chaired the Welfare Council.[74] Following an October 1956 rooming-house fire that claimed two lives, councillor Peter Taraska called for a slum-clearance program for central Winnipeg.[75] A few weeks later, however, the committee's initial report, which called for $15 million in land clearance, was rejected as being too costly.[76]

In a September 1957 report, Triangle Gardens architect Wolfgang Gerson recommended clearing and redeveloping the entire area from Isabel Street to Sherbrook Street.[77] Earl Levin, an architect who served as the chief planner for the Metropolitan Corporation of Winnipeg in the 1960s, later wrote that the 1957 Gerson report, was the first of a series of urban renewal studies in which the consultants, inevitably architects, stepped enthusiastically but naively and without any understanding of the realities of urban poverty, into the realm of the city's urban blight, made jejune and trite inventories of the conditional criteria of blight conditions, proposed massive, sweeping clearance and redevelopment measures which were quietly shelved, and never heard from again.[78]

With the release of the Gerson report, an old idea was re-entering the debate: "slum clearance." Amendments to the *National Housing Act* in 1956 shifted the focus away from creating more, better, and affordable housing for people on low incomes, to clearing the slums and subjecting the lands that they once occupied to "urban renewal." The people who lived in the "slums" once more ran the risk of becoming collateral damage. New homes might be built for them, but they might not be in their old neighbourhoods. The amendment, for example, did not require that new housing be built on the land that was being cleared.[79] According to historian John C. Bacher, the 1956 amendments,

> which opened up a veritable Pandora's box of local greed and boosterism, had complex and contradictory impacts. While it brought social housing to such previously impenetrable fortresses of hostile real estate reaction such as Winnipeg and Calgary, it accomplished this worthy social aim at a heavy price. The local business elites... frequently combined their urban-renewal schemes with the razing of historic neighbourhoods, underpaying expropriated homeowners, and the construction of over-large public-housing projects, devoid of needed complementary recreational spaces.[80]

But in 1958, it was far from clear if any projects would be undertaken. The housing committee of the Welfare Council of Greater Winnipeg called on the City to make more land available for limited dividend projects such as Triangle Gardens, raise and enforce housing standards, and appoint the urban renewal and urban conservation boards called for in the Gerson report.[81]

At the time, Bernie Wolfe also accused notoriously thin-skinned Mayor Stephen Juba of misleading the public with claims that a slum clearance project would soon be underway in the region of the then-proposed Disraeli Freeway. He pointed out that a council committee appointed to address the Gerson Report recommendations had only held one meeting the previous year.[82] In the face of the constant prodding from the Welfare Council, the City established an eleven-member Urban Renewal Board in July 1958.[83]

Over the following three years, the board produced six studies. There were two key areas that it focused on: the area west of Main Street between Notre Dame and the CPR yards and the area north of the CPR yards between Salter and Main and south of Selkirk.[84] In 1960, the Urban Renewal Board delivered a report calling for the renewal of the Selkirk-Jarvis area north of the Canadian Pacific Railway tracks. This urban renewal project included both the Lord Selkirk Park housing project and what was initially termed the Burrows-Fife, later Burrows-Keewatin Project.[85] These projects would be the first Manitoba public-housing projects to make it from the drawing board to reality.

Council granted in-principle approval to the Lord Selkirk Park project in February 1960.[86] It was said at the time that the City had passed the point of no return regarding slum clearance. The cost of the $10 million project was to be split between the federal government and the City, with an expectation that the Province would also contribute. 1,651 people were living in the Lord Selkirk area. It was proposed that the renewal would take the form of demolition, renovation, and leaving some homes untouched, as well as adding 495 units of new housing to the area. The project depended on the Province amending the city charter to exempt the City from a ratepayers' vote on the public housing and urban renewal money bylaws.[87]

This was an historic departure. Credit must be given to those who had been pushing for the creation of public housing since the beginning of the century: the churches, the labour movement, and social-democratic politicians and their constituents. The carpenter John Tooth was one of the labour leaders of the period who supported public housing. In 1959, as the Winnipeg labour council's delegate to the Urban Renewal Board, Tooth attended twenty

Board meetings. The following year, he called on the labour council to give its full support to urban renewal. In his report, he noted that the construction of the Midtown Bridge and the Disraeli Freeway had destroyed up to 450 units of low-cost housing. "The replacement of these, if it can be so-called, has been in apartment blocks whose rental price is quite out of reach of the tenants displaced." To those who said that the cost of public housing was prohibitive, Tooth said, "I feel sure those 15 woman [sic] who called on our Mayor last week would support me when I say 'WE CANNOT AFFORD NOT TO AFFORD IT!'"[88]

Tooth knew whereof he spoke. He had been born in England in 1889 and was obliged to leave school when the farm his father worked on went bankrupt. He came to the Canadian west in 1910 and made his living as an itinerant carpenter, travelling across the west for two years, working on cottages, railway stations, and hotels. While he eventually built small houses for himself in St. James and later Charleswood, his life had been full of financial uncertainty and included stints driving horse-drawn delivery wagons, digging ditches, working as a carpenter, and teaching vocational studies, before taking a job with the carpenters' union.[89] He ran as a CCF candidate for council, saying urban renewal was "the most important undecided issue in Winnipeg." He said that the City had been attempting to deflect the failure to undertake urban renewal to other levels of government, but he felt that "responsibility for failure to act" lay with the City.[90]

By the end of the 1950s, pressure for improved housing was beginning to come from the people who lived in what was increasingly referred to as "slum" housing. In November 1960 a fifty-member committee of residents of "blighted areas" formed the Citizens' Committee for Low Cost Housing. The committee was supported by Juba, alderman A.E. Bennett, Winnifred Noble (often described as a volunteer social worker), and representatives of the Winnipeg ministerial association and business community. The Committee's president was Doris Binding, Olga McLean was vice-president, Lee Gawryluk was secretary, and D. Unrau was treasurer. Two of the participants, Noble and Gawryluk, were involved in the Anglican Church's Old Christ Church Mission. Nobel was also active in the Women's Progressive Conservative Association.[91] In 1960 group of women from what was described as "Winnipeg's slum areas" met with Juba on at least two occasions to urge him to proceed with urban renewal.⁹² Several women's organizations, including the Council of Jewish Women, the Ukrainian Women's League, and the Catholic Women's League, called for a start on what was described as the city's "much-discussed slum-clearing program."⁹³

POLITICAL DISRUPTION

The failure of Triangle Gardens made it clear that the private sector could not address the city's shortage of low-cost housing. The 1956 amendments to the *National Housing Act* made the business community more amenable to the economic potential of urban renewal (which promised more than the construction of low-cost housing). The media and senior municipal officials worked together to highlight the extent of the housing crisis and to underscore the fact that the question was not whether to subsidize, but who should be the beneficiaries of the subsidization of the housing of the city's poorest citizens. Two crucial developments were the election of Stephen Juba to the office of mayor in 1956, leading to a temporary disruption of the political status quo at city hall, and the business community's determination to capture federal urban renewal funds for Winnipeg projects.

In the 1954 municipal election, veteran Citizen councillor George Sharpe was elected mayor. The son of a previous mayor, an electrical engineer by training, the owner of a family-run auto-electric business, and the son-in-law of the University of Manitoba's Dean of Arts and Science, he was a prominent member of the city's establishment. Having garnered the support of the *Free Press*, the *Tribune*, former mayor Garnet Coulter, and premier Douglas Campbell, Sharpe was expected to have no trouble winning re-election in 1956.⁹⁴ His only challenger was brash upstart Stephen Juba. Born in the working-class suburb of Brooklands, Juba had been unable to afford to complete Grade 10 and had failed in his early business enterprises before establishing a successful plumbing-supply firm. He was also politically ambitious, weathering several defeats at the federal, provincial, and municipal levels before being elected to the legislature as an independent in 1953.

There he enhanced his public reputation through a series of well-conceived public relations stunts that endeared him to the city's working class. Positioning himself as the populist challenger to a smug elitist, Juba won a smashing upset victory in the 1956 mayoral election and would hold office for twenty-one years. Popular, and beholden to neither the Citizens nor the Socialists, Juba was a wild card in Winnipeg politics.[95] Earl Levin attributed Juba's success to his having "a shrewd, unerring political instinct, the sensibilities of a gutter-fighter, a mastery of political manipulation, and a flair for publicity." This would allow him to maintain a fragile coalition in favour of urban development. But Juba had no time for coherent planning or sharing credit; as Levin observed, Juba was "ruthless and unprincipled."[96] Juba's victory contributed to the CEC falling into a period of temporary disarray, riven with internal dissent.[97] CEC stalwart and archenemy of public housing, Charles Simonite, chose not to run in the 1956 election. The CEC had withdrawn its endorsement of one councillor, Slaw Rebchuk, only to see him run and win as an independent, while another councillor, Paul Parashin, withdrew from the CEC, citing his unhappiness with secret meetings. One CEC faction was briefly referred to as the "Chocolate milk" caucus after a councillor claimed that he and a group of councillors had just met for "chocolate milk in my basement."[98] Editorialists criticized the CEC for failing to provide leadership, complaining how "CEC aldermen and school trustees thus come to council and the school board without platforms, programs or strong convictions."[99] As a disillusioned Parashin noted, "where there is no platform" councillors were "pushed around by newspaper editorials."[100]

And while Juba had defeated the establishment candidate, there was, in the end, little that was anti-establishment about his politics. Political scientist David Walker observed that Juba:

> was very conservative in his economic, social and governmental policies. This provided a linkage between the north end (ethnic working class) and the south end (wealthier and more WASP) political bases because he was by no means a threat to the corporate and family concerns in the city. Businessmen may have thought Juba to be eccentric

or they may have resented his administrative irrationality but in the end, he was one of them, a pro-development entrepreneur.[101]

The loss of confidence on the part of the Citizens, coupled with the establishment's eventual recognition that Juba, while unpredictable, was not radical, meant that he would succeed where many others, more qualified and more committed, had failed in getting public housing built in Winnipeg.

While he certainly did not run as a supporter of public housing, over the years he portrayed himself as the driving force behind urban renewal. In the 1962 election, Juba said that slum clearance and the promotion of low-cost housing were two of his top three priorities.[102] Others took a dimmer view of his commitment to the issue. His opponent in the 1960 mayoral election, Gloria Queen-Hughes, the daughter of John Queen, with considerable accuracy castigated Juba for "chasing after trivialities like that one-shot Roman Circus, the Pan-American games, at a time when poverty-stricken families were being evicted by the city." The proposed urban renewal projects were, she said, "too slow, too small, too picayune for the emergency on our doorstep."[103]

By the mid-1950s, business leaders were experiencing their own frustrations with the requirement for a ratepayers' vote on major capital projects. Ratepayers were not only turning down public housing, but they were also rejecting bridges and fire halls. In December 1959 council approved CCF councillor Art Coulter's motion that council ask the Province to amend the city charter and the *Manitoba Housing Act* to allow the council to develop *National Housing Act* projects without having to conduct a ratepayers' vote. Among the councillors supporting the motion was engineer, magician, and freeway advocate A.E. Bennett, who was reported to have said, "firsthand tours of slum areas proved to him fast action was needed on public housing."[104] Such votes would still be required for other major capital projects, but they would only need to receive a simple majority as opposed to three-fifths of the votes cast. And the franchise on these votes would be restricted to ratepayers.[105] In defending these restrictions Citizen councillor Walter Crawford said tenants had "less right" than ratepayers to create debt. Another Citizen councillor, Edith Tennant, was blunter, saying, "People living in apartments want all the privileges of voting without the responsibility of homeowning."[106]

Burrows-Keewatin and Lord Selkirk Park were the only two public-housing projects developed in Winnipeg in the 1960s. Given the long struggle to get any public housing built in the city, the construction of these projects should be seen as close to miraculous. However, the type of thinking that allowed councillors Crawford and Tennant to denigrate tenants of all sorts dominated the key decisions around these two projects. The City was happy to get federal money, but was parsimonious with its own, keeping investment in recreation and social services to a minimum. Creative options such as co-operative housing were rejected, the experiences of other cities with bulldozer-led development were ignored, and poor people were demeaned. Public housing advocates could never be certain that a suddenly recalcitrant municipal, provincial, or federal government—whose support was always tepid, contradictory, and half-hearted—might not rescind its commitment to the two projects.

NOTES

1.   Bob Preston, "Winnipeg has long way to go," *Winnipeg Tribune*, April 25, 1961.
2.   Stephen Sweeney, "Communist influence," *Winnipeg Tribune*, January 19, 1961. See also Stephen Sweeney, "Housing for need vs. new city hall," *Winnipeg Tribune*, July 29, 1961. For crest, see: "He listened for 8 years, now city listens to him," *Winnipeg Free Press*, December 21, 1954.
3.   G. McMullen, "Slum clearance," *Winnipeg Free Press*, December 2, 1961.
4.   Nick Hills, "Slum clearance, three-way job," *Winnipeg Tribune*, April 2, 1962.
5.   Harold Kaplan, *Reform, Planning, and City Politics: Montreal, Winnipeg, Toronto*, Toronto: University of Toronto Press, 1982, 506–507, 512–517.
6.   Harold Kaplan, *Reform, Planning, and City Politics: Montreal, Winnipeg, Toronto*, Toronto: University of Toronto Press, 1982, 512–517.
7.   Earl Levin, "City History and City Planning: The Local Historical Roots of the City Planning Function in Three Cities of the Canadian Prairies," PhD thesis, University of Manitoba, 1993, 288.
8.   "Chamber makes spectacular gains," *Winnipeg Free Press*, March 28, 1961; "He's behind many plans of Chamber," *Winnipeg Free Press*, March 28, 1961.
9.   Cy Gonick, "The Manitoba economy since World War II," in James Silver and Jeremy Hull (eds.), *The Political Economy of Manitoba*, Regina: Canadian Plains Research Centre, 1990.
10. "Duff wants to get down to business" and "He sees our city decaying," *Winnipeg Free Press*, February 6, 1959.

11. "Time for action," *Winnipeg Tribune*, April 22, 1959.
12. "Pilot housing backed," *Winnipeg Tribune*, December 21, 1955.
13. "Housing group uses its spurs," *Winnipeg Free Press*, June 18, 1958.
14. Earl Levin, "City History and City Planning: The Local Historical Roots of the City Planning Function in Three Cities of the Canadian Prairies," PhD thesis, University of Manitoba, 1993, 264.
15. Allan Levine, "Stephen Juba," in Allan Levine (ed.), *Your Worship: The Lives of Eight of Canada's Most Unforgettable Mayors*, Toronto: James Lorimer and Company, 1989, 95.
16. "Rent project in Elmwood urged to replace slums," *Winnipeg Tribune*, October 20, 1955; Bob Metcalfe, "City paves way for slum clearance," *Winnipeg Tribune*, February 14, 1956; David G. Burley, "Winnipeg's landscapes of modernity, 1945–1975," in Serena Keshavjee (ed.), *Winnipeg Modern: Architecture, 1945–1975*, Winnipeg: University of Manitoba Press, 2006, 66.
17. "Rent project in Elmwood urged to replace slums," *Winnipeg Tribune*, October 20, 1955; "Pilot housing backed," *Winnipeg Tribune*, December 21, 1955"; "Group wants more land to provide rental housing," *Winnipeg Free Press*, May 20, 1958; John Bacher, *Keeping to the Market: The Evolution of Canadian Housing Policy*, Montreal and Kingston: McGill-Queen's University Press, 1993, 188.
18. Horace L. Seymour, "The National Housing Act 1938," in *Public Affairs*, 2, 3 (March 1939): 129.
19. John Bacher, *Keeping to the Market: The Evolution of Canadian Housing Policy*, Montreal and Kingston: McGill-Queen's University Press, 1993, 108.
20. "Pilot housing backed," *Winnipeg Tribune*, December 21, 1955; "Group wants more land to provide rental housing," *Winnipeg Free Press*, May 20, 1958; John Bacher, *Keeping to the Market: The Evolution of Canadian Housing Policy*, Montreal and Kingston: McGill-Queen's University Press, 1993, 188.
21. Central Mortgage and Housing Corporation, Economic Research Department, *Housing in Canada: A Factual Summary*, First Quarter, 7, 1 (1952): 55.
22. "Rent project in Elmwood urged to replace slums," *Winnipeg Tribune*, October 20, 1955.
23. "Free land offer has no takers," *Winnipeg Tribune*, September 15, 1959; "Triangle Gardens housing project, Elwood, Winnipeg, Manitoba," *Royal Architectural Institute of Canada Journal*, 35, 7 (July 1958): 275–278.
24. "Rental experiment ready for test in Elmwood." *Winnipeg Free Press*, January 31, 1957.
25. Frank Jones, "Low-rent tenants satisfied," *Winnipeg Tribune*, August 3, 1959.
26. "Council of Women asks government guidance to cope with inflation," *Winnipeg Free Press*, April 27, 1957.
27. "Urban renewal report hits two big snags," *Winnipeg Free Press*, April 17, 1958; Jim Hayes, "Mother of seven finds a new life," *Winnipeg Tribune*, October 24, 1959.
28. "Welfare group says private rents in city are too high," *Winnipeg Tribune*, July 13, 1959.
29. "Welfare group says private rents in city are too high," *Winnipeg Tribune*, July 13, 1959; "Free land offer has no takers," *Winnipeg Tribune*, September 15, 1959.
30. Bob Preston, "Three plans for houses don't help," *Winnipeg Tribune*, May 4, 1960.

31. Aldo Santin, "Tenants call eviction notices illegal, vow fight," *Winnipeg Free Press*, February 28, 2005.

32. Re/Max 624 Herbert Avenue. At <remax-winnipeg.com/officelistings. html/listing.1929545-624-herbert-avenue-winnipeg-r2l-1g2.90599090>, accessed January 18, 2020; Realty Executives 646 Herbert Avenue. At <re-altyexecutivesfirstchoice.com/officelistings.html/listing.202000365-646-herbert-avenue-winnipeg-r2l-1g2.91148937>, accessed January 18, 2020.

33. "Suspended term in fire charges," *Winnipeg Tribune*, May 15, 1956.

34. "Policemen praised for heading off fire," *Winnipeg Tribune*, June 19, 1956.

35. "$450 fire damage," *Winnipeg Tribune*, July 20, 1956.

36. "Two jump to safety," *Winnipeg Tribune*, August 22, 1956.

37. "Occupants flee two city blazes," *Winnipeg Free Press*, August 22, 1956.

38. "Woman child die in roominghouse fire," *Winnipeg Tribune*, October 27, 1956: "They live on borrowed time in dirty, cluttered fire-traps," *Winnipeg Free Press*, October 31, 1956.

39. "Ask fire hazard check for all rooming houses," *Winnipeg Free Press*, December 18, 1957.

40. "Unconscious man rescued," *Winnipeg Tribune*, December 14, 1956.

41. "A place to live: Problem for aged," *Winnipeg Free Press*, January 28, 1958.

42. "Zoning law flouted alderman declares," *Winnipeg Tribune*, August 24, 1956.

43. "Fire leaves 12 people homeless," *Winnipeg Free Press*, March 27, 1958.

44. "Night visit to foreign district," *Manitoba Free Press*, May 30, 1913.

45. "Licensing of houses," *Winnipeg Tribune*, November 8, 1956.

46. "Flames so bright at blaze, they didn't need electricity," *Winnipeg Free Press*, September 26, 1957; "Rooming house fire kills blind man," *Winnipeg Free Press*, August 1, 1957; "We need our own fire code, says chief," *Winnipeg Free Press*, August 2, 1957.

47. "Elderly woman dies in fire," *Winnipeg Free Press*, December 10, 1957; "Stiffer fire curbs sought for city rooming houses," *Winnipeg Free Press*, December 12, 1957; "Room check might have saved 2 lives: Dunnett," *Winnipeg Free Press*, December 17, 1957.

48. "Fined for 3rd time over rooming house," *Winnipeg Free Press*, April 27, 1957.

49. "Ask stiffer fines on city landlords," *Winnipeg Tribune*, October 15, 1959.

50. Val Werier, "A 1905 terrace Isn't the answer," *Winnipeg Tribune*, April 30, 1960.

51. "Rooming house policy shapes," *Winnipeg Tribune*, May 19, 1960.

52. "Fire jury sees need for code," *Winnipeg Tribune*, May 5, 1960.

53. Val Werier, "A 1905 terrace Isn't the answer," *Winnipeg Tribune*, April 30, 1960.

54. "Fifty flee night fire," *Winnipeg Tribune*, April 25, 1956.

55. "33 flee as flames hit block," *Winnipeg Free Press*, February 3, 1959.

56. "Three city firemen injured in stubborn apartment blaze," *Winnipeg Free Press*, March 10, 1959.

57. "Fire forces 40 to flee apartment," *Winnipeg Free Press*, August 17, 1959.

58. "Girl lives after fall," *Winnipeg Tribune*, August 15, 1959.

59. "Think of the man who cleans cars," *Winnipeg Tribune*, March 28, 1956.

60. "Probe bares city slum profit: Taxes subsidize big landlords," *Winnipeg Tribune*, October 14, 1959.

61. "Taraska demands slums be cleared," *Winnipeg Free Press*, November 9, 1956.

62. "Won't pay rent for unfit houses," *Winnipeg Tribune*, December 8, 1959.

63. Jim Hayes, "City funds helped draw this portrait of a slum," *Winnipeg Tribune*, October 17, 1959.

64. Jim Hayes, "Rules halt cure of slum cancer," *Winnipeg Tribune*, October 15, 1959.

65. Erik Watt, "Life in the slums," *Winnipeg Free Press*, October 17, 1959.

66. "Congestion in city tenement," *Winnipeg Tribune*, February 26, 1909; Hayes, Jim Hayes, "Rules halt cure of slum cancer," *Winnipeg Tribune*, October 15, 1959.

67. "Homeless family is helped," *Winnipeg Free Press*, August 5, 1959.

68. "$60 rent money claimed too low," *Winnipeg Tribune*, December 15, 1959.

69. "Welfare rent hike is urged," *Winnipeg Tribune*, December 8, 1959.

70. Jim Hayes, "Rules halt cure of slum cancer," *Winnipeg Tribune*, October 15, 1959.

71. "'Subsidized' slums," *Winnipeg Tribune*, October 18, 1959.

72. Jim Hayes, "Rules halt cure of slum cancer," *Winnipeg Tribune*, October 15, 1959.

73. "City action urged on $18 million slum plan," *Winnipeg Free Press*, September 17, 1957.

74. "Special committee studies redevelopment," *Winnipeg Free Press*, July 31, 1956; "Mayor blasts slum plan critic," *Winnipeg Tribune*, June 21, 1958; Burley, "Winnipeg's landscapes of modernity," in Serena Keshavjee (ed.), *Winnipeg Modern: Architecture, 1945–1975*, Winnipeg: University of Manitoba Press, 2006, 59.

75. "Taraska demands slums be cleared," *Winnipeg Free Press*, November 9, 1956.

76. "Plan found too costly," *Winnipeg Free Press*, November 30, 1956.

77. "City action urged on $18 million slum plan," *Winnipeg Free Press*, September 17, 1957.

78. Earl Levin, "City History and City Planning: The Local Historical Roots of the City Planning Function in Three Cities of the Canadian Prairies," PhD thesis, University of Manitoba, 1993, 288.

79. Thomas B. Yauk, "Residential and Business Relocation from Urban Renewal Areas: A Case Study—The Lord Selkirk Park Experience," Master of City Planning thesis, University of Manitoba, 1973, 29.

80. John Bacher, *Keeping to the Market: The Evolution of Canadian Housing Policy*, Montreal and Kingston: McGill-Queen's University Press, 1993, 213.

81. "Housing group uses its spurs," *Winnipeg Free Press*, June 18, 1958.

82. "Says Mayor Juba misleading city on his slum plan," *Winnipeg Free Press*, June 20, 1958.

83. "Housing group uses its spurs," *Winnipeg Free Press*, June 18, 1958; "New board suggested to clear away slums," *Winnipeg Tribune*, July 4, 1958; "Slum clearance speedup sought," *Winnipeg Tribune*, July 1, 1958.

84. Deborah Lyon and Robert Fenton, "The development of downtown Winnipeg: Historical perspectives on decline and revitalization," Winnipeg: Institute for Urban Studies, University of Winnipeg, 1984, 70–73.

85. "Board sets area for city renewal," *Winnipeg Free Press*, February 29, 1960.

86. "Clearing the slums," *Winnipeg Free Press*, March 2, 1960.

87. "$10 million slum plan gets go-ahead in city," *Winnipeg Tribune*, March 1, 1960.

88. John E. Tooth, *Report re Urban Renewal*, Winnipeg and District Labour Council, CLC, August 15, 1960.

89. John E. Tooth, "Sixty years in Canada: By an immigrant of 1910," handwritten manuscript, circa 1972–1973.

90. For position on the Winnipeg Labour Council executive, see: Dudley Magnus, "Press ban vetoed," *Winnipeg Free Press*, October 5, 1960. For 1960 election, see: "Candidate says city at fault on delay in urban renewal," *Winnipeg Free Press*, October 15, 1960.

91. "Slum dwellers unite," *Winnipeg Free Press*, November 30, 1960; H.H.W. Egler, "Housing conditions are as bad as refugee camps," *Winnipeg Free Press*, June 3, 1961; "Tuesday is date for coffee party," *Winnipeg Tribune*, May 27, 1961; "North centre focal point P-C women are told," May 14, 1962.

92. "Slum wives heard," *Winnipeg Free Press*, August 12, 1960.

93. "Women want slum answers," *Winnipeg Tribune*, March 6, 1961.

94. Robert Collins, "The rough and always ready mayor of Winnipeg," *Maclean's Magazine*, November 23, 1957; "Former mayor Sharpe dies," *Winnipeg Free Press*, November 21, 1985.

95. Robert Collins, "The rough and always ready mayor of Winnipeg," *Maclean's Magazine*, November 23, 1957.

96. Earl Levin, "City History and City Planning: The Local Historical Roots of the City Planning Function in Three Cities of the Canadian Prairies," PhD thesis, University of Manitoba, 1993, 256, 265.

97. "Council vote upsets CEC," *Winnipeg Free Press*, January 4, 1961.

98. "Harvey seeking CEC, Independent caucus," *Winnipeg Tribune*, December 8, 1959; "CEC warned to be more discrete," *Winnipeg Tribune*, December 15, 1959; "CEC member hits CEC rule by caucus," *Winnipeg Tribune*, December 29, 1959.

99. "What's the matter," *Winnipeg Tribune*, October 26, 1961.

100. Mary Bletcher, "Bring politics to council table," *Winnipeg Free Press*, January 22, 1963.

101. David Walker, *The Great Winnipeg Dream: The Re-Development of Portage and Main*, Oakville, ON: Mosaic Press, 1979, 20–21.

102. "It's Moffat vs. Juba," *Winnipeg Tribune*, October 3, 1962.

103. "Mayor Juba chided on budget, slums," *Winnipeg Free Press*, November 19, 1960.

104. "Move to bypass ratepayer," *Winnipeg Free Press*, December 29, 1959; Ted Byfield, "Last interview recalls lifetime of fighting," *Winnipeg Free Press*, April 13, 1968.

105. "Charter change bid in three weeks," *Winnipeg Free Press*, February 20, 1960; "A 'no' from the bureau," *Winnipeg Free Press*, February 20, 1960; "Approve charter changes," *Winnipeg Free Press*, March 16, 1960; Warner Troyer, "By-law vote may be the last," *Winnipeg Free Press*, November 7, 1960; "60 percent rule on city bylaws to be scrapped," *Winnipeg Tribune*, April 14, 1961. For the rearguard action, see: "Money vote question is tabled," *Winnipeg Free Press*, December 15, 1959.

106. "Vote for all called a great mistake," *Winnipeg Free Press*, December 15, 1959.

Chapter 8

A FALSE DAWN: 1960–1969

By 1960 it was apparent that some form of low-rent, federally funded housing was going to be built in Winnipeg. After decades of opposing such development, the Chamber of Commerce had come around to the idea, having been won over by changes to the *National Housing Act* that allowed urban renewal money to be used for more than housing.[1] Similarly, a relatively new provincial government, "Conservative" by name but financially expansive by nature, was finally prepared to fund public housing. A mayor with no direct connections to either the Citizen or labour faction on council was determined to take advantage of available federal funding. The media were largely supportive of public housing, as were the usual suspects: unions, churches, and social agencies.

The existence of this broad consensus of support for public housing was essential. Mark Danzker, a Citizen member of Winnipeg city council from 1960 to 1968, credited the change in the political atmosphere during 1953–1961 to the work done by "church, labour, women's clubs and the chamber of commerce." He said in the past, public housing had been blocked by the "idea that a man trying to provide a home for himself should not become liable through taxes for part of the cost of his neighbor's house."[2] Broad consensuses can, however, fracture or dissolve; and public housing, while on the agenda, was not inevitable. As a result, housing advocates needed to apply continuous pressure to ensure that the momentum that had been created for public housing did not falter.

A Citizens' Committee for Low-Rental Housing, formed in 1960, arranged a tour of poor housing for federal public works Minister David Walker that left the minister shocked.[3] In March 1961, the Winnipeg Council of Women established what it termed a continuing committee on low-rental housing. The decision was

Over 100 women showed up at the March 6, 1961, Winnipeg City Council meeting to show their support for public housing. "$8.4 Million Housing Approved by Council: Decision Follows 5 Women's Briefs," Winnipeg Tribune, March 7, 1961.

made after the organization's president, Leslie Hancock, took a tour of the city's "slum" areas. She and the women who accompanied her visited families "paying $60 a month for very inadequate houses where there were fire hazards, poor lighting and heating. These homes could have been condemned 30 years ago."[4] At that month's city council meeting "some 100 women, armed with briefs and indignation urged council to throw off its indifference to the plight of slum families by making an immediate start on public housing."[5]

Among those who lobbied the provincial government in the spring of 1961 to make sure it lived up to its commitment to public housing were Arthur Johnston (the president of the housing committee of the Welfare Council of Greater Winnipeg), representatives of the United Church's Winnipeg Presbytery, Alex Robertson of the Winnipeg Chamber of Commerce, P. Dunphy of the Roman Catholic Archdiocese of Winnipeg, and Sam Goodman of the Winnipeg Labour Council.[6]

The media, particularly the *Winnipeg Tribune*, played an important role in drawing attention, if in sometimes melodramatic terms, to low-income housing needs. At times, the paper focused on the civic shame that arose from having poor housing located just "five minutes from Portage and Main." The caption on *Tribune* cartoonist Jan Kamienski's line drawing of one such house spoke of it being "too old to repair, the sagging wood frame is scarcely able to hold the walls together. The house is old and tired, and everything about it is old, too; old tires, old food cans, old cardboard litter the unfenced yard. The doors won't close and the garbage lids won't stay in place. Nobody cares."[7] The tagline "only five minutes" from downtown was also used to end a *Tribune* report on the city's "hobo jungle" along the banks of the Red River between the Provencher Bridge and Bannatyne Street where a shifting population spent the summer in "crude cardboard shelters."[8]

Tribune columnist Val Werier, in a less sensationalistic vein, regularly made the economic case for public housing, pointing out that while the rents in public housing units would be $21 a month more than the City paid for welfare clients living in slum housing, a housing project would be paying more in property taxes than slum owners, bringing the actual difference down to twelve dollars a month. The cost dropped even further if one considered the fact that the Province paid 60 percent of the City's welfare bill, bringing the monthly cost to the City down to an extra five dollars a unit a month.[9] Werier, the child of socialist immigrants from Czarist Russia and an admirer of Saskatchewan's Co-operative Commonwealth Federation premier T.C. Douglas, was to prove a passionate and constant supporter of quality low-cost housing.[10]

A more surprising convert to public housing was H.W. Egler, the pastor of First English Evangelical Lutheran Church and the outspoken host of a radio call-in show ("Ask the Pastor"), who wrote at least four columns for the *Free Press* in 1961 supporting public housing while defending the mayor against charges for failing to have moved the project forward.[11]

When long-time Communist city councillor Jacob Penner retired from city council in 1961, his place was taken by another Communist, Winnipeg lawyer and school trustee, Joseph Zuken. Raised in the North End by parents who had immigrated from Eastern Europe, Zuken would prove to be as dogged a champion of public housing as Penner had been. While Zuken supported public housing projects, he did not hesitate to question the quality of construction and the authoritarian way in which property was expropriated to make way for the projects, or the lack of recreational facilities in the redeveloped areas. But of even greater concern to Zuken was the fact that the projects undertaken in the 1960s did not begin to meet the city's housing needs. As he said of the work being contemplated in 1962, "The whole project is too little, too late."[12] New Democratic Party councillors such as Isadore Wolch raised similar concerns about the need to increase the number of public housing units under construction.[13] Even as he put pressure on council, Zuken acknowledged that the City was "handcuffed to two senior governmental partners so much that we could hardly move, even on small things."[14]

Despite this broad base of support, only two public housing projects were undertaken in Winnipeg in the entire decade of the 1960s: the Burrows-Keewatin project and the Lord Selkirk Park project. The Burrows-Keewatin and Lord Selkirk Park housing projects were two parts of the same urban renewal plan intended to redevelop the land north of the Canadian Pacific Railway yards. The first step was the construction of Burrows-Keewatin on undeveloped property at the edge of the prairie in the city's northwest. The second step was Lord Selkirk Park, which was part of a larger urban-renewal initiative that targeted the area north of the Canadian Pacific Railway yards between Main and Salter and south of Selkirk. This was a bulldozer-led "slum clearance" that focused on renewing both housing and businesses in the area.

Burrows-Keewatin and Lord Selkirk Park were the subjects of criticism at the time of their construction and in the years following. There was a lack of community consultation coupled with a belief that development should be limited to the physical construction of housing as opposed to the meeting of social needs. Over time, a commitment to retaining the projects as mixed-income communities was abandoned and spending on maintenance was limited. The lack of investment in recreation, social supports, and a mixed community reflected the dominant group on council's underlying hostility to the people who would benefit from low-cost housing. There were options—such as co-operative housing—that the Citizens turned down, and lessons—such as the need to emphasize mixed-income development—that they refused to learn.

CO-OPERATIVE HOUSING: A ROAD NOT TAKEN

In late 1959, the Saskatchewan government sponsored a meeting on co-operative housing in Regina that drew participants from across the country. The participants concluded that it would take at least five years to develop a co-operative housing project. They also recognized that it would be very difficult for "the people who need and want housing" to hold a group together for that long. What was needed was a larger organization, one that would develop housing co-operatives and then recruit residents. It is, of course, one thing to identify a need and a completely different thing to fill it.

Two of the people at that meeting in Regina were Skapti (Scotty) Borgford, an engineer with Green Blankstein Russell and Associates, and Dan Slimmon, who worked for the Manitoba Co-op Wholesale.[15] On their return to Winnipeg, Borgford and Slimmon invited fifteen people to a meeting in the lunchroom of the Manitoba Honey Producers to "discuss the need for—and the possibility of Co-op Housing in Manitoba." Alex Laidlaw, the secretary of the Co-operative Union of Canada and a director of the Central Mortgage and Housing Corporation, was to be a featured speaker at the meeting.[16] A committee headed by Borgford was struck to study the prospect of co-operative housing in Manitoba. The committee went much further, and it moved very quickly. Borgford came from a family of builders. His father, an immigrant from Iceland, worked in construction and had sought to bring up all four of his sons to become engineers. In the case of three of them, he succeeded. Like many Icelandic families, the Borgfords lived in the city's West End, where they adhered to the Unitarian Church. The church's strong teachings of social responsibility and equality were significant in shaping the family's values. One of the engineer sons left the profession to take up a position as a Unitarian minister, while the non-engineer, Gil, was a prominent trade union activist. Aside from making a considerable contribution to his profession and serving as an NDP school trustee, Scotty Borgford would be the driving force behind the creation of Canada's first permanent housing co-operative.[17]

The first step was to create a central organization that could serve as a "Mother Hen." This was based on the Swedish model of housing co-op development in which a "mother" organization established "daughter" co-operatives. In Sweden, the Tenants' Saving and Building Society served as an overall umbrella organization in this process.[18] The Co-operative Housing Association of Manitoba (CHAM) incorporated on January 23, 1960, intending to play that role in Manitoba. CHAM's founding members included Borgford, Slimmon, Art Coulter (the secretary-treasurer of the Winnipeg Labour Council), Ruth Struthers (who was active in the Provincial Council of Women), A.W. Wood (University of Manitoba faculty of agriculture), R. Kapilik (Manitoba Pool Elevators), A.D. Ramsay (future president of the Co-operative Credit Society of Manitoba), T.W. Robinson (future president of the Co-operative Housing Association of Manitoba), D.J. Wood, and R.F. Penner (the Co-op Union of Manitoba). The six organizational founding members were Federated Co-operatives Limited, Manitoba Pool Elevators, United Grain Growers Limited, Co-operative Life Insurance Company, Co-operative Fire and Casualty Company and the Winnipeg and District Labour Council.[19] The drive of individuals such as Borgford and Slimmon was important, but co-operative housing could not have been established without the economic and organizational resources that the broader co-operative movement had developed in the previous half century.

They were working quickly because they wished to seize an opportunity. After decades of delay, the City of Winnipeg had finally committed itself to the redevelopment of the area between Selkirk

Avenue and the Canadian Pacific rail yards. The first step in this process would be the creation of low-income housing at Burrows-Keewatin in the northwest corner of the city to house some of the people displaced by the redevelopment of the Selkirk area.[20]

When the City issued a call for proposals for the area, CHAM was ready. With the assistance of Green Blankstein Russell and Associates (which had prepared the designs for the unbuilt public-housing projects of the 1930s), CHAM proposed the construction of close to one thousand units of low-cost housing in Burrows-Keewatin.[21] Initial meetings with the city's Urban Renewal Board and its housing committee went positively, and planning continued apace throughout the year.[22]

At the beginning of 1962, under the impression that it had the support of council, CHAM unveiled its ambitious proposal: a $10 million, 980-unit project on 950 acres of land. The development would include parks, a shopping centre, senior-citizen housing, and a community centre. CHAM's lawyer, C.N. Kushner, told the *Winnipeg Tribune* that the plan included "the best features of European low-cost housing and an 80 million [dollar] project in New York City." CHAM had been particularly impressed with the extensive series of housing co-operatives the labour movement had developed in New York City in the first half of the twentieth century. The proposal depended on the sale of the land from the City and CMHC granting a 25-year, 90-per-cent mortgage.[23] The proposal had the support of the Winnipeg and District Labour Council, the United Church, the Greater Winnipeg Welfare Council, and the Jewish Welfare Council.[24] Even the city's Urban Renewal Board recommended that unless the City was prepared to develop its own housing in Burrows-Keewatin, it should accept the CHAM proposal.

Peter Taraska, chair of the city's finance committee, emerged as a fierce opponent of the development. Borgford described Taraska as "a confirmed private entrepreneur in a large insurance business," who strove to "thoroughly condemn the co-operative at both ends."[25] Taraska, an accountant who worked in both the insurance and construction industry, said he opposed the co-op plan because it would only provide housing to a "limited class" of people."[26] The co-op responded that the City was preparing to repeat the mistakes of earlier housing projects in other jurisdictions by failing to integrate public housing into the type of affordable housing a co-operative could create.[27]

Despite this, Taraska succeeded in his campaign to have the City turn down the co-operative proposal. CBC commentator Bob Preston noted that the showdown between Taraska and Borgford had forced the City to "take a stand on public housing or give in to the Co-op housing request."[28] After rejecting the CHAM proposal, the council had to commit itself to public housing. In the spring of 1961, council approved an $8.4 million project intended to house 817 families on the Burrows-Keewatin site.[29] Borgford was suspicious at the time of the size of the City's commitment, referring to it as a "tongue in cheek" proposal.[30] He was correct, in the end, the City built only 165 of the proposed 817 housing units in Burrows-Keewatin.[31]

Borgford was not easily deterred. In November 1961, the city finance committee, over the opposition of Taraska, recommended that CHAM be allowed to purchase 21.4 acres of land in the Burrows-Keewatin area for the same price that CMHC was paying for the land.[32] This time CHAM was proposing to build 376 row-housing units for families who made less than $4,500 a year. Citizens city council member Lillian Hallonquist opposed it because it would be crowded. She also felt that the housing being built in Burrows-Keewatin should be reserved for those in the greatest need. CHAM spokesperson T.W. Robinson responded that it was "sociologically undesirable" to restrict an area solely to public housing, adding that the housing the co-op was proposing would be superior in quality to the CMHC housing, which he said would be "just the essentials."[33] Council rejected the proposal by a vote of ten to eight.[34] The margin of defeat was declining, and while CHAM would not win the right to develop the public housing being proposed for Winnipeg in the early 1960s, it did develop Canada's first permanent non-profit housing co-operative, Willow Park, which opened in 1966.[35]

"I HOPE THAT WINNIPEG CAN
LEARN FROM OUR MISTAKES"

The one advantage of Winnipeg's delayed entry into the world of public housing was that the City could have learned from the experiences of other jurisdictions. In the spring of 1961, Pat Brady, the director of Metro Toronto's Housing Authority, warned the Winnipeg Kiwanis Club that Winnipeg was simply going to repeat the errors that Toronto had made in developing Regent Park. "I hope we never see another high-rise unit. Imagine 14 storeys, 96 families. Think of the regimentation required with one laundry." In Toronto, he said, "We are now opposed to large institutional-sized projects. We made mistakes in Toronto and I hope that Winnipeg can learn from our mistakes." It was important, he said, that public housing be integrated into the general community, rather than as a ghetto.[36] Similarly, Albert Rose, a long-time housing activist from Toronto, noted that while Winnipeg lagged fifteen years behind Toronto, it had the opportunity to benefit from that city's experience. Rose said Toronto had erred by concentrating public housing geographically. Unfortunately, he said, the Lord Selkirk Park planners had not absorbed this lesson. He thought "No public housing project should have more than 250 to 300 units in one place." University of British Columbia social scientist Leonard Marsh expressed similar concerns, stressing the need to link social programs with housing programs.[37]

James Cowan, who had been campaigning for public housing since the late 1930s, was by 1961 a Conservative backbencher in the provincial legislature. He criticized the Lord Selkirk Park proposal, pointing to studies that said large-scale projects "tend to segregate low-income people in concentrated areas." Instead, he called for smaller, "mixed-income developments."[38] CCF Metro council member Art Coulter expressed similar concerns: "I was hoping there would be an integration of these units in the area with others. They are going to be isolated and will be easily identified as low-rental units. I don't think this is desirable."[39] As an alternative to largescale "projects," journalist Heather Robertson pointed to what she referred to as the "Myers cure," since it was being promoted by Gerry Myers, Winnipeg's director of welfare. According to Robertson, Myers and others believed that "slums can be wiped out by only one method—a comprehensive program of government-subsidized housing." This would not necessarily require the City to build new homes or develop large projects. "It simply has to rent or purchase existing older homes, renovate them, and rent them to low-income families for whatever the family can pay."[40]

FINALLY GETTING SHOVELS IN THE GROUND

While Duff Roblin's provincial government had given support to urban renewal in principle, it was slow to move from principle to practice. The Province's initial urban renewal priority was to get the City to drop plans to build a new city hall near the legislative building. By early 1961 it had committed $800,000 to a downtown development plan that would provide no new housing.[41] At a key point, the Province held off on making a financial commitment to the acquisition of land or the construction of any housing until a survey of provincial needs was completed.[42] Jean James, one of the women who went on the Winnipeg Council of Women's 1961 tour of "slum housing," wrote she was haunted by the provincial government's delay, calling it "false logic and false economy."[43] Members of the Women's Club , angered by provincial footdragging, endorsed a motion calling on the Province to commit to funding "slum clearance and low cost housing."[44] The Catholic Women's League of Manitoba also endorsed a resolution calling for provincial support for municipal slum clearance projects.[45] The Province continued to vacillate on the extent of its financial contribution throughout 1962, with city officials at one time claiming that the Province had, in effect, killed the project.[46]

While the provincial government perseverated, city council and the federal government slowly put together a development plan. In March 1961, the council approved what was then described as an $8.4 million Burrows-Keewatin project and adopted a four-step urban-renewal plan for the Selkirk area.[47] In October 1961 the federal government committed $3 million to the purchase and clearing of 48.8 acres of land. The federal government also made a $1.65 million commitment to the 10-acre Burrows-Keewatin project.[48] The City's commitment to the actual look and feel of these projects was always limited. To speed up the development process, for

Lord Selkirk Park consisted of a seven-storey seniors' residence and a series of row houses with 192 three-, four-, and five-bedroom units. It was intended to provide housing for 1,350 people on an 11.5-acre site. University of Manitoba Archives & Special Collections. Henry Kalen fonds, PC 219 (A2005-100), item # UM_pc219_A05-100_001_0026_003_0001.

example, council requested that CMHC simply make use of plans for a Regina housing project for Burrows-Keewatin.[49] City council gave final approval to a pared-down $2 million Burrows-Keewatin project in August 1962.[50] In total there were to be ten buildings, with two- to five-bedroom suites. In addition, there were plans for a shopping centre, a recreation centre, and a park in the neighbourhood.[51] With the federal government committed to providing 75 percent of the funding, the Province agreed to split the remaining 25 percent on a fifty-fifty basis with the City of Winnipeg. CMHC had awarded the construction contract by December 1962, sod was turned in January 1963, and the first residents moved in October 1963.[52]

Because over two years were devoted to the acquisition of land, construction of the $4 million Lord Selkirk Park housing project did not start until January 1967. The first residents began to move in December 1967.[53] The project consisted of a seven-storey seniors' residence that had 137 bachelor, one-bedroom, and two-bedroom units and a series of row houses with 192 three-, four-, and five-bedroom units. It was intended to provide housing for 1,350 people on an 11.5-acre site. In addition to the housing, a local elementary school was expanded and a vocational junior high school, named for 1919 General Strike leader R.B. Russell, was planned for the area.[54] Because federal urban renewal agreements did not provide funding for parks, cities were obliged to pay the full cost of any park or recreation projects included in Lord Selkirk.[55] In 1966 the City, always very cost-conscious when dealing with public housing, rejected a proposal for a larger park in the Lord Selkirk development even though the project's landscape architects believed that the planned recreational facilities were not adequate for so large a project.[56] Lord Selkirk was, in many ways, the type of project that Toronto housing advocates had warned the City against.

Both Burrows-Keewatin and Lord Selkirk Park were managed by the Winnipeg Housing Authority, which was headed by Alex Robertson, the former Chamber of Commerce president who was also the driving force behind Triangle Gardens.[57] Rental rates for both projects were income-based, and as a family's income increased its rent also increased. When it opened in 1963, Burrows-Keewatin sought to limit residence to households with incomes below $3,500 a year. Families were encouraged to move out as their income increased.[58] In this way, public housing was very much seen as a trampoline, rather than a safety net: families would move into it, and once they achieved a measure of financial stability they would move out. This disregarded the fact that living in secure, well-maintained housing could be one of the factors that contributed to a household developing some financial security. The initial recruitment policy set aside only one-quarter of the units at Burrows-Keewatin and Lord Selkirk Park for families on welfare. There was also an effort to limit the number of what were called "multi-problem" families admitted to Burrows-Keewatin.[59] Newspaper columnist Ann Henry, who knew from first-hand experience how difficult it was for a single mother to obtain public housing, wrote critically of the "'screening' processes that allow moving into new housing based on 'social adaptability.' Surely the least desirable person—the lowest income groups and the most damaged people are the ones most in need of rehabilitation."[60]

Both projects were the subject of ongoing public controversy. The top-down development approach in the Lord Selkirk area had led to the destruction of good quality as well as poor quality homes, while the City's expropriation policy meant that payments to people who were forced to sell their homes were so low that they were not able to buy equivalent homes in other parts of the city.[61] In the end, while the projects increased the quality of housing, they did not increase its quantity or necessarily reduce its costs.[62] Families that were displaced by the project were often met with hostility and suspicion by the neighbours, who believed the newcomers "were all welfare delinquents, slum dwellers and drunks."[63] Largely focused on the bricks-and-mortar elements of the project, the City and Province were slow to address the social issues that arose in the wake of such a significant neighbourhood redevelopment.[64] Belatedly, the City appointed William Courage, its former head of Emergency Housing, to address the human side of the project, and it was not until 1968 that the provincial government established Peoples' Opportunity Services (POS) to address the social needs of people affected by the relocation.[65]

EARLY DAYS IN THE PROJECTS: "BOTH THE GOOD AND THE BAD"

As the city's first public-housing development, Burrows-Keewatin was the subject of considerable media interest. Rhoda Mulvaney, her husband, and her seven children moved into Burrows-Keewatin on September 30, 1963. Their previous home had been on Derby Street, just around the corner from Jarvis Avenue. She felt the move was of greatest importance to her children. "Environment," she said, "doesn't make much difference to the adults—our minds are made up on things. But it's important for the kids. That's why we are here."[66]

By 1964, she was the president of the tenant association, and the following year she made a presentation pointing out that some of the work on the project was done poorly and some had never been completed. The association also objected to the fact that rents were calculated based on gross rather than net income and did not adequately consider family size. But she was also philosophical: residents, she said, had experienced "both the good and the bad" that can arise in public housing and hoped that planners would make use of their experience in other buildings.[67]

When interviewed in 1969, Mulvaney remained positive about the opportunities that life in the development had given her children, saying, "The kids didn't seem to have as much chance downtown as they do out here." That said, while she did not feel personally stigmatized, she said she was "not really in favour of this type of development. I'd rather see older homes renovated, and families on low incomes scattered in different communities." When asked why, she told *Tribune* reporter Michael McGarry, "Just because of the questions you ask, about ethnic groups and vandals and what are the people like in this community."[68] Upon her death in 2014, many of the comments on the online memorial page spoke of the close links that developed between families that lived in the Burrows-Keewatin project.[69]

Winnipeg Tribune columnist Val Werier wrote in 1963 that the quality of the housing at Burrows-Keewatin was a tribute to the planners. Of one family's unit he wrote: "The kitchen is bright and efficient with new equipment and ample cupboards. It is not elaborate, for an eye was kept on costs. But there is nothing of the appearance of cheap row housing. It has an air of solidity. And it has more space outdoors than many commercial blocks."[70] In 1967, Werier revisited Burrows-Keewatin, writing, "A stranger would not know it as public housing for it appears as an attractive development with buildings of dark red brick and white stucco, green lawns and flowers. The grounds are more spacious than expensive townhouse developments." He did note that tenants had to "cope with its remoteness from shopping centres and other activities of city life." Ninety-nine families left in the first two years of operation: fifteen left town, five left because of distance from work, ten families broke up, two heads of families died, thirteen families were evicted, eleven separated, and seventeen left for other reasons, seven bought homes, and nineteen moved because their rents had risen to the point where they could rent elsewhere. Werier believed "The development has been a tremendous step forward in the provision of good housing for 900 people who would otherwise be living in mean, crowded quarters."[71]

In the fall of 1966 *Tribune* reporter Heather Robertson filed a profile on life in Burrows-Keewatin. The story was framed by the question "has the slum simply moved out to new quarters on the city's fringe?" It is not clear where her data came from, but she reported that truancy was down and school performance was up, homes were better maintained, delinquency and crime were down, employment was high, and alcoholism was under control. People were still poor, but she wrote, "Burrows-Keewatin is not a poverty ghetto." Robertson did, however, liken life at Burrows-Keewatin to living in a goldfish bowl: "Violent feuds develop. Nothing is secret and many things get shouted across courtyards with accompanying profanity. Housing units are built in a court-square formation which enables a dozen or more families to see and hear everything that happens in each other's homes." She also identified racial prejudice as a contributor to the "high-voltage" emotional climate of life in Burrows-Keewatin.[72]

A 1968 academic study of Burrows-Keewatin conducted by William Morrison, the head of the University of Winnipeg sociology department, reached similarly positive conclusions. Morrison told the media that the people he interviewed were nearly unanimous in their "intense dislike for their old living quarters." The location, in his opinion, was a "success." At the same time, he urged planners to "stay away from large apartment complexes."[73] His report noted that 75 percent of the people he surveyed said that they would recommend the project to their friends.[74]

Housing research carried out by the Manitoba Indian Brotherhood in early 1971 reported that while "Registered Indians" living in Burrows-Keewatin and Lord Selkirk Park "expressed a general satisfaction with their dwelling units, there is some divergence of opinion with regard to subsidiary features." Lord Selkirk residents expressed dissatisfaction with the limited playground facilities, the deteriorating nature of the surrounding community, and a lack of pre-occupancy orientation and maintenance that led to the deterioration of the housing units. Burrows-Keewatin respondents were more positive, saying that they felt themselves to be part of a "community unto itself rather than merely constituting an updated extension of a slum."[75]

Not everyone was as positive. By 1968, John Tooth—the carpenter who, in the 1950s, had been a strong advocate of the Lord Selkirk and Burrows-Keewatin projects—had become so disillusioned with the projects that he resigned from the Winnipeg Housing Authority. He said the development had been designed by planners who had never lived on the prairies and had failed to take the city's climate into account. More significantly, he accused the City of destroying more homes than it built. As a result, the supply of homes in Winnipeg was worse than it had been forty years earlier. Tooth said of Burrows-Keewatin and Lord Selkirk Park that they were "expensive... ghettos" that failed "to blend in and conform with surrounding property of any age or period. In this respect, it's self-defeating because all of our surrounding cities and municipalities reject it, leaving our city to assume the entire load of providing housing for the less fortunate one third of the province." He was also critical of row-housing designs, saying that destroyed privacy and dignity.[76] That same year, residents of Lord Selkirk Park told a federal task force on housing that they objected to the "loss of privacy, barracks-type living, complete lack of recreational facilities and the feeling of being on display for a more affluent public." One resident said little was gained by moving "a family wracked with social problems from an old house to a new."[77]

In 1970, *Winnipeg Tribune* reporter Eugen Weiss wrote a lengthy profile on the Lord Selkirk housing project. Many of the people he spoke with were critical of the project. Residents of the seven-storey senior citizens' residence said they were scared about going out in the evening after seven o'clock. Many also felt isolated because they spoke only Ukrainian or Polish.[78] Juan Gomez-Perales, who worked for Peoples' Opportunity Services, told Weiss, "Lord Selkirk was built on the basis of cost per unit, family size. They considered the costs of beams, stoves, and room functions. All this is good information." But he said the project should have been preceded by "community involvement and planning, for recreational facilities, schools, health and community services."[79] While many of the people Weiss spoke with had specific criticisms of life at Lord Selkirk, they all agreed that "more public housing has to be built." The only questions were as to its location and density and the level of community involvement.[80] Why, then, it is legitimate to ask, were no more projects built in the 1960s?

WHY ONLY TWO PROJECTS IN A DECADE?

In 1964 the newly elected federal Liberal minority government, which was dependent on support from the New Democratic Party, amended the *National Housing Act* to allow CMHC to lend provincial and municipal non-profit housing corporations up to 90 percent of construction costs for public housing. In addition, the federal government would pay up to 50 percent of operating costs.[81] From the provincial perspective, this deal was too good to pass up: by 1967 six provinces, including Manitoba, established provincial housing corporations.[82] Winnipeg city council began to consider more projects: in August 1965 the council approved an application to the federal and provincial government for a 690-acre urban renewal project that would straddle Main Street south of the CPR yards and provide housing for 11,500 people, while a 200-unit development was planned for the Main and Stella area.[83]

In 1968, a new Liberal leader, Pierre Trudeau, won a commanding parliamentary majority and appointed Paul Hellyer, a former Toronto housing developer, as minister with responsibility for the CMHC. In August of that year, Hellyer, controversially, appointed himself as the chairperson of a seven-person Federal Task Force on Housing and Urban Development.[84] Hellyer set himself a six-month timeline: four months of study, two months of writing. The task force received five hundred briefs and held twenty-seven meetings across the country. And it kept to its deadline, submitting its final report in January 1969.[85] Given the short timeline, there was little opportunity to commission new research. Indeed, Hellyer distrusted experts.[86]

The task force report's harshest criticisms were reserved for public housing, saying that no other issue had "aroused more concern within the Task Force than the present scheme of public housing." This was in large measure because public housing did not fit with Hellyer's goal of permitting "all but the most deprived families to select and finance accommodation of their own choice within the private market." Grudgingly, Hellyer acknowledged that the public housing projects were decent, safe, and sanitary and "in that sense, it has been an improvement on the slums." But in Hellyer's opinion—and it was little more than an opinion—the real problems were psychological and social. He then conflated all public housing with "big housing projects" and recommended a halt to federal public housing development until the government conducted a "thorough research program into the economic, social and psychological issues of public housing." Biased and incomplete as it was, the report brought all public-housing projects, including those in development in Winnipeg, to a halt.[87] While the federal government conducted yet one more examination of its housing policy, conditions in Winnipeg worsened.

"POOR, UNSANITARY AND DANGEROUS": THE PROBLEM REMAINED

Between them, Burrows-Keewatin and Lord Selkirk Park created just over five hundred units of housing. As everyone recognized, this barely put a dent in the city's housing problems for low-income people. In 1962, George Rich, the planning director for the Metropolitan Corporation of Winnipeg (a regional level of government created in 1960 that coordinated regional issues for Winnipeg and its surrounding municipalities), reported that there were several thousand buildings in Winnipeg in need of repair.[88] The following year, E.G. Simpson, the city's director of housing, said there was a need for an additional 5,000 units of low-rental housing in the city. In addition, 3,451 families were deemed to be living in overcrowded conditions and there were 1,000 cases where more than one family was living in a unit intended to house a single family.[89]

In the spring of 1967, Toronto consultant James A. Murray pointed out, in a survey of Winnipeg housing conditions, that the local housing industry was focused on meeting the housing needs of approximately 50 percent of the population. The other 50 percent of the population was either living in housing that was overcrowded, substandard, or more than they could afford—or all three. 35,000 families needed some form of housing subsidy—and there were only 2,000 housing units that met their needs. Seniors were particularly hard hit, 43 percent of the single seniors were living on less than $1,500 a year, the figure that the Age and Opportunity Bureau had concluded in 1966 that a person needed to live independently on their own.[90] Murray called for the creation of a metropolitan housing corporation that would supply public housing when the private supply of housing failed to meet the housing needs of low-income Winnipeggers. He felt that the initiative had to include Winnipeg and its surrounding suburbs to ensure that low-income people were not housed in remote and segregated ghettoes.[91]

The following year, a report from the Neighbourhood Services Centre spoke of the "poor, unsanitary and dangerous" condition for seniors living in the areas bounded by Princess, Main, Alexander, and the CPR tracks. The suites and rooms were not "maintained adequately by the landlords and most of the residents complain of bugs."[92] The rooms were often "dirty, unsanitary, badly in need of redecorating and the residents have to use a community wash-room as private washrooms do not exist in most of these accommodations." According to the report, "Many of the senior citizens have a real fear of living in this area because of the disturbance and discomforts caused by the frequency of fighting, lawlessness, drunkenness and problems that arise out of the high incidence of prostitution in the area."[93]

Even in the 1960s, tenants did not enjoy full voting rights. The system of plural voting by which a property owner could vote in every ward in which he or she owned property was only repealed in 1965.[94] NDP member of the legislature Saul Cherniack said that he was pleased to see "the passing of an archaic principle which provided that property had the right to vote for aldermen." He said he hoped that other "principles of this type would gradually find their way out of our legislation and the sooner the better and not gradually."[95] But progress was slow. The following year, the Conservatives turned down an NDP proposal to allow people who owned houses on leased land to vote on money bylaws. Municipal Affairs Minister George Smellie said that such a move would "be opening the door for tenants to vote on money bylaws. That is something we are not prepared to consider at this time."[96] In 1967, city council defeated an attempt made by NDP councillors Donovan Swailes and Lloyd Stinson to petition the legislature to allow tenants to vote on money bylaws.[97] The *Free Press* said that the decision "flew in the face of all common sense." By restricting the vote to property owners, "the majority of city electors have no say in the city's major capital expenditures."[98] In April 1969, when debating proposed amendments to the municipal Act, NDP MLA Saul Miller, then sitting in opposition, said he regretted the retention of the provision that limited the right to vote on money bylaws to property owners. "We seem to want to retain the old idea that unless a man owns something he is not a solid citizen."[99]

It was also acceptable for politicians to express contempt for tenants on welfare. Winnipeg school trustee George Frith owned eleven rooming houses and was an outspoken critic of tenants. He said they were the main cause of the poor upkeep of many of the city's rooming houses. Welfare workers, he wrote, should be empowered to drop in on families daily to make sure that floors were scrubbed by noon. "Failure to do so should result in a sentence to scrub the Legislative Building stone floors during evenings for three months, such scrubbing to be without use of kneeling pads." He also called for the return "of what Dickens describes as debtors' prisons."[100] Del. T. Starr was sufficiently angered by Frith's suggestion to write in a letter to the editor: "If we had police officers as social workers, if we had police officers paddling around behind bottle pickers, then, my friend, we would also have police officers ordering landlords to tear down those wrecks board by board, nail by nail, as punishment for having caused people to live in such filth in the first place."[101]

The sort of class hatred that Frith exhibited was being reinforced by racism by the 1960s. In 1958 *The People of Indian Ancestry in Manitoba Report*, prepared by Jean Lagasse, estimated that 1,200 "Indians" lived in Winnipeg, compared with 22,000 in rural Manitoba. Similarly, he estimated that 3,500 Métis lived in Winnipeg, compared to 27,000 in rural Manitoba. This was the beginning of a period of increasing movement of Indigenous people to urban centres. Housing conditions on reserves and off-reserve Indigenous communities were deplorable and employment opportunities were limited and shrinking. In response, Indigenous people moved to cities in search of jobs, education, and better housing. By 1968, the First Nations and Métis populations in Winnipeg had increased to 4,200 and 7,800, respectively.[102] Urban Indigenous people were subject to demonization and vilification. In particular, they were blamed for the deterioration of the community south of Selkirk Avenue between Salter and Main Street. Jarvis Avenue, a street that ran parallel to the CPR yards, became the focus of public debate, much of which was conducted in what can only be described as racist terms.

Jean Kryshka, a former resident of Charles Street (which intersected Jarvis Avenue) and whose parents owned four houses on Charles Street, wrote a letter of complaint to the Winnipeg police in 1962, apparently at the suggestion of Mayor Stephen Juba. In the letter, she wrote of how she had left Charles Street because she was scared of the "Indians" who had moved into the neighbourhood. She said her father's tenants were talking of moving out and it would not be possible to get "nice people to move in." She wondered why the government did "not send these Indians to a reservation where they belong."[103]

In response, Winnipeg police inspector Robert Young reported, "the immediate vicinity of Charles Street has been a problem district to the police for some years but in recent months, the problem has been increasing with the arrival of more and more persons of Indian racial origin." Conditions in the Jarvis Street area would, he wrote, continue to decline as long as "these people are maintained by public funds and are not required to seek employment."[104] Communist city councillor Joe Zuken called the police report a "blanket condemnation of a racial group," adding that the police were "throwing around racial tags. Indians get a raw deal— there isn't a people in the world more exploited."[105]

A follow-up article in the *Tribune* claimed that Jarvis was often referred to as "Tomahawk row." According to reporter Dave Kemp, "Down here the houses are rotting wrecks tottering above the garbage-strewn sidewalks, and all seems clutched within a smothering decay. Things seem to happen on Jarvis St. that make decent people sick. It was here a social worker found an eight-year-old suffering from venereal disease, he reported this week." Kemp approvingly quoted Magistrate Isaac Rice, who, after dealing with family cases from the inner city, said, "families who make welfare an occupation should be sterilized." One police officer held out little hope for the Burrows-Keewatin project, saying, "These people down there are animals. They don't know how to live. They won't work and they won't take care of anything. They'll turn anything into a slum in six months." The story told of drinking parties that went on for over a week and children left to fend for themselves. The article ended with a series of harsh rhetorical questions: "Will Burrows-Keewatin mean the end of Jarvis, with all one thinks of on hearing that name? Or does it merely mean that Jarvis is to be resurrected, a tattered and shameful Phoenix, further away from City Hall?"[106]

There were no services in the 1950s for Indigenous people coming to Winnipeg. Dorothy Betz, who came from Pine Creek Reserve and went on to establish the Native Court Communicator Program, recalled, "We didn't have a place of our own—all we had was Main Street, but we weren't too ecstatic about it."[107] Mary Guilbault, who came from the Fisher River Reserve and would become a social worker, participated in the Urban Indian Association study of inner-city housing carried out in the 1950s. Years later she recalled, "It was sad, very sad, the housing situation was deplorable to say the least... whenever we went to see people while we were doing our study there used to be these great big house rats—how our people survived through that was that they took turns sleeping so that the rats would not attack the kids."[108]

Lack of housing led to people being charged with vagrancy—to deal with this, Betz acquired six bunk beds from the military, set them up in her basement, and arranged with the courts to have young women arrested on vagrancy released into her custody.[109] Starting in the mid-1950s a group of Indigenous people, including Guilbault and Betz, established the Urban Indian Association, meeting in one another's homes to discuss the issues facing Indigenous people who were moving to the city. The Association worked with various church and social welfare groups to establish the Indian-Métis Friendship Centre.[110]

While Celestin Guiboche, one of the co-founders of the Manitoba Métis Federation, moved to Winnipeg in the mid-1960s, he quickly discovered that the only housing available to most Indigenous people was of shockingly poor quality. In 1970, he gave *Winnipeg Tribune* reporter Eugen Weiss this picture of his first home in the city.

> For $75 a month here's what he got: 2 ½ rooms, with the half room the hallway leading downstairs.
>
> Wood was used in the furnace, which wasn't designed for wood, and constant smoke came through apartment vents so that people had to sleep with pillows over their faces and to contend with the fire department, attracted by the heating system. "The walls were black from smoke— but they're moving."
>
> Cockroaches.
>
> Four suites shared one washroom with bad plumbing. Four calls to the health department about that produced no results.
>
> There were no switches on the walls, and the wiring was bare.[111]

A 1968 survey conducted by the Indian and Métis Women of Greater Winnipeg found "faulty wiring, leaking gas stoves, poor outlets, leaking roofs, no screens on doors or windows" to be common in homes that were rented to 130 Indigenous households that they surveyed. Amy Clemons, a leading figure in the Indian-Métis Friendship movement told city council, "In this slum community many live in constant fear of fire traps."[112] The 1971 Manitoba Indian Brotherhood (MIB) housing survey found that "the average income of the urban Indian is insufficient to provide an adequate level of accommodation." Specifically,

> Apartments that are within the scope of the average Indian's financial resources are usually cramped and/or in a state of disrepair. Houses that are sufficiently spacious either command exorbitant rents or offer conditions unfit for human habitation.[113]

Newly arrived Indigenous people were soon caught up in a labyrinthine welfare system. "We contend that the chain of circumstance by which the newly-arrived Indian is confronted often irrevocably shackles him to an existence of hopelessness and degradation. We further contend that the first link in this blighted chain of events is forged by the type of accommodation into which he is thrust" said the MIB.[114]

* * *

With the construction of Burrows-Keewatin and Lord Selkirk Park, a barrier had been breached. After sixty years of struggle, public housing had been built in Winnipeg. But for housing advocates, the 1960s was more of a false dawn than a glorious victory. The decade ended as it began, with thousands of Winnipeggers living in poor-quality housing that they could not afford. Despite the efforts of Joe Zuken and Isadore Wolch, rooming houses remained unregulated and rooming house fires were regular occurrences. In rejecting a call to make smoke detectors mandatory, Citizen councillor Leonard Claydon said, "There are some big and powerful people in this city who would get awfully mad if we forced such legislation down their throats." In 1969, John Masyk, a pensioner from the North End, reminded members of a civic committee that thousands of pensioners were "living in crowded dirty rooming houses with stairs we can't climb and rents we can't afford."[115] In 1970, seven-hundred households were on the Lord Selkirk Park waiting list. On the day in 1970 that *Winnipeg Tribune* reporter Eugen Weiss interviewed Jack Spence, who worked for the city welfare department, Spence was looking for housing for fifty families. Spence said that the City had a list of forty addresses to which it would not refer families because of the poor quality of housing—and that did not include the houses that the City had condemned as being unfit for habitation but were still being inhabited.[116]

But the tide was about to turn. Paul Hellyer may have temporarily brought the expansion to a halt, but Robert Andras, the newly appointed Minister of State for Urban Affairs, took a much more expansive approach to the federal role in funding low-cost housing.[117] Additionally, six months after the Hellyer Report was released, Manitoba voters elected an NDP government. For the first time, Manitoba had a provincial government that was determined to play a leadership role in the construction of public housing; the change in the pace of construction of public housing would be dramatic.

NOTES

1. "Urban renewal," *Winnipeg Tribune*, May 23, 1962.
2. "Bad public view stalled public housing: Danzker," *Winnipeg Free Press*, October 10, 1961.
3. "Minister shocked by city's slums," *Winnipeg Tribune*, May 23, 1962.
4. "Women's club endorses slum clearance stand," *Winnipeg Free Press*, April 11, 1961.
5. "$8.4 million housing approved by council," *Winnipeg Tribune*, March 7, 1961.
6. "Roblin pledges housing aid," *Winnipeg Free Press*, May 9, 1961.
7. Jan Kamienski, "Within five minutes of Portage and Main," *Winnipeg Tribune*, July 25, 1961.
8. "Their home is the jungle just off Portage and Main," *Winnipeg Tribune*, August 2, 1961.
9. Val Werier, "Out of the slums for another $5," *Winnipeg Tribune*, January 27, 1962.
10. Percy Rowe, "It's your business," *Winnipeg Tribune*, January 21, 1950; Susan Ferrier MacKay, "Winnipeg was Val Werier's beat for 75 years," *Globe and Mail*, May 11, 2014.
11. H.H.W. Egler, "Slum clearance means cleanliness, less crime," *Winnipeg Free Press*, May 6, 1961; "Slums are result of vicious circle," *Winnipeg Free Press*, May 12, 1961; "Indirectly slum clearance costs all of us money," *Winnipeg Free Press*, May 27, 1961; "Housing conditions are as bad as refugee camps," *Winnipeg Free Press*, June 3, 1961. For Egler's background, see: Jane Becker, "Radio's public confessors: The air is full of secrets," *Maclean's Magazine*, September 9, 1961, 82.
12. "Plan switch means OK on housing," *Winnipeg Tribune*, March 20, 1962; "To debate Lord Selkirk recreation," *Winnipeg Free Press*, November 3, 1966; "Govt. aid sought on renewal parks," *Winnipeg Free Press*, November 25, 1966; "Fight to hold homes," *Winnipeg Free Press*, December 22, 1967.
13. "To set up body for city renewal," *Winnipeg Free Press*, December 22, 1961; "City owes $129 million: Crawford," *Winnipeg Tribune*, December 22, 1964.
14. Eugen Weiss, "Lord Selkirk Park: Is it good or bad?" *Winnipeg Tribune*, March 7, 1970.
15. Provincial Archives of Manitoba, Co-operative Housing Association of Manitoba, Papers re: Willow Park Housing Co-operative, P 299, File: Co-operative Housing Association of Manitoba, 1959-1966, S.J. Borgford, "Co-operative housing in Manitoba: The story of the Co-operative Housing Association of Manitoba and the development of Willow Park Housing Co-operative in Winnipeg," undated, unpublished paper, 2; interview with Karen Botting, July 28, 2020; Don Slimmon, *People and Progress: A Co-op Story*, Brandon: Leach Printing, undated, xiii–xv.
16. Provincial Archives of Manitoba, Co-operative Housing Association of Manitoba, Papers re: Willow Park Housing Co-operative, P 299, File: Co-operative Housing Association of Manitoba, 1959–1966, D.H. Slimmon to S.J. Borgford and others, November 2, 1959.
17. Family background information from interview with Karen Botting, July 28, 2020; Winnipeg Architectural Foundation, "Skapti 'Scotty' Josef Borgford" <winnipegarchitecture.ca/skapti-borgford/>, accessed September 4, 2020. Gil Borgford's story is recounted in Brian Borgford, *Gil*, North Charleston,

South Carolina: CreateSpace Independent Publishing Platform, 2013.
18. J.W. Ames, "Co-operative Housing in Sweden," *Irish Monthly*, 77, 913 (1949): 312–314.
19. Provincial Archives of Manitoba, Co-operative Housing Association of Manitoba, Papers re: Willow Park Housing Co-operative, P 299, File: Co-operative Housing Association of Manitoba, 1959–1966, S.J. Borgford, "Co-operative housing in Manitoba: The story of the Co-operative Housing Association of Manitoba and the development of Willow Park Housing Co-operative in Winnipeg," undated, unpublished paper. For A.D. Ramsay biographical information, see: "Proclamation," *Brandon Sun*, October 21, 1966. For Ruth Struthers biographical information, see: Gordon Goldsborough, "Ruth Heyes Struthers," Manitoba Historical Society <mhs.mb.ca/docs/people/struthers_rh.shtml>, accessed August 27, 2020. For R. Kapilik, see: "Pool meet opens," *Winnipeg Free Press*, October 30, 1962. For R.F. Penner, see: "25 Manitobans leave for meet," *Winnipeg Tribune*, April 12, 1961. For Art Coulter, see: "Political activist a tireless advocate for labour rights," *Winnipeg Free Press*, April 12, 2005. For T.W. Robinson, see: "Co-op housing plan revealed," *Winnipeg Free Press*, February 2, 1960.
20. "Board sets area for city renewal," *Winnipeg Free Press*, 29 February 1960.
21. Provincial Archives of Manitoba, Co-operative Housing Association of Manitoba, Papers re: Willow Park Housing Co-operative, P 299, File: Co-operative Housing Association of Manitoba, 1959–1966, Borgford, "Co-operative Housing in Manitoba," 2.
22. Provincial Archives of Manitoba, Co-operative Housing Association of Manitoba, Papers re: Willow Park Housing Co-operative, P 299, File: Co-operative Housing Association of Manitoba, 1959–1966, D.H. Slimmon to Gentlemen, February 24, 1960; Provincial Archives of Manitoba, Co-operative Housing Association of Manitoba, Papers re: Willow Park Housing Co-operative, P 299, File: Co-operative Housing Association of Manitoba, 1959–1966, Co-operative Housing Association of Manitoba, Directors Minutes, February 6, 1960.
23. "Co-op plans big housing project," *Winnipeg Tribune*, January 24, 1961; Co-op housing plan revealed," *Winnipeg Free Press*, February 2, 1960; Provincial Archives of Manitoba, Co-operative Housing Association of Manitoba, Papers re: Willow Park Housing Co-operative, P 299, File: Co-operative Housing Association of Manitoba, 1959–1966, Co-operative Housing Association of Manitoba, Directors Minutes, January 6, 1961. For information on New York co-operatives, see: Joshua Freeman, *Working Class New York: Life and Labor Since World War II*, New York City: New Press, 2000.
24. "Approve $8.4 million in public housing," *Winnipeg Free Press*, March 7, 1961.
25. Provincial Archives of Manitoba, Co-operative Housing Association of Manitoba, Papers re: Willow Park Housing Co-operative, P 299, File: Co-operative Housing Association of Manitoba, 1959–1966, Borgford, "Co-operative Housing in Manitoba," 3.
26. "Co-op bid on housing is rejected," *Winnipeg Tribune*, March 1, 1961; "Co-ops rap refusal on public housing," *Winnipeg Tribune*, March 2, 1961; Manitoba Historical Society, Memorable Manitobans, "Peter Stanley Taraska" <mhs.mb.ca/docs/people/taraska_p.shtml>, accessed November 24, 2021.
27. "Housing boss sees flaws in Burrows-Keewatin plan," *Winnipeg Tribune*,

March 29, 1961; "He favors 'integrated' housing," *Winnipeg Free Press*, March 31, 1961.

28. Provincial Archives of Manitoba, Co-operative Housing Association of Manitoba, Papers re: Willow Park Housing Co-operative, P 299, File: Co-operative Housing Association of Manitoba, 1959-1966, "Co-op housing is down, but not out," *Winnipeg Co-op News*, March 13, 1961.

29. "$8.4 million housing approved by council," *Winnipeg Tribune*, March 7, 1961.

30. S.J. Borgford to Jack Midmore, March 25, 1962. Personal possession of author.

31. Garry Lahoda, "5,000 low-rent units urgently needed—city," *Winnipeg Tribune*, December 27, 1963.

32. "Low-rent land sale backed," *Winnipeg Tribune*, November 16, 1961.

33. David Pulver, "Co-op housing likely to fall before council," *Winnipeg Tribune*, November 25, 1961.

34. "We're not defeated—Co-op," *Winnipeg Tribune*, November 30, 1961.

35. "The Willow Park story," *Willow Park News*, November 1967. Personal possession of the author.

36. Housing boss sees flaws in Burrows-Keewatin plan," *Winnipeg Tribune*, March 29, 1961.

37. "Winnipeg can serve as social test area," *Winnipeg Free Press*, June 7, 1962; Nick Hills, "Some sober second thoughts on the welfare conference," *Winnipeg Tribune*, June 14, 1962.

38. "Slum clearance plan criticized by speaker," *Winnipeg Tribune*, May 16, 1961.

39. "Low-rental housing plan approved," *Winnipeg Free Press*, June 8, 1961.

40. Heather Robertson, "Urban renewal not the answer for the really poor," *Winnipeg Free Press*, October 22, 1966.

41. "Disgraceful," *Winnipeg Tribune*, March 2, 1961; "Backbencher flays Govt. on housing," *Winnipeg Free Press*, March 8, 1961; "Housing record," *Winnipeg Tribune*, April 17, 1961.

42. "Province slum aid is delayed," *Winnipeg Tribune*, March 21, 1961.

43. Jean James, "False economy," *Winnipeg Free Press*, April 1, 1961.

44. "Women's club endorses slum clearance stand," *Winnipeg Free Press*, April 11, 1961.

45. "Among CWL concerns, dubious films and slums," *Winnipeg Tribune*, September 13, 1961.

46. John Dafoe, "Province will share slum costs," *Winnipeg Free Press*, October 6, 1961; "Roblin orders estimates cut," *Winnipeg Tribune*, December 11, 1961; "Aid for public housing," *Winnipeg Free Press*, April 17, 1962; "Winnipeg rips into housing bill," *Winnipeg Free Press*, April 30, 1962; Laszlo Bastyovanszky, "Repeal of closing law was '62 city highlight," *Winnipeg Free Press*, January 2, 1963.

47. "Housing plans," *Winnipeg Tribune*, March 7, 1961; "Four-step slum cleanup okayed," *Winnipeg Free Press*, March 17, 1961; "First slum project start is ordered," *Winnipeg Tribune*, March 17, 1961.

48. Victor Mackie, "$9 million to erase city slums," *Winnipeg Free Press*, October 2, 1961.

49. "Early talk sought by CMHC," *Winnipeg Tribune*, October 19, 1961.

50. "Minister declines slum talk," *Winnipeg Tribune*, March 9, 1962; "Burrows-Keewatin approved," *Winnipeg Tribune*, August 8, 1962.

51. "40 low-rent units ready by Oct. 15," *Winnipeg Free Press*, September 19, 1963.
52. Laszlo Bastyovanszky, "Ol' Jarvis Avenue gets ready for a facelift," *Winnipeg Free Press*, January 15, 1963; "40 low-rent units ready by Oct. 15," *Winnipeg Free Press*, September 19, 1963.
53. Bob Lisoway, "$4,098,700 housing job gets rolling," *Winnipeg Free Press*, January 6, 1967; Hubert Beyer, "Lord Selkirk Park scheme starts urban renewal wheels in motion," *Winnipeg Free Press*, December 9, 1967.
54. Bill Morriss, "329 unit, $525 million plan for Lord Selkirk Park unveiled," *Winnipeg Free Press*, April 27, 1966.
55. Catherine Macdonald, *A City at Leisure: An Illustrated History of Parks and Recreation Services in Winnipeg, 1893–1993*, City of Winnipeg, 1995, 160.
56. "Too late for bigger play area," *Winnipeg Free Press*, December 9, 1966; Catherine Macdonald, *Making a Place: A History of Landscape architects and Landscape Architecture in Manitoba*, Manitoba Association of Landscape Architects, 2005, 115.
57. "Housing authority," *Winnipeg Free Press*, May 10, 1967.
58. "40 low-rent units ready by Oct. 15," *Winnipeg Free Press*, September 19, 1963.
59. Heather Robertson, "Burrows—not a new slum," *Winnipeg Tribune*, October 15, 1966; Eugen Weiss, "Lord Selkirk Park: Is it good or bad?" *Winnipeg Tribune*, March 7, 1970.
60. Ann Henry, "Biting indictment of sick mixture," *Winnipeg Tribune*, November 6, 1963.
61. "City solicitor claims many land claims deliberately high," *Winnipeg Tribune*, November 6, 1964; Wally Dennison, "Expropriation," *Winnipeg Free Press*, August 17, 1965; "Winnipeg city council rejected petition from home owners," *Winnipeg Free Press*, August 19, 1965.
62. "City launches study of two areas for downtown conservation plan," *Winnipeg Tribune*, November 6, 1965; Thomas B. Yauk, "Residential and Business Relocation from Urban Renewal Areas: A Case Study—The Lord Selkirk Park Experience," Master of City Planning thesis, University of Manitoba, 1973, 94, 100, 101.
63. Michael McGarry, "Happiness is the sunset at Burrows-Keewatin," *Winnipeg Tribune*, February 8, 1969.
64. Thomas B. Yauk, "Residential and Business Relocation from Urban Renewal Areas: A Case Study—The Lord Selkirk Park Experience," Master of City Planning thesis, University of Manitoba, 1973, 109, 144.
65. Thomas B. Yauk, "Residential and Business Relocation from Urban Renewal Areas: A Case Study—The Lord Selkirk Park Experience," Master of City Planning thesis, University of Manitoba, 1973, 77, 109; "Operation '63 wants furniture," *Winnipeg Free Press*, October 19, 1963; "Welfare seekers treated like dirt," *Winnipeg Free Press*, June 20, 1968; "Area programme director for urban renewal areas," *Winnipeg Free Press*, October 17, 1968.
66. "Big step out of the slums into a bright new world," *Winnipeg Free Press*, October 17, 1963.
67. "Home repairs—tenants," *Winnipeg Free Press*, September 3, 1965; "Manitoba's first low-rent housing officially opened," *Winnipeg Free Press*, June 26, 1964.
68. Michael McGarry, "Happiness is the sunset at Burrows-Keewatin," *Winnipeg Tribune*, February 8, 1969.

69. "Rhoda Sarah-Ann Mulvaney," *Winnipeg Free Press* Passages <passages.win-nipegfreepress.com/passage-details/id-209386/MULVANEY_RHODA>, accessed November 19, 2021.

70. Val Werier, "Now they have a 'decent place to live,'" *Winnipeg Tribune*, December 28, 1963.

71. Val Werier, "Four years of low rental housing," *Winnipeg Tribune*, October 4, 1967.

72. Heather Robertson, "Burrows—not a new slum," *Winnipeg Tribune*, October 15, 1966.

73. "Slums not just shifted: Prober," *Winnipeg Free Press*, April 26, 1968.

74. William A. Morrison with Donald MacFarlane, *A Study on Some of the Social Aspects of Urban Renewal: A Detailed Investigation of the Social Effects of Relocation upon Selected Families from a Renewal Area in Winnipeg*, Winnipeg: Community Welfare Planning Council of Winnipeg, 1967, 72.

75. Manitoba Indian Brotherhood, *Manitoba Indian Brotherhood Urban Housing Survey*, Winnipeg: Manitoba Indian Brotherhood, 1971, 87–90.

76. "A concrete nightmare," *Winnipeg Free Press*, November 29, 1969; "Urban renewal projects "expensive... ghettos," *Winnipeg Free Press*, May 7, 1968.

77. Mac Keillor, "An earful, an eyeful, on housing," *Winnipeg Free Press*, October 29, 1968.

78. Eugen Weiss, "Lord Selkirk Park: Is it good or bad?" *Winnipeg Tribune*, March 7, 1970.

79. Eugen Weiss, "Lord Selkirk Park: Is it good or bad?" *Winnipeg Tribune*, March 7, 1970.

80. Eugen Weiss, "Lord Selkirk Park: Is it good or bad?" *Winnipeg Tribune*, March 7, 1970.

81. Alvin Finkel, *Social Policy and Practice in Canada: A History*, Waterloo: Wilfrid Laurier University, 2006, 232.

82. Gregory Suttor, "Canadian Social Housing: Policy Evolution and Impacts on the Housing System and Urban Space," PhD dissertation, University of Toronto, 2014, 124; "$8,7550,000 renewal plan goes ahead," *Winnipeg Free Press*, October 11, 1967.

83. Peter Raeside, "Giant renewal plans rolling," *Winnipeg Free Press*, August 20, 1965; "Beehler letter riles urban group," *Winnipeg Free Press*, November 26, 1969.

84. Canada and Paul Hellyer, *Report of the Federal Task Force on Housing and Urban Development*, Ottawa: Queen's Printer, 1969, 78.

85. Lloyd Axworthy, *The Housing Task Force: A Case Study*, University of Winnipeg: Institute of Urban Studies, 1970.

86. Michael Wheeler, "Illusion to think the private market can house all decently," *Financial Post*, February 8, 1969; Humphrey Carver, "'Like a cavalry charge,' says expert, criticizing Hellyer housing report," *Ottawa Journal*, February 4, 1968; Albert Rose, "Paul Hellyer on housing: fact or fiction?" *Globe and Mail*, February 5, 1969.

87. George Anderson, *Housing Policy in Canada: Lecture Series*, Canada Mortgage and Housing Corporation, 1992, 34–36; Peter Raeside, "Giant renewal plans rolling," *Winnipeg Free Press*, August 20, 1965; David G. Burley, "Winnipeg's landscapes of modernity, 1945-1975," in Serena Keshavjee (ed.), *Winnipeg Modern: Architecture, 1945-1975*, Winnipeg: University of Manitoba Press,

2006, 67.

88. "Metro wants new power to hit slum landlords," *Winnipeg Tribune*, December 4, 1962. For background on the Metropolitan Corporation, see: Earl Levin, "City History and City Planning: The Local Historical Roots of the City Planning Function in Three Cities of the Canadian Prairies," PhD thesis, University of Manitoba, 1993, 258–259.

89. Garry Lahoda, "5,000 low-rent units urgently needed—city," *Winnipeg Tribune*, December 27, 1963.

90. Wade Rowland, "Housing report to cause political storm," *Winnipeg Free Press*, March 14, 1967.

91. "Housing agency urged to end slum living," *Winnipeg Free Press*, August 2, 1967.

92. Pieter Van Bennekom, "Bugs, dirt and fear plague old people downtown: Report," *Winnipeg Free Press*, August 23, 1968.

93. Pieter Van Bennekom, "Bugs, dirt and fear plague old people downtown: Report," *Winnipeg Free Press*, August 23, 1968.

94. "Voting change backed," *Winnipeg Free Press*, April 21, 1965.

95. Debates of the Manitoba Legislature, Fourth Session of the 27th Legislature, April 14, 1965, 1578.

96. "Leaseholder votes out: Smellie," *Winnipeg Tribune*, March 22, 1965.

97. "Group would cut number of city aldermen to 12," *Winnipeg Free Press*, February 22, 1967.

98. "Civic reform," *Winnipeg Free Press*, February 25, 1967.

99. "Provincial urban affairs department urged," *Winnipeg Free Press*, April 18, 1969.

100. "Jarvis landlords defended by Frith," *Winnipeg Tribune*, October 13, 1962.

101. Del T. Starr, "Views by Firth rapped by reader," *Winnipeg Tribune*, November 3, 1962.

102. Donald M. McCaskill, "Migration, adjustment, and integration of the Indian into the urban environment," Master of Arts thesis, Carleton University, 1970, 98.

103. "Jarvis-Charles area termed 'unbearable,'" *Winnipeg Free Press*, August 16, 1962.

104. "Slums hit by police," *Winnipeg Free Press*, September 25, 1962.

105. "Clean up on Jarvis sought," *Winnipeg Tribune*, September 25, 1962.

106. Dave Kemp, "The first glimmer of light on Jarvis Ave.," *Winnipeg Tribune*, August 25, 1962.

107. Dorothy Betz, interview #1 with Leslie Hall, Winnipeg, Manitoba, March 3, 2004, quoted in Leslie Hall, "'A Place of Awakening': The Formation of the Winnipeg Indian and Métis Friendship Centre 1954–1964," Master of Arts thesis, University of Manitoba, 2004, 32. For background on Dorothy Betz, see: "Dorothy Betz," *Winnipeg Free Press* Passages <passages.winnipegfreepress.com/passage-details/id-124740/Betz_Dorothy>, accessed November 6, 2021.

108. Mary Guilbault, interview #3 with Leslie Hall, Winnipeg, Manitoba, April 2, 2004, quoted in Leslie Hall, "'A Place of Awakening': The Formation of the Winnipeg Indian and Métis Friendship Centre 1954–1964," Master of Arts thesis, University of Manitoba, 2004, 33–34. For background on Mary Guilbault, see: "Mary Jane Guilbault," *Winnipeg Free Press* Passages <passages.

winnipegfreepress.com/passage-details/id-203365/Guilbault_Mary>, accessed November 6, 2021.

109. Leslie Hall, "'A Place of Awakening': The Formation of the Winnipeg Indian and Métis Friendship Centre 1954-1964," Master of Arts thesis, University of Manitoba, 2004, 34.

110. Leslie Hall, "'A Place of Awakening': The Formation of the Winnipeg Indian and Métis Friendship Centre 1954-1964," Master of Arts thesis, University of Manitoba, 2004, 58-59.

111. Eugen Weiss, "Lord Selkirk Park: Is it good or bad?" *Winnipeg Tribune*, March 7, 1970.

112. "Indians here have to live in slums, city council told," *Winnipeg Free Press*, March 26, 1968.

113. Manitoba Indian Brotherhood, *Manitoba Indian Brotherhood Urban Housing Survey*, Winnipeg: Manitoba Indian Brotherhood, 1971, 93.

114. Manitoba Indian Brotherhood, *Manitoba Indian Brotherhood Urban Housing Survey*, Winnipeg: Manitoba Indian Brotherhood, 1971, 7.

115. "Fire damages rooming house," *Winnipeg Free Press*, January 31, 1967; "Questions stall fire alarm bill," *Winnipeg Free Press*, March 22, 1967; "Unnecessary rejection," *Winnipeg Free Press*, April 24, 1967; "City douses safety measures," *Winnipeg Free Press*, October 11, 1967; "Fire alarm law urged, *Winnipeg Free Press*, February 3, 1968; "Detector alarm confusion seen," *Winnipeg Free Press*, February 15, 1968; "Fire bylaw plan kindles arguments," *Winnipeg Free Press*, March 12, 1968; Hubert Beyer, "Around city hall," *Winnipeg Free Press*, April 13, 1968; Stephen Riley, "Housing for elderly championed by committee," *Winnipeg Free Press*, October 2, 1969.

116. Eugen Weiss, "Lord Selkirk Park: Is it good or bad?" *Winnipeg Tribune*, March 7, 1970.

117. George Anderson, *Housing Policy in Canada: Lecture Series*, Canada Mortgage and Housing Corporation, 1992, 34-36.

EPILOGUE

The New Democratic Party's surprise victory in the June 1969 Manitoba provincial election marked a historic turning point in the history of public housing in Manitoba. The Liberal government of Douglas Campbell had passed what it termed "enabling" legislation in the 1950s but did nothing to actually enable the construction of public housing. The Progressive Conservative government of Duff Roblin had brought money to the table, but it was content to let the federal and municipal governments take the lead. While the Roblin government exempted the City of Winnipeg from the requirement to get ratepayers' approval before proceeding with any public housing program, the provision still held for all other municipalities in Manitoba. The requirement to hold a ratepayers' vote was not the only barrier to the development of public housing: under the 1964 amendments to the *National Housing Act*, public housing capital costs were to be split on a nine to one basis between federal and provincial governments, while operating subsidies were to split on a fifty-fifty basis between the federal and provincial governments. The Roblin government, like many other provincial governments, had been insisting that municipalities cover half of the provincial costs of any development. The results were predictable: by the end of the 1960s, no public housing had been built outside Winnipeg. Studies conducted by the government had identified the need for public housing in Brandon, Selkirk, St. James, Flin Flon, The Pas, Selkirk, and Churchill. Burrows-Keewatin and Lord Selkirk Park, with just over five hundred units of housing, were the only two projects developed in Manitoba during the eleven years the Conservatives held power.[1]

NDP Premier Ed Schreyer and his government took a far more aggressive approach. It did away with the ratepayers' vote and it stopped asking municipalities to cover any portion of capital and operating costs. At the same time, the Schreyer government also did away with the last of the provisions restricting the rights of tenants to run for council.[2] In 1970, the Manitoba Housing and Renewal Corporation (MHRC) committed itself to building between 900 and 1,000 units of public housing in the coming year, almost double what had been built in the previous decade. In the financial year of 1970-71, 2,409 units of public housing were put into construction: these included seniors and family housing. Public housing was built in Selkirk, Carman, Brandon, Morris, The Pas, Flin Flon, Winkler, Killarney, and Swan River, as well as in Winnipeg. The scale of increase in the investment in construction is staggering: $3,273 in 1969, $848,371 in 1970, $7,583,939 in 1971, and $31,499,744 in 1972. Projects tended to be small in scale: in 1971-72 only one of the projects was larger than 100 units.[3] Several of the projects were innovative for their time: 1010 Sinclair was the first public housing project for people living in wheelchairs, while the Kiwanis Centre for the Deaf was also a new step in housing for people with disabilities.[4] The government was also supportive of the Co-operative Housing Association of Manitoba (CHAM), renting land at 5 percent of cost to co-operatives in exchange for a guarantee of reduced rents for low-income members. The government also provided interim loans to help co-operatives conduct pre-construction studies and technical work.[5]

The expansion of public housing in Manitoba was fueled by changes at the federal level. In 1973 the federal Liberal government of Pierre Trudeau established ten new housing programs that focused on the provision of social and co-operative housing and planning. Non-profit organizations—usually church groups, service clubs, or residents' groups—were granted long-term low-cost federal mortgages to build what came to be termed "social housing." Operating subsidies were also established to allow rents to be geared to income. CMHC hired staff to promote the formation of social-housing projects and startup funding was provided.[6] By 1978 this social housing sector, which depended largely on federal funding, was producing 19,000 units of housing a year nationally; and by the mid-1980s public and non-profit housing jointly amounted to 5 percent of the Canadian housing stock.[7] This was the golden age of public and social housing in Canada.

At the end of the eight-year Schreyer administration, the Manitoba Housing and Renewal Corporation (MHRC) could report that there were 11,187 units of public housing in the province.[8] MHRC's activities generated controversy and criticism: in its efforts to quickly increase housing supply it was forced to overpay for land, and projects were not always well integrated into communities. At one point, issues were so heated that housing minister Len Evans appointed himself to the position of chair of the MHRC board of directors.[9] In his 1980 assessment of Canadian housing policy, Canadian public housing scholar Albert Rose commented, "Manitoba's record in a variety of housing assistance programs, with particular emphasis upon public housing, is all the more impressive when its population of just over 1 million persons is considered."[10]

Indigenous housing organizations took advantage of the expansionist policies of the federal and provincial governments during the 1970s and 1980s to provide housing directly. The Manitoba Indian Brotherhood's 1971 research paper demonstrated Indigenous people faced the worst housing conditions in the city and the province. A 1983 study of Winnipeg housing conditions concluded that Indigenous people were more likely than other Winnipeggers to be living in poor-quality, overcrowded housing and paying more than a third of their income on housing.[11] The Manitoba Métis Federation and the Indian-Métis Friendship Centre led the way on housing. In 1969, the CMHC and MHRC agreed to cost-share a Manitoba Métis Federation project that built fifty homes for Métis people in Manitoba. One hundred houses were constructed the following year and another one hundred were built in 1971.[12] A housing working group of Winnipeg's Indian-Métis Friendship Centre, with the support of the Institute of Urban Studies at the University of Winnipeg, organized Kinew Housing as a non-profit housing corporation in 1970. While it eventually received funding from CMHC, Kinew purchased its first three houses with money lent to it by private individuals. Kinew bought single-family homes throughout the city and hired Indigenous people to repair them. After a decade in operation, Kinew owned 140 homes, which were rented to Indigenous tenants, with the long-term goal of the tenants purchasing the house. After 1976, rent subsidies were made available to the tenants. Much of Kinew's early work was carried out by volunteer board members, particularly Marion Meadmore and Delia Opekokew. Kinew made two important contributions to national housing policy. Its example led to the creation of similar organizations in other cities and the establishment of the Native Urban Housing Association of Canada.[13] The Kinew model also prompted the federal government into establishing an Urban Native Housing Program. This commenced as an informal commitment to ensuring that 10 percent of the government-sponsored low-cost housing built in Canada was reserved for Indigenous people. Over the years, a formal program was created that produced approximately 11,000 units of housing.[14]

Payuk Inter-Tribal Housing Co-operative, another major Indigenous housing initiative, was the outgrowth of Winnipeg Native Family Economic Development Inc., which brought together Indigenous social agencies and businesses. Having developed a set of principles that focused on meeting local needs with local resources, the coalition and its members played important roles in the establishment of the Ma Mawi Chi Itata Centre, Children of the Earth School, and Neechi Food Co-operative. Payuk was incorporated in 1985 to provide housing for single Indigenous parents.[15] With financial support from both the provincial and federal governments, Payuk was able to open a new forty-two-unit co-op on Balmoral Street with CMHC in 1989.[16] Kathy Mallett, one of the early board members, told the *Free Press*, "Taking control is the answer. We no longer have to beg at the doors of landlords to give us accommodation."[17] These were but two of many innovative Indigenous housing initiatives from this period.

The crucial role a sympathetic provincial government can play is underscored by the fate of public housing under alternating NDP and Conservative administrations. The Schreyer government was defeated in 1977 by a Conservative party whose leader, Sterling Lyon, was committed to a policy of "acute, protracted restraint." This included throttling the construction of public housing. After four years of Conservative administration, the number of units under public administration increased by only 393, totaling 11,580.[18]

A resurgent New Democratic party, led by Schreyer's former attorney general Howard Pawley, returned to power in 1981. During its six years in office, the Pawley government increased public and social housing to 23,192 units. In its last year in power, the Pawley government committed to the construction of 670 units of housing.[19] Gary Filmon's Conservative government, elected in 1988, oversaw a dramatic reduction in investment in public housing.[20] In the mid-1990s, changes in federal policy brought the development of public housing in Canada to a standstill, from which it has never recovered.

* * *

The golden age of public housing came to an end in 1993, when the Conservative federal government headed by Brian Mulroney announced that it would no longer provide or guarantee loans for the construction of new social housing.[21] The implications of the federal government decision are starkly reported in Manitoba Housing's annual report for 1994–1995: "due to the federal government's decision to terminate funding for new social housing across Canada effective January 1, 1994, there were no new commitments of family and elderly non-profit housing units in 1994/95."[22] Despite an election commitment to the contrary, the Liberal government of Jean Chrétien continued this federal retreat as it transferred all responsibility for administrating public housing that it had created and funded to the provinces.[23] The result was the growth of homelessness as thousands of families found themselves priced out of the housing market. By 2001, 20 percent of Canadian households were paying more than 30 percent of their pre-tax income on housing.[24]

Since 2001, a succession of federal governments has done little to address the plight of low-income Canadians who are victimized by the failure of the Canadian housing market. Federal housing programs have been ad hoc in nature and limited in their funding. They have relied heavily on provincial cost-sharing and the participation of non-profit organizations to create "affordable housing." This housing is often not affordable for low-income households and does not provide anything close to the level of federal funding that was available between 1973 and 1993. From 1991 to 2016, annual investment in affordable housing declined by 46 percent.[25] Organizations that seek to build low-cost housing must cobble together projects making use of a patchwork of often short-lived funding programs. Instead of addressing low-income needs, the primary concern of federal housing policy has been the stimulation of housing construction and the spread of homeownership. Low-cost mortgages, government-insured mortgages, first-time homeowner supports, and the capital gains exemption all serve to subsidize the homeowners and homebuyers. These subsidies, provided with little in the way of means-testing, continue to dwarf government spending on social housing.[26]

* * *

Public housing developments represented a real improvement in the lives of the people who moved into them from the city's slums and boarding houses. Modest as these developments were, they constitute a valuable social legacy, one that must be defended against provincial policies of privatization and neglect. The market continues to fail low-income Manitobans (and low-income Canadians). In each year of the past decade, the *Winnipeg Free Press* has carried stories that speak of the ongoing affordable housing "crisis" in the city.[27] Conservative politicians, lenders, and the property industry remain militant, united in their opposition to public housing. Indeed, when Sam Katz was mayor from 2004 to 2014, Winnipeg city hall was little more than a branch office of the real-estate industry and its planning capacity was gutted.

Arrayed against the powers of private property one finds the usual suspects: social democrats, socialists, urban reformers, research agencies, academics, service organizations, leaders of faith communities, and journalists. To this can be added a host of Indigenous- and community-led organizations through which the residents of poorly housed communities have channeled their energies. What is needed from the federal government is a commitment to guarantee long-term low-cost mortgages for non-profit housing and to provide rent subsidies to those households that cannot afford the rents required to pay down those mortgages. Wrestling such a commitment of out the federal government and ensuring that provincial and municipal governments are prepared to facilitate any opportunities, rather than block them, was and is an uphill battle. As the history of the struggle to create public housing in Winnipeg demonstrates, property will cede none of its privileges without a challenge. And today's public-housing advocates can take pride, and be celebrated, for shouldering their share in a long struggle to place the rights of people to have a safe and decent roof over their head before the rights of property.

NOTES

1. Manitoba Housing and Renewal Corporation, *Annual Report 1968-69*, Winnipeg: Manitoba Housing and Renewal Corporation, n.d.
2. Arlene Billinkoff, "Decision delayed on bid to give tenants money vote," *Winnipeg Free Press*, December 3, 1969; Bob Culbert, "Manitoba may abolish tenant ban," *Winnipeg Free Press*, March 9, 1970.
3. Manitoba Housing and Renewal Corporation, *Annual Report 1968-69*, Winnipeg: n.d.; Manitoba Housing and Renewal Corporation, *Annual Report 1969-70*, Winnipeg: n.d.; Manitoba Housing and Renewal Corporation, *Annual Report 1970-71*, Winnipeg: n.d.; Manitoba Housing and Renewal Corporation, *Annual Report 1971-72*, Winnipeg: n.d.; Manitoba Housing and Renewal Corporation, *Annual Report 1972-73*, Winnipeg: n.d.; Manitoba Housing and Renewal Corporation, *Annual Report 1973-74*, Winnipeg: n.d.
4. Albert Rose, *Canadian Housing Policies (1935-1980)*, Toronto: Butterworths, 1980, 87.
5. Manitoba, Manitoba Housing and Renewal Corporation, *1976-77 Annual Report*, Winnipeg: n.d., 4; Harry Finnigan, "The Role of Co-Operative Housing Resources Groups in Canada: A Case Study of the Co-operative Housing Association of Manitoba (CHAM)," Master of City Planning thesis, Department of City Planning, University of Manitoba, 1978.
6. George Anderson, *Housing Policy in Canada: Lecture Series*, Canada Mortgage and Housing Corporation, 1992, 37; John Bacher, *Keeping to the Market: The Evolution of Canadian Housing Policy*, Montreal and Kingston: McGill-Queen's University Press, 1993, 245.
7. Gregory Suttor, "Canadian Social Housing: Policy Evolution and Impacts on the Housing System and Urban Space," PhD dissertation, University of Toronto, 2014, 225.
8. Manitoba Housing and Renewal Corporation, *1977-78 Annual Report*, Winnipeg: 1978.
9. "MHRC drops proposal calls for public housing projects"; "Housing Corp. manager backs Evans' position," *Winnipeg Free Press*, July 2, 1977.
10. Albert Rose, *Canadian Housing Policies (1935-1980)*, Toronto: Butterworths, 1980, 87.
11. Stewart J. Clatworthy, *Native Housing Conditions in Winnipeg*, Winnipeg: Institute of Urban Studies, 1983, 88; Josh Brandon and Evelyn Peters, *Moving to the City: Housing and Aboriginal Migration to Winnipeg*, Winnipeg: Canadian Centre for Policy Alternatives-Manitoba, 2014.
12. Lawrence J. Barkwell, *The History of the Manitoba Métis Federation*, Winni-

peg, Manitoba Métis Federation, 2018, 23; Manitoba Housing and Renewal Corporation, *1969-70 Annual Report,* Winnipeg: n.d.; Manitoba Housing and Renewal Corporation, *1970-71 Annual Report,* Winnipeg: n.d.

13. Stanley A. Fulham, *In Search of a Future,* Winnipeg: no publisher, 1981, 15-24; Ryan C. Walker, "Aboriginal self-determination and social housing in urban Canada: A story of convergence and divergence," *Urban Studies,* 45, 1 (January 2008): 194; Randal McIlroy, "Program helps natives to adjust to city," *Winnipeg Free Press,* June 8, 1990.

14. Ryan C. Walker, "Aboriginal self-determination and social housing in urban Canada: A story of convergence and divergence," *Urban Studies,* 45, 1 (January 2008): 197.

15. John Loxley, *Aboriginal, Northern, and Community Economic Development Papers and Retrospectives,* Winnipeg: Arbeiter Ring Publishing, 2010.

16. James Thunder and Mark Intertas, *Indigenizing the Co-operative Model,* Winnipeg: Canadian Centre for Policy Alternatives–Manitoba, 2020, 31; Janet McFarland, "Group seeks funding," *Winnipeg Free Press,* December 30, 1988; Mary Ann FitzGerald, "Province funds different plans for same site," *Winnipeg Free Press,* May 15, 1987; "Street widening threatens plan for new school," *Winnipeg Free Press,* June 24, 1987; Gerald Flood, "Dress kills project," *Winnipeg Free Press,* June 27, 1987; Tyler Craig and Blair Hamilton, *In Search of Mino Bimaadiziwin: A Study of Urban Aboriginal Housing Cooperatives in Canada,* Winnipeg: Partnering for Change: Community-based Solutions for Aboriginal and Inner-city Poverty, a SEED Winnipeg Inc. research report in conjunction with Manitoba Research Alliance, 2014, 23.

17. Ruth Teichroeb, "Racism compounds woes of poverty," *Winnipeg Free Press,* July 25, 1989.

18. Manitoba Housing and Renewal Corporation, *Annual Report 1976-1977,* Winnipeg: n.d.: 8; Manitoba Housing and Renewal Corporation, *Annual Report 1980-1981,* Winnipeg: n.d.

19. Manitoba Housing, *Annual Report 1987-1988,* Winnipeg: n.d.: 26; Manitoba Housing and Renewal Corporation, *Annual Report 1982-1983,* Winnipeg: n.d.: 20; Manitoba Housing, *Annual Report 1987-1988,* Winnipeg: n.d.: 26.

20. Manitoba Housing, *Annual Report 1990-1991,* Winnipeg: n.d.: 18-19.

21. Steve Pomeroy, "Discussion paper: Envisioning a modernized social and affordable housing sector in Canada," Ottawa: Carleton University Centre for Urban Research and Education, 2017.

22. Manitoba Housing, *Annual Report 1994-1995,* Winnipeg: n.d.: 14.

23. Michael Shapcott, "Where are we going? Recent federal and provincial housing policy," in J. David Hulchanski and Michael Shapcott (eds.), *Finding Room: Policy Options for a Changing Rental Housing Strategy,* Toronto: Centre for Urban and Community Studies Press, 2004, 198; Sharon Chisholm, *Affordable Housing in Canada's Urban Communities: A Literature Review,* Ottawa, Ontario: Canada Mortgage and Housing Corporation 2003, 5-12.

24. Jacqueline Luffman, "Measuring housing affordability," *Perspectives on Labour and Income,* 7, 11: 16.

25. The Canadian Housing and Renewal Association, the Co-operative Housing Federation, the Canadian Alliance to End Homelessness, the British Columbia Non-Profit Housing Association, the Ontario Non-Profit Housing Association, le Réseau québecois des OSBL d'habitation, and the New Brunswick

Non-Profit Housing Association, *Affordable Housing: A Foundation for Social Inclusion*, 2016. <chra-achru.ca/wp-content/uploads/2016/02/pre-budget_2016_housing.pdf>, accessed September 6, 2022.

26. John R. Miron, *Housing in Canada: Demographic Change, Household Formation, and Housing Demand*, Kingston and Montreal: McGill-Queen's Press, 1988; Marion Steele, "The Canadian Home Buyers' Plan: Tax benefit, tax expenditure, and policy assessment," *Canadian Tax Journal, Revue Fiscale Canadienne*, 55, 1 (2007): 3–4; John Sewell, *Housing and Homes: Housing for Canadians*, Toronto: James Lorimer and Company, 1994, 88–95; Robert G. Dowler, *Housing-Related Tax Expenditures: An Overview and Evaluation*, Toronto: Centre for Urban and Community Studies, University of Toronto, Major Report No. 22; Bacher, *Keeping to the Market*.

27. Mary Agnes Welch, "Rooming-house loss a crisis," *Winnipeg Free Press*, July 12, 2013; Mary Agnes Welch, "People before parks," *Winnipeg Free Press*, June 15, 2014; Mary Agnes Welch, "Group touts cure to affordable housing woes," *Winnipeg Free Press*, June 23, 2015; Christina Hryniuk, "Housing can be harrowing," *Winnipeg Free Press*, November 27, 2016; Kirsten Bernas, "Falling behind on homelessness," *Winnipeg Free Press*, October 25, 2017; Dylan Robertson, "Budget fails to speed up funding," *Winnipeg Free Press*, February 28, 2018; Tessa Vanderhart, "Lockers to rescue city homeless and their carts," *Winnipeg Free Press*, June 22, 2019; Joyanne Pursaga, "City report considers supports to address homelessness," *Winnipeg Free Press*, September 15, 2020; Joyanne Pursaga, "City keeps tax hike plans intact," *Winnipeg Free Press*, November 26, 2021; Ben Waldman, "A hand up in St. B," *Winnipeg Free Press*, January 24, 2022.

INDEX